Rawlsian Political Analysis

PAUL CLEMENTS

Rawlsian Political Analysis

RETHINKING THE
MICROFOUNDATIONS
OF SOCIAL SCIENCE

University of Notre Dame Press

Notre Dame, Indiana

Library of Congress Cataloging-in-Publication Data

Clements, Paul, Ph. D.
  Rawlsian political analysis : rethinking the microfoundations of
social science / Paul Clements.
      p.   cm.
  Includes bibliographical references and index.
  ISBN: 978-0-268-02371-3 (pbk. : alk. paper)
  ISBN: 0-268-02371-9 (pbk. : alk. paper)
  E-ISBN: 978-0-268-07696-2
  1. Political science. 2. Rational choice theory. 3. Social justice.
4. Rawls, John, 1921–2002—Political and social views. I. Title.
  JA71.C535   2012
  320.01'1—dc23
                                                    2012014876

To Aedín

contents

acknowledgments

I am particularly grateful to Emily Hauptmann for working with me on earlier stages of this project, for collaborating on the critique of rational choice theory, and for friendship and support throughout. Peter Stone provided very helpful comments on early drafts of several chapters. Email communication with Lucinda Dhavan helped me to get started on the analysis of Bihar. I received very helpful comments on a draft of the first chapter from John Hare, and discussion with Christine Moser helped me to frame the discussion of the economic analysis of climate change. I am grateful to Jonathan Allen for wide-ranging discussions, some in areas touched on here. My chief intellectual debt is, of course, to John Rawls, but I also owe a great deal to Atul Kohli, for his example as a scholar and for what I learned from his books and lectures. I am also very grateful to two anonymous reviewers, one of whom gave particularly helpful suggestions for extensions of the argument found mainly in chapter 2, and to Ann Delgehausen for excellent editing.

Some ideas in chapter 3 are found in "The Reasonable and the Rational Capacities in Political Analysis," an article I co-authored with Emily Hauptmann that appeared in *Politics & Society* in 2002, and much of the analysis in chapter 5 is found in "A Rawlsian Analysis of the Plight of Bihar," my article that appeared in *Studies in Comparative International Development* in 2005.

My sister Crispin read early drafts of several chapters and provided many helpful comments. It is hard to express my gratitude to my parents, as it extends in so many directions. I am grateful to my daughter Anna for her interest in Kant and Rawls and for many helpful discussions. More than anyone, I am grateful to my wife, Aedín.

Rawlsian Political Analysis

chapter one

Introduction

Why Rawlsian Political Analysis?

Ontology precedes methodology.

New Microfoundations for Social Science

Good and bad and right and wrong are our most fundamental moral concepts. We are instructed from early childhood to "be good," we want what is good for ourselves and for our families and friends, and we like to be good at our jobs and at other tasks that are important for us. For Americans, the right to the pursuit of happiness, associated with achieving the good, is enshrined in our Declaration of Independence. We all know, too, that we should try to do what is right. Learning right from wrong is an important part of growing up, and to be right with one another is to have our relationships in good order. In our political discourse, no value exceeds doing what is right.

The distinction between the good and the right, and the consequences of this distinction for social analysis, is the topic of this book. Since the 1950s, Anglo-American political scientists, economists, and other social scientists have been trying to found political and social analysis on the analytics of the good, neglecting or relegating to a subsidiary order the analytics of the sense of right. I argue, however, following Immanuel Kant and John Rawls,

1. that the sense of right is just as fundamental as is the sense of the good,
2. that these two senses are somewhat independent from one another and operate according to different dynamics, and
3. that these two senses and only these two are consistently fundamental to our practical decision making.

These senses and no others form the basis for practical reason. If these claims are true then we need a new political analysis, and this is the analysis this book aims to launch.

Some social scientists have argued that decision making can be modeled in terms of rational utility maximization, which boils down to each person (rationally) maximizing the satisfaction of his or her interests (including the interest we take in the good of others). To satisfy our interests, in this view, is to achieve what we take to be our good. This model lies at the foundation of rational choice theory and of neoclassical economics, and it stands as the only established microfoundations for political or social analysis. When contemporary political scientists or economists speak of microfoundations, this is the model to which they refer.

Among neoclassical economists this model is completely normative and uncontroversial. Almost every economic analysis relies on the assumption of rationality, implying that the decisions and choices of the people under consideration can be modeled as aiming to maximize the satisfaction of their interests. Among political scientists, however, (and among sociologists and historians as far as their disciplines use this model) it is a very different story. Here rational utility maximization as a model of choice is highly controversial, and although most political scientists probably use some findings from rational choice theory, only a minority could be considered adherents to this theory and most consider it inadequate as a basis for the work they do.

I argue that rational choice theorists and economists have simply got their model of choice wrong. To the extent that the model works, it is because the sense of the good (represented by our interests) is one of the two foundations for practical decisions.[1] It is serviceable enough to assume rational utility maximization when analyzing some kinds of voting patterns and power politics, rates of inflation, and changes in prices.

This assumption is not much use, however, for analyzing the social and political dynamics underlying most social problems. In fact, our practical decisions are influenced as much by our principles, the cognitive objects of the sense of right, as by our interests, the main cognitive objects of the sense of the good. For this reason, social analysis based on both the right and the good, on principles as well as interests, will provide accounts of social relations that are more coherent, more satisfying, and more true. Rawlsian political analysis, as I call it, provides the firmer basis for understanding our social world, and, understanding it, for changing it.

I appreciate that these are rather audacious claims. This introductory chapter will lay out the forms of evidence I offer to support them and summarize the main points of my arguments. The model of choice that I propose, however, borrowed from Kant and Rawls, means more for political science than just showing how better empirical arguments can be developed. It also has consequences for how we understand the role of political science, what we are doing when we do political science, and for the ethical frameworks from which we should approach social analysis. That it should have these kinds of consequences will come as no surprise to anyone familiar with the work of Kant and Rawls.

I should state at the outset that adopting their model of choice does not imply accepting their ethics or epistemologies wholesale, much less accepting all of Kantian metaphysics (some of which Rawls rejects). However, I think it does require accepting the main lines of the structures of their ethical theories as plausible. We have to take many of their conclusions seriously even if we do not completely buy them.

In particular, I will argue that adopting his model of choice requires that we accept Kant's view that our experience of the world is based as much on our own cognitive capacities and on the concepts and categories we bring to perception as on the nature of external reality. When we do political analysis, one thing we are doing is constructing (reinforcing, revising, deepening) our conceptions of right, conceptions that form a basis for our engagement with subsequent practical problems.

I will also argue that accepting this model of choice leads to accepting Rawls's "original position," the viewpoint he establishes for selecting principles of justice, as appropriate for approaching problems of social justice generally. In the original position, we consider questions of social justice as if from behind a "veil of ignorance," that is, as if we did not know our level of wealth or our position in the distribution of natural talents, political power, and so on. Excluding this kind of knowledge, we arrive at a perspective from which we can consider social problems fairly, free from biases that might arise from our individual interests. As vulnerable social agents with compelling interests and regulative senses of right, when we are going to address questions of social justice, this is the appropriate place to start.

Kant is widely regarded as the preeminent philosopher of the Enlightenment, and Rawls, who largely adopts and extends Kant's ethics, is the preeminent political philosopher of the last half century. Kant, of course, wrote long before Darwin, but Rawls does not engage with evolutionary theory or the associated science either. Writing on models of choice today, however, in the first decade of the new millennium, as the science advances and evolutionary perspectives have begun to seep into common sense, this connection needs to be made. From an evolutionary perspective, interests can be explained straightforwardly in terms of desires for food, sex, and territory, but how can an equal place in choice for principles or sentiments of right be reconciled with evolution? I build on Marc Hauser's account of sources for the sense of right particularly in primate evolution to argue that the sense of right is grounded in our cognition of expectations, that is, of the regularity of the natural world.[2] However, this and other components of the sense of right could not produce moral emotions such as guilt and resentment until language came to be well developed. Both interests and principles are basic cognitive objects that we can alter through reflection and that contribute to constructing our world, but although interests are grounded in natural desire, principles are associated with conceptions of the shape and structure of social worlds infused with agency.

When I say that principles and interests are cognitive objects, I mean literally that they are embodied in structures of neurons in our brains. To say they are fundamental to decision making is to say that these structures are engaged when we make decisions, contributing to their content. To say that they operate according to different dynamics is to state the hypothesis that the structures of neurons that embody principles and interests operate according to distinct sets of patterns, probably located in different regions of the brain (and probably with some overlap). Although there are differences in dynamics among principles and among interests, the differences between the sets are greater than the differences within the sets.

One might have interests in getting a job or a promotion, in reading the *New York Times*, in keeping one's weight down, or in going to a party. When economists assume that people are interested, say, in maximizing their incomes, formally they may only imply that people's behavior can be expected (on average, to some extent, in specified contexts) to be consistent with this assumption. This formal assumption, however, must eventually be made good in particular choices and these choices in patterns of neural activity. Also, it is hard to keep the formal use of terms such as "rational self-interest" rigorously distinct from common, everyday self-interest. We sometimes say that someone has an objective interest (in studying to do well in a class, for example) that may differ from their subjective sense of their interests (when they want to go out with friends instead) or that they may not properly understand (say when a young person rides a motorcycle without a helmet). The tension between so-called objective and perceived interests is, of course, one of the basic justifications for scholarship and education.

My use of the term "principle" is broader, and more formal, than the way the term is often used in common speech. Many people might recognize responding aggressively to a threat or giving credit where credit is due as principles, but they might not think of stopping at red lights or greeting neighbors cheerfully when meeting them on the street as principles. But the cognitive processes underlying all these actions fit the pattern of a principle. Principles underlie our senses of right, justice, fairness, appropriateness, legitimacy, and propriety, so when something strikes us as, say, appropriate, it is because an event has conformed to our principle. When we feel indignant, resentful, or vengeful it is due to the violation of a principle, and principles are invoked by sentiments of loyalty, honor, and obligation. The fixed ideas someone might refer to as "my principles" are a subset of that person's principles as I understand them.

The Kantian Model of Choice

I follow Rawls's example in appropriating central features of Kant's model of choice. Whereas Rawls builds a theory of justice on this model,

I build a new form of social analysis. Of course Rawls's application of the model changes it,[3] and mine does too, but in both cases the essential features of the model remain. Kant takes practical reason to consist of two parts, one empirical and the other pure. Empirical practical reason always involves an object in the world, and it is on this basis that it is defined. For example, if I hurry to a performance in order to find a good place to sit, I am employing empirical practical reason. Since interests normally involve objects (the object in which the interest rests), insofar as rationality supports the pursuit of interests it falls within empirical practical reason. In Kant's lexicon, "pure" refers to an operation of the mind that does not involve impressions from the senses. Our reason is practical when it is employed in guiding our actions. It is practical and pure when we choose an action because it accords with a principle.[4] For example, if after my partner cooks the dinner I choose to wash the dishes because that is fair, I am employing pure practical reason.

In Kant's model the imperatives of empirical practical reason are hypothetical and those of pure practical reason are categorical. A hypothetical imperative of empirical practical reason (an interest) is one we follow depending on the configuration of conditions in the world, and as a means to something else. Kant defines a categorical imperative as "one which represents an action as objectively necessary for itself, without any reference to another end."[5] Here he has in mind an imperative of morality (a principle), which has to do "not with the matter of the action and what is to result from it, but with the form and the principle from which it results."[6]

Kant's pure practical reason becomes "the reasonable" for Rawls, while empirical practical reason becomes "the rational." Rather than defining "the reasonable," Rawls specifies two of its aspects as virtues of persons. First,

> persons are reasonable . . . when, among equals say, they are ready to propose principles and standards as fair terms of cooperation and to abide by them willingly, given the assurance that others will likewise do so.[7]

Second, reasonable persons are willing

to recognize the burdens of judgment and to accept their consequences for the use of public reason in directing the legitimate exercise of political power in a constitutional regime.[8]

Here we see that the cognitive capacity that underlies the reasonable is
the sense of fairness.[9] The reasonable involves the ability to generate an
idea of what is fair in particular circumstances (necessarily a generalized
idea) and to use such an idea to guide one's behavior. The second aspect
of the reasonable, the willingness to recognize the burdens of judgment,
involves the demands that are placed on the sense of fairness in the political life of citizens in a constitutional regime. While this aspect gives an
idea of the scope of application of the sense of fairness, and it helps to
express the role of the reasonable in Rawls's idea of political liberalism, it
is not essential to the cognitive capacity per se.

The capacity that we call "the sense of fairness" is also expressed in
our senses of right, justice, legitimacy, appropriateness, and propriety.
We can think of these as a family of senses expressing the same cognitive
capacity, or as terms that describe applications of one underlying sense in
different contexts. They all operate on the basis of a logic of principles,
and their principles work by ruling some actions or states in and others
out. If an action strikes us as, say, unjust or illegitimate, we can explain
this sense by naming the principle that we take to have been violated.
We may also sometimes take an action simply because it is fair or right,
and to do so is not to act from self-interest. In such a case it would be
incorrect to say that we are acting in order to promote any particular
interest, whether ours or another's, although the action may indeed serve
particular interests. One might say that a just action promotes the interest
of justice, but this is metaphorically to personify justice.

To include the reasonable within the microfoundations of political
analysis is to take motivations associated with the sense of fairness—
those discussed above and related sentiments such as guilt, indignation,
resentment, and vengefulness—to be no less central to political decisions than motivations associated with interests and notions of the good.
This requires an analysis that can account for manifestations of these
senses in our political and social world, one in which explanations for
political phenomena may be worked out in terms of these senses and

their associated motivations. It bears noting that while Kant and Rawls hope to help us to clarify our reflections on principles, perhaps so that we might lead more ethical lives or so that a more just society might be attained, a practical political analysis must come to grips with the actual principles upon which political action is based, however unsavory these may sometimes turn out to be.

In order to model the relationship between principles and interests in cognition, however, it is useful to start from what Rawls calls "ideal theory." In *Groundwork for a Metaphysics of Morals* Kant presents *the* categorical imperative, which he thought to be the supreme principle of morality, in several formulations. A familiar one is, "act only in accordance with that maxim through which you can at the same time will that it become a universal law."[10] In his lectures on Kant, Rawls argues that the principles in *Groundwork* are those "from which a fully ideal reasonable and rational agent would act, even against all object-dependent desires, should this be necessary to respect the requirements of the moral law. Such an ideal (human) agent, although affected by natural inclinations and needs, as we must be belonging to the natural world, never follows them when doing so would violate the principles of a pure will."[11] Here Rawls sets up a framework for the relationship between categorical and hypothetical imperatives, or principles and interests. He views one function of principles as essentially negative in the following way: they exclude the pursuit of some interests. We have no moral reason not to act on those interests that the categorical imperative does not exclude.

Rational choice theory conceives of the person as possessing a set of interests, which in a given practical situation yields a schedule of preferences.[12] Given the person's beliefs about a practical situation, this schedule in turn yields an ordering of options and, possibly, the selection of a unique utility-maximizing choice. The sequence can be schematically represented as:

Figure 1.1   **Rational Choice Model**

Interests → Preferences → Choice

In the Rawlsian view of the person, however, both the reasonable and the rational, principles and interests, are sources of volition. I follow Rawls in identifying rational choice theory's interests as hypothetical imperatives.[13] Let us call them "Interests$_h$." It is also possible for the person to adopt the promotion of a principle as an interest (e.g., when one takes an interest in promoting justice).[14] Let us call such interests "Interests$_c$." However, the reasonable, as cognitively represented in our principles, also excludes from consideration some interests associated with hypothetical imperatives that we would otherwise affirm. Therefore the significance of our principles for our interests can be represented as:

Figure 1.2   **The Reasonable Guides and Restricts the Rational**

Principles $\rightarrow$ Interests$_c$, ~~Interests$_h$~~

Even for Kant's ideal agent, however, there are some hypothetical imperatives that the categorical imperative does not exclude. Also, the categorical imperative sometimes leads directly to choice, without establishing an interest.[15] Therefore the Kantian model of choice can be represented as:

Figure 1.3   **Kantian Model of Choice**

Interests$_h$

Principles $\rightarrow$ Interests$_c$, ~~Interests$_h$~~

Interests$_{h \text{ (remaining)}}$, Interests$_c$ $\rightarrow$ Preferences $\rightarrow$ Choice

Principles $\rightarrow$ Choice

The person starts with interests and principles. Principles lead to the establishment of certain interests and to the exclusion of others. The remaining interests based on hypothetical imperatives as well as those (perhaps few) interests based on categorical imperatives serve as the basis for a schedule of preferences, which (as in rational choice theory), in a particular situation yields a choice. As in rational choice theory, choice is also informed by the person's beliefs, but this can be omitted here because there is no difference between the two models in this respect. Finally, the Kantian model includes a pathway to choice that is foreign to rational choice theory, which is when a person makes a choice because it is consistent with a principle. Clearly, it is this feature of the model that distinguishes it absolutely from the rational choice model. The deliberation in the choice made in accordance with a principle is not one of maximization.[16]

In cognition, the separation of principles from interests is not always clear and distinct. I think we should take Kant as indicating that principles and interests represent distinct forms of thought or deliberation that are central to practical reason. In some cases a decision may be influenced by both principles and interests. Indeed, Kant argues that reasoning is not necessarily transparent to the reasoner, and an action that one takes to be motivated by a principle may be influenced by an interest in ways that one may not acknowledge or even comprehend.[17] The philosophical challenge has been to demonstrate that principles can be independent of interests. In the well-known scenario he uses to support this point, Kant argues that a man must admit that when threatened with execution if he fails to give false testimony against someone whom his prince would like to destroy under a plausible pretext, it would be possible for him to overcome his love of life.[18] Granting the fundamental and distinct roles of principles and interests in cognition, for the purposes of social analysis we can then relax the constraints on principles imposed by ideal theory; a husband may hold the principle that his wife should both cook and wash dishes because that is a wife's role, and a parent may hold that a child should obey the parent unquestioningly. If self-interest enters more strongly into the formulation of the principle than perhaps it should, that does not much affect how the principle functions in cognition.

Principles, Norms, Values, and Identity

A defining feature of the model I propose is that principles form the basis for social norms. A norm is nothing more than a widely shared principle. The norms that shape our culture are implicit in our language, and we learn them in childhood by hearing them asserted and by observing how they order social relations (i.e., how they are interpreted and applied). Once we have learned them, they shape our expectations for the behavior of others, and we interpret others' behavior in terms of the norms/principles we have already adopted. If we think of particular principles as important to our identity, they are specific principles that we have selected or on which our actions have been based in important life events and that we have chosen to affirm.

In ordinary speech it is not unusual for the terms "values" and "principles" to be used as synonyms. Someone may place a high value on telling the truth, and also affirm telling the truth as a principle. The concept of "values," however, as it is derived from the concept of value, occludes the distinction between principles and interests. If we hold to a principle, it translates into one of our values, and we also value what we see to be in our interest. We generally have deeper and more considered attachments to values than to interests, and to interests than to mere preferences. (A preference is the residual, so to speak, after applying our relevant principles and interests to a given case, or one of a set of options in the event of a tie.) Compared to a principle, however, a value has a more individualistic connotation. A principle has a warrant to recognition beyond that it belongs to someone. While both values and principles express identity, our links to society are more likely to be expressed by principles.

Despite their connecting us with others, we think of our principles as very much our own. When we identify a norm, however, we are acknowledging that it is held by "most people," or by a particular group. There are two ways in which we are likely to encounter a norm, from the outside and from the inside. As a visitor to a foreign country, we are likely to remark on how local norms differ from the ones with which we are familiar. "To think that the drivers stop here when they see a pedestrian in the cross walk!" or "If you don't 'tip' the customs officer here you are likely to spend several hours at the airport!" When we encounter norms from the outside, it is like learning the rules of a new game (particularly if we plan to participate for some time) and/or it is part of coming to understand a complex external phenomenon (a society, an organization).

When we encounter a norm from the inside, it is likely that we are becoming aware of its present force or significance for us or for someone else. It may be a minor realization leading to routine compliance, such as when I recall the way I should address the president of my university when I meet him in the library. Or it may involve a twinge of guilt and an effort to compensate, such as when I realize how long it has been since I extended hospitality in my circle of friends. Often our compliance with social norms is barely conscious; we know and follow many complex rules that we might not be able to articulate. Although it may strike us that they are externally imposed (e.g., by expressions of favor or disfavor), and we may find them burdensome, it is clear that cognitively we impose them on ourselves. Unless we are told what to do, it is our own conception of the norm with which we comply.

It would be a mistake to think of identity narrowly or reductionistically, given that it seems to involve our entire person as it is expressed in our various relationships, the projects we undertake, and our experience up to the present. Nevertheless, our principles make up a substantial part of our identity, perhaps the most important part. Kant has a particular idea of freedom that emphasizes not being a subject to material causality. He takes it that it is in adherence to the principles of a moral law of which we are ourselves the author that we find our freedom. One can admit the centrality of principles to identity, however, without accepting the whole cloth of Kantian ethics. Note that we have to learn many of our society's principles (norms) before we are in a secure position for identifying our own, and to a considerable extent we choose and define our principles over and against the context constituted by those of our family, communities, and society. Although we habitually comply with many principles, it is the ones we choose ourselves, those that become central to our decision making, that we often value most highly. This is not to say that we normally adopt principles *qua* principles with heroic clarity of choice. On the contrary, we often adopt them in the course of the give-and-take of a relationship, or we make a choice and then gradually adopt the principles that follow from it. The way in which principles become layered with one another and with experience over time contributes importantly to our identity.

Interests and Norms Are Widely Accepted Bases for Social Analysis

In order to demonstrate the plausibility of Rawlsian political analysis I pursue several strategies. First, in this introductory chapter, I show that the distinction between interests and norms is widely accepted as fundamental in the social sciences, with each forming the basis for different schools of social analysis. If one accepts that norms are shared principles, then principles and interests really are the uniquely correct microfoundations for social analysis, which suggests that Rawlsian analysis could unify hitherto disparate strands. Following this discussion I outline the principal arguments in the remaining chapters.

The noted organizational theorist James G. March argues that there are two approaches to analyzing decisions, one based on a logic of consequences (i.e., interests) and the other on a logic of appropriateness (i.e., norms).[19] For March these are simply two different approaches, the former associated with rational choice theory and the latter with certain traditions in sociology. Each approach is found in a systematic and established tradition of social analysis, so it seems plausible that each of their respective logics captures something that is fundamental to practical reason. Yet surely our reason is the same, regardless of the perspective from which it is analyzed. If each logic is indeed fundamental, should not social analysis be responsive to both?

As distinguished a rational choice scholar as Jon Elster finds himself similarly compelled to take recourse to two social theories. In discussing problems of bargaining and of collective action, he employs two main conceptual tools: rational choice theory and the theory of social norms. He notes that he has "come to believe that social norms provide an important kind of motivation for action that is irreducible to rationality or indeed to any other form of optimizing mechanism."[20] These conceptual tools, in turn, correspond to the two sides of "[one] of the most persisting cleavages in the social sciences . . . the opposition between . . . lines of thought conveniently associated with Adam Smith and Emile Durkheim, between *homo economicus* and *homos sociologicus*. Of these, the former is supposed to be guided by instrumental rationality, while the behavior of the latter is dictated by social norms."[21] Elster therefore adopts an eclectic view, taking it that some behaviors "are best explained by the assumption that people act rationally, whereas others can be explained by something like the theory of social norms," or else that many actions are influenced by both rationality and social norms.[22] It is certainly better to take an eclectic approach than to ignore the reasonable, but from a theoretical perspective this is unsatisfactory. We should aim for a unified theoretical apparatus based on the best available conception of social reason.

In her influential book *Governing the Commons*, Elinor Ostrom develops a model of rational choice that incorporates norms. Rational action, she argues, involves an "internal world of individual choice" consisting of four variables: expected benefits, expected costs, discount rates, and internal norms.[23] In a given situation, the first three variables, which interpret the present value of the net benefits from a choice, correspond to interests in Kant's model, and the fourth variable, internal norms, corresponds to principles. Ostrom argues that communities that develop norms involving high levels of trust and reciprocity possess social capital, and these communities are more likely to succeed in building institutions that resolve dilemmas associated with common pool resources (such as groundwater or fisheries). She reverts to a maximization model, however, to account for how people change their rules.[24]

Recall that one aspect of the reasonable involves the readiness to propose principles and standards as fair terms of cooperation and to abide by them willingly. Given Rawls's idea of the person, one can no longer imagine choice—even, or particularly, choices about rules for managing common resources—merely in terms of a process of individual maximization. Rather we see that such decisions are routinely and often sincerely based at least in part on notions of fairness. This leads to a view of social institutions that is quite different from those found in rational choice theories; the analyst must now attend to the specific nature of the principles of fairness that are employed.

This distinction between rational choice and Rawlsian views of institutions is a fundamental one, with implications not only for how social analysis should be carried out but also for how citizens in a constitutional regime should (or are likely to) regard one another. Thus, as Jack Knight develops theoretical foundations for rational choice institutionalism, he is bound to view individuals as locked in conflict. Like Elster (whom he cites), Knight sees a basic cleavage in the social sciences, although Knight places Adam Smith along with David Hume and Herbert Spencer on the side of theorists who emphasize the collective benefits produced by social institutions, while he counts Karl Marx and Max Weber as theorists who emphasize conflict in the distribution of these benefits.[25] Like Elster, Knight takes it that it is "reasonable to assume that both norms and rational calculation motivate action in different contexts."[26] Knight argues, however, that "most social outcomes are the product of conflict among actors with competing interests," and that "rational choice theory is better able to capture the strategic aspects of that social conflict."[27]

Knight takes it that social institutions are formed out of a "standard bargaining problem," a situation where "there are benefits to be gained from social actors working together, sharing resources, or coordinating their activities in some way. These actors need rules to structure their independent activities. More than one set of rules can satisfy this requirement, and the rules differ in their distributional properties. Because of this, people have conflicting preferences regarding the institutional alternatives."[28] Since there is nothing in Knight's model to ameliorate these conflicts and each resolution yields ongoing inequalities, the conflict will persist. Yet this is the very same problem that Rawls takes to define the circumstances of justice:

> There is an identity of interests since social cooperation makes possible a better life for all than any would have if each were to try to live solely by his own efforts. There is a conflict of interests since men are not indifferent as to how the greater benefits produced by their collaboration are distributed, for in order to pursue their ends they each prefer a larger to a lesser share. Thus principles are needed for choosing among the various social arrangements which determine this division of advantages and for underwriting an agreement on the proper distributive shares.[29]

While Rawls acknowledges the conflict that Knight identifies, he thinks people are capable of adopting principles that are fair as the basis for a constitutional regime. Hence, we need not perpetually regard one another as potential adversaries. We can hope to establish a society in which all benefit from one another's natural gifts and productive projects.

Although Knight initially acknowledges that norms influence choice independently from interests, he later attempts to derive norms from interests, saying he aims to build "microfoundations for the informal network of rules, conventions and norms that capture some of the principal ideas of macro-level accounts in the Weberian and Marxian tradition."[30] He argues that informal institutions arise in a decentralized manner as "a by-product of strategic conflict over substantive social outcomes,"[31] the results of which hinge on *"the fundamental relationship between resource asymmetries, on the one hand, and credibility, risk aversion, and time preference, on the other."*[32] Principles play such a major role in social relations, however, that any social theory will be substantially defined by how it accounts for them. Since rational choice theory is based on interests, it is perhaps inevitable that it eventually finds interests to provide the basis for principles.

Although a Rawlsian view does not discount the force of interests, it implies that even principles that affect large-scale social outcomes can arise from our free reason. Moreover, principles and interests have distinct roles in cognition that require different forms of analysis. Principles are significantly independent from interests, and their sources and the way they influence choice are different. They have different links with the emotions, and certain sentiments (e.g., indignation, resentment) depend directly upon principles. If principles and interests follow different logics, and they are each fundamentally involved in choice, and if neither principles nor interests can be reduced to the other, then both should be included in the microfoundations of social and political analysis.

Grounding and Demonstrating Rawlsian Political Analysis

As this brief discussion has shown that it is common for theorists to base different forms of social analysis on principles and on interests, chapter 2 grounds the concepts of principles and interests in the work of Kant and Rawls and discusses their roles in their respective philosophies. This is to give a richer understanding of the meaning of principles and interests and of their roles in cognition. Also, given Kant's and Rawls's positions in Western social thought, to see the architectonic place of principles and interests in their corpuses aids an appreciation of the importance of these concepts. Little attention in the scholarship on Rawls has been devoted to the way the reasonable and the rational are represented in the original position, so it is helpful, too, to bring this representation out.

Chapter 2 proceeds to discuss several accounts of the origins and development of principles. One set of accounts, as noted above, takes an evolutionary perspective. Interests are so clearly central to cognition in the context of evolution that the task here is to explain how principles could possibly be coequal to interests in the microfoundations of social analysis. Scientists have recently uncovered considerable evidence that some primates and other mammals possess many component parts of a sense of fairness. Expectations, a sense of status, the recognition that other animals' actions are affected by what they can see (implying some kind of appreciation that other animals can think), and other cognitive capacities of primates provided materials for what became the sense of right. In this chapter I argue, however, that the development of language deepened humans' appreciation of consequences and their understanding that other people think and feel like them. Language also made it possible for humans to make commitments. All of these capacities together provided the platform from which the sense of right emerged.

Granted evolutionary sources for the sense of right, the questions remain how the sense of right develops in each person and how we should understand the historical development of norms that embody complex political principles. These are deep and complicated questions that can only be addressed here in a limited way. In regard to the individual person's development of a sense of right, chapter 2 discusses three stages of morality, from childhood through adulthood, that Rawls presents in *A Theory of Justice*. The roles and significance of principles change as a person passes through what Rawls describes as the morality of authority and the morality of association to, in full maturity, the morality of principles. It is notable that this discussion lies at the intersection of philosophy and psychology, as Rawls links his account not only with those of Jean-Jacques Rousseau, Kant, and John Stuart Mill, but also with that of child psychologist Jean Piaget.

For another view on the development of principles in children and for an account of the historical development of norms, chapter 2 turns to Axel Honneth's notion of reciprocal recognition. A student of Jürgen Habermas and Georg Wilhelm Friedrich Hegel, Honneth's ideas are not easily encapsulated. However, he presents a threefold schema based on love, rights, and solidarity that is both psychologically and historically grounded. Although each schema is based on a different form of recognition, I argue that they can be reframed in terms of principles. Linking our discussion of the evolutionary sources of principles to Honneth's account of the transition from traditional (medieval) to postconventional morality helps to round out this account of the development of principles.

After chapter 2 fleshes out the ideas of principles and interests, chapter 3 addresses the legacy of rational choice theory. Given the widespread applications of rational choice theory, if rational choice theorists have indeed got their model of choice wrong they must have found ways to accommodate principles outside the core of their analyses. This chapter presents several examples of rational choice theorists encountering evidence of the sense of right and shows how they have accommodated it in rationality-centered accounts. Recall that microfoundations provide models of choice that are said to underlie decisions and social events that we observe in the world. There are two possible patterns: either (1) rational choice theorists will exclude patterns of reasonable choice (including resentful and vengeful choice as well as choices based on ideas of fairness or appropriateness) from their core analyses, or (2) they will incorporate them but reframe them in terms of rationality. In the first case, they will either (a) account for observed choices wrongly or (b) include reasonable choices in their discussions but fail to explain them. In the second case (such as Ostrom's model of choice described above), as they force the reasonable into models based on the rational, their models will lack a certain elegance and at some point they must inevitably impose a consequentialist framework onto deontological material (actions based on principles). In either case, they will fail to reach fully adequate explanations for social patterns based on principles.

Chapter 3 begins with the historical record of prisoner's dilemma experiments, where the behavior of human subjects apparently motivated by a sense of fairness diverged consistently from predictions informed by rational choice theory. This is an example of pattern 1a: because their models excluded reasonable choice, the experimenters explained certain behaviors that they observed wrongly. Next, the chapter considers Robert Bates's account of the Mau Mau Rebellion in Kenya and Margaret Levi's account of compliance and noncompliance with military conscription in Canada. The former is an example of 1b: Bates identifies behavior arising from resentment, which he actually explains quite well, but he fails to ground his explanation in his theory. The latter is a second example (after Ostrom's model of choice) of pattern 2: Levi builds a model including ideas based on fairness but forces it to conform to a utilitarian framework by way of the so-called dual utility hypothesis.

Besides addressing rational choice theory's limits as a positive theory, chapter 3 also discusses what we might describe as the theory's constructive limitations. From a Rawlsian perspective, social and political analysis cannot be merely positive, since to analyze the social world is also to take part in constructing it. Rational choice theory's focus on interests leads it to overemphasize conflict, and in light of the constructive role of social analysis this is deeply problematic. Moreover, although Knight argues that rational choice theory is better at explaining the strategic aspects of social conflict, this theory also fails to recognize many of the grounds for cooperation (as well as long-standing resentments that sometimes undermine it). But as vulnerable social beings in changing environments, we need an analysis that can help us to thrive collectively as well as individually. Rational choice theory's limitations in this regard constitute a serious analytic shortcoming.

Chapters 4 through 6 present different kinds of applications of Rawlsian political analysis—a program analysis, a political history, and an analysis of a social problem, in each case comparing them to neoutilitarian[33] alternatives. Changing microfoundations leads to two kinds of changes in social analysis. First, although economics and rational choice theory (in their internally consistent applications) explain social events and patterns of social change based only on interests, Rawlsian analysis explains events and patterns based also on principles. At the micro level, Rawlsian analysis can register dynamics involving the promotion of new principles—and resentments and power plays based on old ones—to which neoutilitarian analyses tend to be blind. At the macro level, the Rawlsian approach conceives of patterns of social relations and social change that are based on principles, and combinations of principles and interests, as well as patterns based mainly on interests. Since principles are internal to the person and interests have external objects (usually subject to change from various forces), analyses of social patterns based on principles tend to require longer time frames. These patterns are also prone to violent eruptions. Norms and principles often define and are expressed by orientations and frames of reference, and when these conflict they seem to be harder to negotiate than conflicting interests.

The second structural change in social analysis due to the change in microfoundations is found in its evaluative standards and frameworks. Neoutilitarian analyses, not surprisingly, involve utilitarian evaluations of one kind or another, that is, evaluations based on some idea of maximizing the satisfaction of interests (sometimes including interests in the well-being of others). In addition to the satisfaction of interests, Rawlsian analyses, by contrast, take account of changes in principles, and are oriented to autonomy and social justice. Thus, Rawlsian political analysis rests directly on Rawls's original position.

This change in evaluative standards works out differently in program analyses from the way it does in political history or problem-based analyses. Program analyses orient strategies of governments or of other agencies with public purposes. Whatever the evaluative standard, these agencies should aim to maximize their impacts subject to their resource constraints (and without violating ethical prohibitions). Rawlsian analysis adds a second spectrum of impacts to those a neoutilitarian program analysis would recognize. While neoutilitarians measure and count up gains such as in income, health, and security, Rawlsian analysts also take account of changes in principles in favor of autonomy and social justice, such as when members of a previously excluded group are empowered to participate in decisions about the allocation of public resources, or when groups build what neoutilitarians refer to as social capital. Changes in principles and in the satisfaction of interests are brought together (possibly summed) and compared to costs, and the result anchors the assessment of the program and its component parts.

A political history or a problem-based analysis, by contrast, orient an individual person or a group, contributing to that individual's or that group's members' conceptions of the social world. It responds to the general assumption of agency and potential engagement, although of course a particular individual who reads and affirms an analysis may not act specifically in response to it. Kantian and Rawlsian ethics, however, do involve an imperfect (wide) obligation to promote social justice (see chapter 2). Political histories and problem-based analyses can be understood as supporting the orientations required to fulfill this obligation.

The program analysis carried out in chapter 4 focuses on the Grameen Bank of Bangladesh, mainly in the period from the late 1980s through the 1990s. The Grameen Bank, established in the early 1980s, provides loans and other financial services to over three million poor people, predominantly rural women. Consistently reporting repayment rates around 98 percent, in the 1990s it gained worldwide acclaim as one of the few successful large-scale microfinance programs serving the poor. In this period, international financial institutions such as the World Bank were promoting so-called market friendly approaches to development in low-income countries. Microfinance programs were often established as a partial substitute for welfare programs that made handouts to the poor,[34] and the Grameen Bank was often proposed and taken as a model.

The Grameen Bank is an appropriate illustration of Rawlsian program analysis for several reasons. First, it is very well studied. Neoclassical economics provided the dominant theoretical orientation within the international development community of the 1990s, and hence the standard framework for analyzing the Grameen Bank, but there are also many rigorous studies informed by other theoretical frameworks. Second, the two central elements of the Grameen Bank's strategy—microfinance and a focus on poor women—offer good materials for substantiating neoutilitarian and Rawlsian approaches both in their causal analyses and in their impact assessments. Third, because the Grameen Bank was widely taken as a model, mistakes and omissions in the neoutilitarian analyses are particularly important. This is a good case for demonstrating the significance of adopting Rawlsian program analysis.

Economists attributed the Grameen Bank's success largely to the structure of incentives resulting from the bank's famous group-lending policy with its so-called social collateral. The bank would lend only to individuals in groups of five, with new loans to any member of the group contingent on all members repaying their loans. Under this policy each borrower has an incentive to help the members of her group to repay their loans and to discourage them from defaulting. While social collateral certainly contributed to the Grameen Bank's success, it is unlikely to have had the central importance often attributed to it. This is partly because the policy was seldom enforced, and indeed it has now been abandoned. Additionally, Rawlsian analysis reveals measures the Grameen Bank took to encourage borrowers and also bank personnel to adopt principles from the bank's ideology. These principles bound the bank's borrowers and personnel in a joint project: poverty reduction and empowerment.

Impact studies of the Grameen Bank informed by neoutilitarian assumptions conceive of the bank's impacts as consisting of a sum of utilities. These include changes in borrowers' incomes, health, nutritional standards, and other goods that enhance the welfare of the borrowers and their families. In neoclassical economic analyses, the borrower's motivation to participate in the program is thought to be a function of her (and her husband's) expected utility gains, such as in these areas.

The logic of accounting for impacts in terms of autonomy and justice is complicated, because Kant's idea of autonomy centers on acting in conformance to (freely generated principles of) the moral law. A heteronomous action, by contrast, is one that seeks to achieve an end or objective. Although material goods often are not immediately necessary for autonomy, the lack of the requirements for a secure subsistence undermines the development of autonomy. It is partly for this reason that Rawls's theory of justice places so much emphasis on securing for all citizens what he calls "primary goods." Having adequate income, education, and health care, as well as rights and liberties, creates conditions that support the development of autonomy. By this somewhat circuitous route Rawlsian analysis accounts for the importance of the program impacts that a neoutilitarian analysis recognizes, and the Rawlsian approach provides the stronger account of the importance of reducing poverty.

Rawlsian analysis also counts certain changes in principles as impacts. While some microfinance programs reinforce a paternalistic status quo, the Grameen Bank helps women who have traditionally been excluded from many household and societal decisions to participate in these decision-making processes. The development community's discourse on the Grameen Bank has given a prominent place to the bank's empowerment of women, so economists who study the bank have also recognized impacts in this area. The notion of empowerment, however, involves women changing their orientations to their families and to their society. These changes of orientation consist of changes in principles, but the neoutilitarian model does not acknowledge such changes. For this reason, economic accounts of the Grameen Bank's impacts have had a hard time dealing with empowerment. In Rawlsian analysis, however, participation in collective will formation is an important part of autonomy. Empowerment has a natural place in Rawlsian analysis, and chapter 4 reveals and explains the Grameen Bank's impacts in this area.

After chapter 4 addresses the nature, causes, and consequences of a famously successful institution, chapter 5 examines an instance of deep government failure. This chapter offers a Rawlsian analysis of the causes of poverty in Bihar, one of India's poorest, and, with a population over one hundred million, second most populous state (prior to Bihar's recent division).[35] Political history is the approach that Rawlsian analysis necessarily takes to explain the conditions of a whole society. Rawls would consider Bihar to be a burdened society, one with historical, social, and economic circumstances that impede the establishment of a public conception of justice that supports the good of all citizens.[36] In light of Bihar's increasing poverty and worsening social conditions, the Rawlsian question is Why has it not been reasonably and rationally governed? To answer this question we look to Bihar's moral traditions and to the structure of the state's political and social institutions.

From this perspective we find that competent governance in Bihar has been undermined by the unfolding politics of caste at the state and village levels in a formally democratic context. Institutions based on an assumption of legal equality were superimposed on a society segmented by caste's hierarchical principles. Governance has been undermined by the aggregation of political loyalties along caste lines and the resulting difficulty of aggregation along functional lines of material interest. For example, relations among the political elite in the twenty years following India's independence in 1947 often took the form of conflict among the upper castes, while they neglected to promote their common interests as landlords and farmers. The application of caste principles sometimes displaced a focus on productivity, such as when some upper-caste landlords' disdain for manual labor left them more likely to squeeze their tenants than to invest in improvements on the land.

Particularly divisive conflicts have arisen from caste resentments. Neoutilitarian views of the person provide no purchase on resentment, because it is not a rational emotion.[37] Resentment arises, rather, from a sense of injury due to the uncorrected or uncompensated violation of a principle. On the face of it, given Bihar's strong caste prohibitions and shockingly inegalitarian social relations, democratic practices were likely to engender resentment among dalits (former untouchables) and the lower castes as they were awakened to their democratic rights. It seems to have been the rage engendered by attempts of recently enriched middle-caste farmers to dominate those below them, however, and by subsequent dalit and lower-caste resistance, that has prompted the most violence in Bihar's countryside. For decades Bihar has suffered marauding caste armies, and the Indian public has become inured to reported massacres of men, women, and children in dalit hamlets and villages. Also, while many factors have contributed to fragmentation and corruption in Bihar's state government, the most precipitous decline in the government's competence has followed from a charismatic politician's mobilization of caste resentments.

This chapter illustrates Rawlsian analytics at both macro and micro levels. We have noted that at the macro level, because a Rawlsian analysis must account for the interacting dynamics of principles as well as interests it tends to adopt a more panoramic perspective than neoclassical economic or rational choice approaches would require. Norms tend to reproduce themselves, and conflicts in Bihar, for example, between hierarchical principles of caste and egalitarian principles of democracy, have evolved over the better part of a century. The causes of the violence in Bihar, similarly, extend deep into the state's colonial history. Examples of analysis at the micro level include investigations of caste principles, civil service appointments based on loyalty rather than merit, and cognitive-level factors influencing Bihar's widespread social violence.

Program analysis lends itself to sharp distinctions between Rawlsian and neoutilitarian approaches, but explanations for a society's social and economic conditions constitute a more diffuse field. To explain conditions in Bihar this Rawlsian analysis takes a narrative approach, establishing the context and developing the various themes that carry out and link the micro- and macro-level parts of the analysis. The analysis overall can be seen as framing Bihar's conditions in terms of social justice, but the chapter does not include a point-by-point comparison with neoutilitarian approaches. This narrative could be compared to the analytic narratives of rational choice theory. The chapter does briefly compare its recommendations for Bihar with those from neoclassical economists.

Whereas the Grameen Bank is very well studied, Bihar's conditions have not received adequate scholarly attention.[38] I became familiar with this case when I taught a class on the political economy of Tanzania and Bihar.[39] The socioeconomic problems in Bihar seemed to lend themselves to Rawlsian analysis; economic analyses of Bihar's conditions have been particularly superficial, and I could not find a good overall synthesis. Although the specific problems would of course be different, this chapter's analytic approach could be applied to countries, and the contrast in analytic method will be apparent to readers familiar with economic and rational choice country studies.

While chapter 4 takes as its point of departure a famously successful program and chapter 5 sets out to explain the extreme poverty of a particular group of people, chapter 6 aims to come to grips with a looming social problem: global climate change. Rawlsian political analysis generally provides an orientation to its subject in terms of social justice on the assumption that it can orient and partially constitute the relevant portion of a person's conception of the social world, and it is always at least implicitly forward looking. In the case of a problem like climate change that involves all living persons, its role is particularly foundational. Rawlsian analysis aims to offer a framework from which a person can approach his or her activities that involve the production of greenhouse gasses and that can orient political reform and institutional construction to respond to climate change. It provides a first answer to the questions What is the problem of climate change? and What should be done about it?

Since Rawlsian analysis shares the neoutilitarian focus on interests, one analytic source for approaching climate change is the theories of externalities and common pool resources already well developed by economists and rational choice theorists. Global warming involves costs of productive activities that producers may not have to bear and that are imposed on others besides those who consume the goods produced. It also involves the atmosphere surrounding the earth (and other goods of nature such as the oceans) as a global commons. Like herdsmen who share a pasture, we all share the atmosphere, so the greenhouse gasses that each person contributes can collectively undermine its value for everyone. While economists approach the resulting regulatory problem by taking existing institutions for granted and applying values based on the concept of utility, the Rawlsian approach starts from the original position and applies values based largely on primary goods. Given the nature of the causes of climate change and the roles of these causes in our productive and political systems, Rawlsian analysis assumes that we need significant institutional reform to reach a just solution. It takes the original position to be the appropriate starting point for considering these reforms, a vantage point from which threats to the livelihoods of certain groups in the present and the future take on particular importance.

Chapter 6 develops Rawlsian analysis of climate change in contrast to analyses by economists Nicholas Stern and William Nordhaus. They both aim to balance marginal costs and benefits, but Nordhaus, following growth economics, arrives at a much higher target for restraining global warming, a temperature rise of about 3.5°C compared to preindustrial times. He discounts harms to future generations quite heavily, but Stern counts future harms the same as current ones, so he arrives at a target range of 2°C to 2.8°C. Both Nordhaus and Stern count up harms in economic terms based on the price system, but Rawlsian analysis aims to defend the livelihoods of those most threatened by climate change (while minimizing the compromise to economic growth). Rawlsian analysis also articulates the challenge of responding to climate change as one of changing principles and institutions. Nordhaus and Stern discuss strategies for reaching targets, but Rawlsian analysis identifies institutional barriers and what it would take to overcome them. Hence, agents in the original position accept a 2°C target for a maximum rise in temperatures, preferring a lower target but finding it institutionally implausible.

The Rawlsian approach analyzes the temperature target in terms of justice between generations. It analyzes the division of rights and responsibilities for reducing greenhouse gas emissions and for addressing harms caused by climate change in terms of justice between the rich and the poor (taking account of different contributions to causing climate change). In this context the international system of nation-states presents significant barriers to a just resolution. Nordhaus and Stern identify carbon taxes as efficient means to reduce greenhouse gas emissions, and Rawlsian analysis concurs. Given the association between greenhouse gas emissions and a country's long-term economic prospects, however, the Rawlsian approach also aims for equal average per capita emissions on an international basis by 2050. Climate change turns out to be (among other things) a mechanism by which wealthy individuals impose harms on poor individuals, and averting and ameliorating these harms is a matter of justice. Chapter 6 explores the institutional barriers to a just solution and indicates directions for reforms, in particular, (1) political constraints on the United States achieving adequate reductions in its greenhouse gas emissions and adequate contributions to developing countries' adaptation costs, and (2) institutional constraints on the effective use of adaptation and transition funds in developing countries.

Political constraints can be understood partly through political history. Chapter 6 discusses, for example, how in the United States, Republican governments and the Senate have usually blocked significant responses to climate change. The substantial and costly changes needed for an adequate response will need widespread public support, however—significantly more than has been demonstrated at this writing. Chapter 6 reflects briefly on some of the factors involved in generating and restraining such public support. The greatest challenge in the United States is probably to reduce greenhouse gas emissions. Even if the United States and other wealthy countries did provide adequate funds for poor countries to adapt to harms from climate change and to support transitions to low-carbon development pathways, however, at present these funds could not be used cost effectively. Adaptation and transition present technical and political challenges largely due to the difficulty vulnerable populations have in securing their interests in the public forum. Given that such difficulties cannot be overcome in the short run, I propose institutional innovations to defend the interests of vulnerable populations. This involves new ways to hold implementing agencies accountable for employing adaptation resources cost-effectively. Poor country governments may be no better positioned to use transition funds effectively than adaptation funds, but agents in the original position would nevertheless place primary responsibility for transitions to low carbon economies on poor-country governments while responsibility for supporting adaptation to climate change would be more widely shared.

Chapter 7 concludes the book by discussing some of the implications of the Kantian model of practical reason for the social sciences. This model views the practice of social science as constructing the social world, so although it must conform to empirical standards, it is inherently engaged in the ethical domain. Political economy and mainstream comparative politics already analyze macrodynamics of principles as well as interests, but they are likely to be enriched by building on microfoundations that heretofore have only been implicit. Also, their leading practitioners have often understood their task as merely empirical and articulated their questions in a critical dialogue with neoclassical economics (and sometimes with rational choice theory). The touchstone for social analysis as an ethical practice, however, is the concept of social justice; social analysis can only fulfill its constructive potential when it is grounded in this idea. Chapter 7 assesses the consequences of this shift in relation to important works by Robert Wade and Atul Kohli.

The Cognition of Principles and the Role of Rawlsian Political Analysis

This chapter aims to secure the place of principles as coequal with interests in the microfoundations of political analysis, and to consider how this recasts the role of political analysis. In order to do these things, it first shows how the proposed political analysis is grounded in the work of Kant and of Rawls and explains how that analysis builds on Rawls's project. Although I noted above that Kant and Rawls are engaged in ideal theory, given the Kantian moral psychology as a foundation, a certain applied analysis becomes both necessary and possible. In order to explore our cognition of principles and the relation of the reasonable to the rational and to other forms of cognition, this chapter considers the role of principles in Kant's and Rawls's philosophies. While Rawls asserts that "justice as fairness" (his conception of social justice) does not rely on Kantian metaphysics,[1] the Kantian moral psychology is at the core of Rawls's constructive procedure. Showing how the reasonable and the rational are represented in the original position and their role in Rawls's idea of political liberalism at once clarifies the concepts of principles and interests and also helps us to see what is required from what I am calling "Rawlsian analysis."

In order to move from ideal theory to political analysis we need to grasp a more prosaic conception of principles than one might normally associate with Kant or Rawls. For this purpose, and also to establish principles as coequal with interests, we consider three accounts of the sources and development of principles; the first is from Rawls, the second is from Honneth, and the third is my own account of possible origins of principles in human evolution. Kant and Rawls work with ideological frameworks that include theistic worldviews, although Rawls does not adopt such a view himself and Kant generally keeps the working area of his philosophy free from deistic considerations.[2] Contemporary common sense, however, is beginning to take evolution more or less for granted. While an evolutionary perspective might appear to suggest that interests are more fundamental than principles, I show how the independence of principles from interests can be consistent with such a perspective.

The sparest justification for a Rawlsian political analysis can be drawn from basic features of Kant's ontology and Rawls's ethics. Given that (1) social relations are constructed from principles and interests and (2) we have an obligation to promote social justice, the need for such an analysis becomes apparent. We can link this spare account with Rawls's project as follows. Rawls views the importance of justice as given.[3] He builds on the contractarian tradition, drawing from John Locke, Rousseau, and Kant, to provide an alternative conception of social justice to those of the prevailing utilitarian tradition.[4] His theory is loosely grounded in history, in that it appeals to what he refers to as "our" considered judgments and political traditions, and he explains a general sequence of implementation (i.e., by way of a constitutional convention),[5] but he does not address how his theory might be adopted, for example, by any particular society.

I would like to emphasize that achieving a society that is just in Rawlsian terms is contingent and perhaps unlikely. Social justice is, after all, the ultimate public good (to borrow from economic theory). As the obligation of all, it is the responsibility of none, and steps to building a just society offend powerful interests. Rawls offers his theory of justice as cohering with and helping to order our considered judgments, but whether it does so depends on the principles that constitute a particular person's political identity. The analysis I propose takes the question of what principles actually constitute our political identities to be an empirical one.

Kant and the Sense of Right

Kant regarded his own philosophy as having solved, once and for all, many long-standing problems in ontology, epistemology, and ethics. A central feature of his solutions in all three areas is the distinction between things in themselves and things as objects of experience, and the concepts from Kant on which Rawls bases the reasonable and the rational employ this distinction in Kant's ethics. The distinction initially arises in Kant's first great book, the *Critique of Pure Reason*, in which he addresses what he calls "theoretical reason," the reason that supports the kind of knowledge found in the natural sciences. According to Kant we can gain knowledge of things in the world only through features revealed by our senses, and it is on this basis that things become objects of experience. There is no way for us to know what things in themselves might be like separate from our sensory experience. Our knowledge of things in the world, however, is based not only on sensory experience but also on how our minds interpret evidence from the senses. For instance, Kant takes it that we bring senses of space and time and the concept of causation to experience. Spatial and temporal relations and notions of cause and effect are forms of order imposed on experience by our minds.

When it comes to objects in the world, the idea of a "thing in itself" expresses an absolutely impenetrable barrier. There is just no way for us to know what a thing in itself might be like. In Kant's view, though, when it comes to our own persons, we can and do have knowledge of ourselves, of our own personalities, distinct from the persons we are as belonging to the world of sense. As it turns out in Kant's philosophy, although he does not express it in these terms, our personalities as "things in ourselves" are constituted by principles,[6] while our natures as persons belonging to the world of sense are constituted largely by interests. Theoretical reason involves our knowledge of external objects; practical reason involves how we decide what to do. As Rawls puts it, "practical reason is concerned with the production of objects according to a conception of those objects— for example, the conception of a just constitutional regime taken as the aim of political endeavor—while theoretical reason is concerned with the knowledge of given objects."[7] And just as our knowledge of things in the world is conditioned by our notions of causation, space, and time, so our experience of practical situations is conditioned by our principles (but also, in the case of practical reason, by our interests).

As noted in chapter 1, practical reason, according to Kant, consists of two parts—one pure, one empirical—and it is in the course of working out this ontological distinction that he develops the main concepts that make up his ethics. Pure reason, whether practical or theoretical, involves concepts or constructs we bring to experience from our own minds; empirical reason involves the activity of and evidence from the senses. As persons belonging to the world of sense, we find ourselves with natural inclinations and desires, and it is empirical practical reason that is moved by these. Pure practical reason, however, has the capacity to establish principles that can guide action without any admixture of an empirical motive, and this describes the central dynamic in Kant's ethics. In Kant's view we should always act in a manner that fulfills or at least that is not inconsistent with our duty, and we know our duty, in the first instance, by the principles that constitute our pure practical reason.

Two central and closely related concepts in Kant's ethics—the categorical imperative and autonomy—are based on the distinction between pure and empirical practical reason.[8] He takes it that every person naturally has a sense of duty, but that philosophy can sharpen or guide this sense and defend it from being undermined by various forms of skepticism. The form of the imperatives that constitute the sense of duty, or morality generally, is categorical, such that, a "categorical imperative would be that one which represented an action as objectively necessary for itself, without any reference to another end."[9] And also, "It has to do not with the matter of the action and what is to result from it, but with the form and the principle from which it results; and what is essentially good about it consists in the disposition, whatever the results may be."[10] Kant offers a universal formula for morality, *the* categorical imperative, which in one statement reads, "*Act only in accordance with that maxim through which you can at the same time will that it become a universal law.*"[11] Thus when we are considering an action, we are to ask if we could affirm everyone in similar circumstances acting according to the same maxim or principle. Note that in establishing principles based on the categorical imperative, we of course take account of consequences, and part of comprehending (and framing) a situation in which we might apply such principles is to appreciate the consequences of different courses of action. To apply the categorical imperative is to match a principle to a case. Once we see that the situation calls for a particular maxim, say, of fairness, we simply apply it, at this point without regard to consequences.

The categorical imperative falls within pure (practical) reason because both the establishment and application of its principles abstract from sensory impulses. By applying principles, we impose an order on the social world that we ourselves have chosen, separate from imperatives arising from our nature as embodied beings. Our natural desires are included in the information involved in forming principles, but since we are choosing as though for a universal law we account for the natural desires of others on an equal footing with our own.

While the moral quality of principles that apply the categorical imperative arises from their suitability for universal application, their cognitive character arises largely from their independence from our nature as persons belonging to the world of sense. These two features—moral quality and cognitive character—together establish the suitability of principles as the basis for autonomy, which then becomes the central ideal for the person in Kantian ethics.

> If the will seeks that which should determine it *anywhere else* than in the suitability of its maxims for its own universal legislation, hence if it, insofar as it advances beyond itself, seeks the law in the constitution of any of its objects, then *heteronomy* always comes out of this. Then the will does not give itself the law but the object through its relation to the will gives the law to it. Through this relation, whether it rests now on inclination or on representations of reason, only hypothetical imperatives are possible: "I ought to do something *because I will something else.*" By contrast, the moral, hence categorical imperative says: "I ought to act thus-and-so even if I did not will anything else."[12]

According to Kant our dignity as persons is due to our capacity to choose and to act from principles consistent with the categorical imperative, and in doing so we establish autonomy from our nature as sensible beings. He takes it that humans, like all embodied or sensible beings, necessarily desire happiness, such as from the satisfaction of interests, yet the principle of one's own happiness is "most reprehensible."[13]

The absolutely good will, whose principle must be a categorical imperative, will therefore, undetermined in regard to all objects, contain merely the *form of volition* in general, and indeed as autonomy, i.e., the suitability of the maxim of every good will to make itself into a universal law is itself the sole law that the will of every rational being imposes on itself, without grounding it on any incentive or interest in it.[14]

This contrasts markedly with utilitarianism, which would orient morality to maximizing the good, largely in the satisfaction of interests (and which Kant critiques in its early form represented by Hume). Utility maximization as understood in economics and rational choice theory is often heteronomous.

Kant uses the terms "principles" and "interests" somewhat differently from my use of them here. He does not make the point that our sense of right is constituted by principles that represent duty and morality for us, but I argue this is evidently the case. Rawls (whom I follow in this matter) is right to associate the rational, which is constituted by interests, with hypothetical imperatives and empirical practical reason.[15] Also, Kant's discussions of political principles generally take some form of monarchy more or less for granted, and distributive justice does not appear in his enumeration of duties. He asserts an obligation of beneficence but not to promote social justice.[16] Nevertheless, Kant is the classical source for the idea expressed in shorthand as "the right has priority over the good," and so heavily does Rawls draw on Kant (although they are separated by almost two centuries) that it is hardly an overstatement to call Rawls's work an extension of Kant's.

The Reasonable and the Rational in Rawls's Theories of Justice and Political Liberalism

While Kant's ethics are largely oriented to providing a secure account of and grounding for morality, Rawls aims to provide an account of social justice. He argues that the social contract tradition, and Kant in particular, provides a better basis for this task than either the utilitarian tradition, which dominated Anglo-American political philosophy before his *Theory of Justice*, or the other established alternatives. While utilitarians aim to maximize happiness or "the good," perhaps as the satisfaction of rational desire, contractarians take it that we should adopt principles of justice that would be selected in some initial situation of equality. Rawls develops the original position to characterize such a situation, revising the categorical imperative as it applies to the problem of social justice. The original position is to carry the contract doctrine to a higher level of generality and to separate it from features of earlier approaches that were widely taken to be fatal weaknesses.[17]

Principles of justice provide a basis for describing institutions that would constitute a just society, and "laws and institutions no matter how efficient and well-arranged must be reformed or abolished if they are unjust."[18] Once one takes the problem of injustice seriously it is clear that the obligation to beneficence translates into an obligation to promote social justice, and Rawls takes this obligation for granted,[19] although how it applies to each individual depends on her own circumstances and opportunities. To identify what should count as a just law or institution in a modern society, however, in the context of multiple and competing claims, can be quite difficult. Yet it is straightforward that just laws and institutions must be based on just principles.[20] Rawls constructs the original position to serve as a framework for identifying such principles, and he does this by applying the reasonable and the rational to the problem of social justice.

Using Rawls's well-known concepts as shorthand, we can say that the reasonable is applied through the veil of ignorance and the rational through the idea of primary goods. In the original position, imaginary agents representing us as citizens are to choose the principles of justice that will then serve as the basis for society's constitution, laws, and institutions. These agents' deliberations take place, however, behind a veil of ignorance, in that although they know that their society is reasonably well off, they do not know which particular individual they represent—and not the person's wealth or income, gender, ethnicity, or natural talents, nor the person's particular aspirations or plan of life.[21] The idea is that when you and I select principles of justice, it would lead to bias if we took factors such as these into account. Through the veil of ignorance the original position excludes all information that would permit any kind of heteronomy in the selection of principles of justice, so the principles selected will be reasonable.

On what basis, then, are agents in the original position to make their decision? They are to select the principles of justice that secure the best combination of primary goods for the person they represent, whoever this person turns out to be. They assume that this person has some plan of life and they select the principles that lead to the best goods to support it, including such goods as income, education, and health care; freedoms of belief, speech, and association; and opportunities to fill society's various positions of responsibility.[22] In securing such primary goods, the original position represents the rational, since justice requires society to provide the wherewithal for each person to secure her interests.

A central argument in *A Theory of Justice* is that agents in the original position would select the following two principles of justice (Rawls's) rather than the principle to maximize the total or average utility of the people they represent.

1.   Each person is to have an equal right to the most extensive total system of equal basic liberties compatible with a similar system of liberty for all.
2.   Social and economic inequalities are to be arranged so that they are both:
     a.   to the greatest benefit of the least advantaged, consistent with the just savings principle, and
     b.   attached to offices and positions open to all under conditions of fair equality of opportunity.[23]

These principles provide a secure basis for each person to develop and pursue a life plan, while under utilitarian principles there is always the danger that a lesser utility for some may be justified by a greater utility for others.

Thus, the original position provides a handy means of representing the reasonable and the rational as they apply to the problem of selecting principles of justice. Moreover, when we act on principles selected in this way, we are acting autonomously. We could clearly will that such principles should become universal laws (if freely chosen by citizens of reasonably well-off societies), and by acting on them we express and consolidate our nature as free and equal rational beings alongside other citizens.

This brief summary of Rawls's arguments is drawn from *A Theory of Justice*. I emphasize Rawls's continuity with Kant and the centrality of the reasonable and the rational for both philosophers. In the years following the publication of *Theory*, however, Rawls found that he needed to distance himself from Kant in a particular way, and this is a central purpose for his second great book, *Political Liberalism*. It became apparent to Rawls that *Theory* expresses, or is grounded in, what he comes to call a "Kantian comprehensive doctrine," and that this undermined the chances that his two principles would be adopted as a basis for political reform. The problem is that one normally finds in contemporary democracies several competing comprehensive doctrines, and indeed this is a natural consequence of sustained freedom of thought in a modern democratic society. Alongside the comprehensive liberalisms of Kant and Mill, one is likely to find Protestant, Catholic, Muslim, Jewish, Hindu and/or other religious doctrines, as well as some worldviews that do not rest on any comprehensive philosophical or religious doctrine, and some of their various adherents are unlikely to accept Kant's autonomy (or Mill's individualism, on the side of utilitarianism) as central values. Hence, in *Political Liberalism* Rawls presents his two principles of justice as the object of an overlapping consensus among adherents to competing—but reasonable—comprehensive doctrines.

After this development in Rawls's thought, the original position still represents the reasonable and the rational as applied to the problem of selecting principles of justice, but now in a circumscribed way. Also, now the idea that to act from principles chosen in the original position is to act autonomously no longer carries the weight that it did in *Theory*. In *Political Liberalism*, Rawls distinguishes between rational autonomy, full autonomy, and ethical autonomy, and he argues that selecting principles of justice from the original position expresses rational and full autonomy. Adherents to religious and to non-Kantian philosophical comprehensive doctrines and to other worldviews are likely to have their own central values in the place Kant reserves for (what Rawls now calls) ethical autonomy, but it is nevertheless decisive that Rawls's principles of justice provide reliable support for them to advance their own notions of the good.

Not all comprehensive doctrines are reasonable, of course. Some promote coercive proselytizing and would use state power to impose their own views on others, and some doctrines are simply mad. Adherents to reasonable doctrines seek to deal fairly with adherents to other doctrines, so they want society's laws and institutions to be based on reasons all can support. In *Political Liberalism,* Rawls emphasizes the role of the original position as the basis for an overlapping political consensus among adherents to reasonable but competing comprehensive doctrines. While each person's idea of the good (and therefore what is rational for her) may be specified in terms of her own comprehensive doctrine, Rawls's two principles of justice provide a reasonable basis for political institutions that will support her liberty and her capacity to advance her idea of the good, whatever it turns out to be. Adherents to reasonable comprehensive doctrines adopt the reasonable constraints imposed by the original position to establish laws that all reasonable people can support.

A central difference between the systems of ideas in *Theory* and *Political Liberalism* is expressed in the distinction in the latter work between rational and full autonomy on one side and ethical autonomy on the other. In *Political Liberalism,* Rawls argues that the original position models citizens' rational and full autonomy and in doing so provides a particular way for citizens to think of themselves as free and equal. Rational autonomy, according to Rawls, is shown in persons "exercising their capacity to form, to revise, and to pursue a conception of the good . . . to deliberate in accordance with it . . . [and] to enter into agreement with others [to support it],"[24] and full autonomy is demonstrated when citizens not only comply with principles of justice but also act from these principles as just.[25] In the original position there is no external standard, such as God's law or a historically established constitution, for determining what is just. The parties themselves have to decide what principles are best, considering what is most likely to advance the good of the citizens they represent. Moreover, the parties recognize that citizens possess a reasonable and a rational capacity, a sense of justice and an idea of the good, and they (the parties) aim to select principles that will support the complete development and full exercise of these capacities. In these ways the original position models citizens' rational autonomy.

Rawls argues that the original position models full autonomy through its structure, that is, with the parties deliberating behind a veil of ignorance so they are fairly situated to select principles for basic laws and institutions. The structure of the original position also fixes what are to count as appropriate reasons for selecting principles of justice and requires that (if possible) the parties should select principles "that may be stable, given the fact of reasonable pluralism; and hence . . . that can be the focus of an overlapping consensus of reasonable doctrines."[26] By establishing conditions in which its parties act justly the original position models the full autonomy of citizens in society.

Note, however, that full autonomy for citizens, as opposed to that modeled by the original position, "is realized in public life by affirming the political principles of justice and enjoying the protections of the basic rights and liberties; it is also realized by participating in society's public affairs and sharing in its collective self-determination over time."[27] In *Political Liberalism,* Rawls emphasizes the distinction between full autonomy and ethical autonomy, "which may apply to the whole of life, both social and individual, as expressed by the comprehensive liberalisms of Kant and Mill."[28] *Political Liberalism* "affirms political autonomy for all but leaves the weight of ethical autonomy to be decided by citizens severally in light of their comprehensive doctrines."[29]

As noted above, the way rational and full autonomy are modeled in the original position supports citizens in thinking of themselves as free and equal. We have seen that citizens appreciate that they are recognized, in the device of representation for selecting principles of justice, "as having the moral power to form, to revise, and rationally to pursue a conception of the good,"[30] and that the parties make it their priority to support all citizens in securing the requisite primary goods. They see that all are recognized equally as having reasonable and rational powers "and other capacities that enable us to be normal and fully cooperating members of society[, and that] all who meet this condition have the same basic rights, liberties, and opportunities, and the same protections of the principles of justice."[31] Hence, citizens see that to live in a society with laws and institutions based on principles selected in the original position would support their self-respect, and that it is a worthy endeavor to work toward establishing such a society.

In order to clarify Rawls's arguments it may be helpful to respond to some challenges to them from Amartya Sen.[32] Rawls's aim in *Theory* and *Political Liberalism* is to identify a few basic principles to guide the design of the main social institutions in reasonably well-off states, aiming to improve on those of the most prominent alternatives, utilitarianism and perhaps perfectionism. He holds that the original position defines the appropriate perspective from which to select such principles, and that from this perspective his two principles would be chosen. Sen, however, is not convinced that there would be any unique choice in the original position. "There are genuinely plural, and sometimes conflicting, general concerns that bear on our understanding of justice. They need not differ in the convenient way—convenient for choice, that is—that only one such set of principles really incorporates impartiality and fairness, while the others do not."[33] Sen argues, in fact, against all "transcendental" approaches that propose particular principles to uniquely define an ideally just society. Rather, he argues, our plural ideas of justice often permit the identification of unambiguous improvements over existing states of affairs, and theories of justice should support just such incremental improvements.[34]

To respond to Sen we need to rehearse the justification for Rawls's two principles and the boundaries to what Rawls expects from them. Given that each of us has a set of interests—a conception of the good, and, in due course, a rational plan of life to achieve it—we need to acknowledge our vulnerability. Casual perusal of current affairs is sufficient to see how easily and often hopes are dashed by poverty, authoritarian government, or domination by powerful economic interests or by ethnic or religious factions. The defense of liberty and of economic opportunity found in Rawls's principles provides critical guarantees, perhaps the best general guarantees society can offer, that each person will have the opportunity to develop and carry out his or her life plan. In a polity dominated by organized interests, the radical demand of the original position is to set aside our individual and group interests when it comes to political fundamentals and to develop a political program based on this conception of our common good, in order that a just society should be built and sustained. Rawls's two principles are favored in the original position because they defend each person's autonomy more robustly than do those of the alternative traditions, and in a manner that adherents to any reasonable comprehensive doctrine have reason to support.

Sen argues that there are many unbiased and impartial principles, maxims consistent with Kant's categorical imperative, that "bear on our understanding of justice," but he does not propose any specific principles for the basic structure of society that agents in the original position would prefer to Rawls's.[35] He argues that the priority Rawls gives to "the most extensive total system of equal basic liberties" over economic gains, and to economic gains for the least well-off over gains to others, is extreme,[36] but he does not show how unmanageable conflicts would arise in plausible arrangements based on these principles.

As noted above, in *Theory* and *Political Liberalism* Rawls aims to develop principles for designing the basic structure of reasonably well-off, contemporary societies. He focuses on principles for individual countries because the nation-state is the primary effective political unit at the present time and for the foreseeable future. The broad parameters of social policy, such as the overall design of the tax scheme, welfare, and social security arrangements, and the regulatory regime for business are established mainly at the national level. This is why the original position is framed initially (in these books) at the national level. Rawls reframes the original position in *The Law of Peoples* to develop principles for international relations, and it can be reframed further based on the moral structure of particular problems, such as climate change (see chapter 6 for discussions of both frames).

Sen argues that Rawls's principles of justice, and the process through which they are derived, does not take into account concerns or perspectives from the rest of the world, or possible adverse effects on the rest of the world.[37] He argues further that the original position is oriented to securing mutual advantage, and he questions "whether advantage-seeking, in either a direct or indirect form, provides the only robust basis of reasonable behaviour in society. A related question is whether mutual benefit and reciprocity must be the foundation of all political reasonableness."[38] But Rawls's two principles of justice are not intended to answer all questions of justice. Sen does not indicate how promoting equal liberties, the interests of the least well-off, or fair equality of opportunity hurts people in other countries,[39] or how these principles express "parochial values."[40] Given that we are vulnerable beings with interests, it is important that principles for the basic structure of society should take into account requirements for securing interests; but these principles do not express a complete social ethics. Rawlsian political analysis, as the present book proposes, is also far short of a complete social ethics, but it should help to address many of the very important matters of incremental social justice that Sen raises.

The Kantian and Rawlsian arguments I have described support the thesis of the present book in several ways. First, of course, Kant's idea of practical reason consisting of pure and empirical forms—moral powers that Rawls reformulates as the reasonable and the rational—is the starting point for Rawlsian political analysis, the form of social analysis this book aims to launch. Second, it is evident from the categorical imperative and its role in Kant's ethics that principles can contribute to practical decisions independently from interests. This is also implied by the role the veil of ignorance plays in selecting principles of justice, and it is explicit in the idea of full autonomy.

Third, the way Rawls develops and supports his two principles of justice and their roles in his theory of justice and in his conception of political liberalism help to clarify the dynamics of principles in cognition. We sometimes arrive at principles after long and careful deliberation, but once we affirm them, they contribute to constituting our sense of right. Indeed, careful deliberation can deepen the grounding of a principle in one's cognition. Principles are linked together with our conception of our social world—in fact, they help constitute it—and studying *A Theory of Justice* or *Political Liberalism* (or political philosophy generally) can deepen our understanding of social dynamics. Studying political philosophy can alter the way we perceive and interpret information about our social world, such as about tax policies or a politician's program proposals. If one were to choose to promote Rawlsian justice, adopting it as an interest, one would incorporate his reasoning (as one understands it) in one's strategic perspective alongside other forms of strategic reasoning.

And fourth, Rawls presents his ideas about social justice in part to support reforms toward a more just society. Once we see that social institutions are constituted by principles and interests, it becomes apparent that the kind of analysis proposed here is needed to guide such reforms.

Three Accounts of the Origins of Principles

According to Kant and Rawls, we choose our principles, and moral philosophy can inform this choice. This does not imply, of course, that we can simply choose whatever principles we like, adopting new ones when it suits our fancy, much less that social institutions can be formed at will to fit some ideal. Although political analysis informed by a Rawlsian view of the person imagines social institutions and individual identities as constructed from principles, it takes it that principles are established in the course of solving particular practical problems. Hence, an institution is a representation of its history.

If principles did not exhibit a high degree of continuity, our social world would be chaotic and political analysis impossible. Principles are not separate from our conception of our social relations—they constitute this conception. Although it is important to our freedom that we conceive of principles as subject to change, at any point in time they constitute part of our practical reality, alongside (so to speak) our physical reality. It may even be that principles are invoked in our conception of objects that we consider part of our physical reality, such as things we own (as it is commonly noted that property relations are relations among persons in reference to things).

Principles may be discovered at any time, and they are subject to rediscovery and to change. Since particular practical contexts and complex verbal formulae are often involved in the establishment of principles, it should come as no surprise that principles can be subtly altered as they are rehearsed or rediscovered. This is another reason for which political analysis is never merely an empirical exercise but always also a moral one: the description and the establishment of principles cannot be completely separated.

For more than fifty years, however, rational choice theorists have constructed political analyses that highlight the dynamics of interests to the exclusion of the dynamics of principles. It is remarkable that principles can cause us to abjure interests that we would otherwise pursue—or cause us not to perceive an interest at all—and this needs to be explained. Since we have started from the perspective of ideal theory, as we move on and consider the mechanics of an applied Rawlsian analysis, we need to acknowledge our banal familiarity with nonideal principles in our actual social world. On one hand, principles that are inconsistent with the categorical imperative and that would not be affirmed in the original position contribute to the constitution of many of our solutions to practical problems. On the other hand, the cognitive and social dynamics of these flawed principles are similar to those of the more legitimate sort. Together they constitute our conceptions of right, separately from our interests and our conceptions of the good.

In due course, we should hope to develop unified and consistent political and psychological conceptions of the origins, development, and dynamics of principles, but the present account of the possibility of Rawlsian political analysis falls far short of this ideal. The first source for such a conception is Rawls's own account of the individual's development of principles beginning in childhood. In working out this account, Rawls's aim, however, is to explain the possible form of a society based on his principles of justice, the well-ordered society of justice as fairness, and to consider the prospects for its stability. His account describes, if not a best-case scenario, at least a very good scenario, and it tends to emphasize the conscious choice of principles. Rawls does, however, acknowledge the possibility of inadequate parenting, and this and his brief historical account of the development of religious toleration offer insight into his view of the social dynamics of nonideal principles.

Another, more historically grounded, account of the development of principles is found in Honneth's analysis of the moral grammar of social conflicts in *The Struggle for Recognition*. Honneth does not explain principles per se, but rather the development of certain forms and moral content of interpersonal recognition, and its contribution to the social and cognitive grounds for self-respect. In his psychologically nuanced model, however, when the person comes to accord herself a certain status, she also accords it to other people, and this leads her to adopt certain principles for her relations with others. Honneth offers an account of the self-respect arising from gains in civil, political, and social rights from the eighteenth through the twentieth centuries, and although he draws largely on Hegel, he is sensitive to Kantian aspects of questions of rights. His account is more socially embedded than Rawls's, and it helps us to see more clearly how principles may be adopted gradually and inconsistently in the flow of social relations.

My own account of the origins of principles in human prehistory is concerned with how we understand the sense of right and its relation to the sense of the good. I am particularly interested in how principles constitute our social world, and I argue that it is plausible that the cognitive origins of the sense of right may be found in our cognition of the material world. If this is true, it helps to account for the independence of principles and interests in cognition and for the appropriateness of their parity in microfoundations for political analysis.

Rawls's Three Stages of Morality

In the well-ordered society of justice as fairness, Rawls imagines the development of morality taking place through three stages, which he designates as the morality of authority, of association, and of principles. The morality of authority describes the child's moral development, while those of association and of principles describe a progression as the individual grows in experience and understanding. Rawls also posits three psychological laws, one for each form of morality, that explain how these forms are possible. He acknowledges that this sequence is schematic and incomplete. He draws from what he calls a rationalist tradition of thought, illustrated by Rousseau, Kant, Mill, and Piaget, that sees moral learning not as a matter of supplying missing motives but as one of "the free development of our innate intellectual and emotional capacities according to their natural bent."[41]

In the morality of authority, the child accepts the injunctions of parents whom she loves and trusts. Lacking her own standards of criticism, since she is not in a position to reject precepts on rational grounds, she accepts her parents' judgments of her, and she is inclined to judge herself as they do when she violates their injunctions. Nevertheless, her desires exceed the boundaries of what is permitted; she has no reason to do as she is told, because their instructions are, from her perspective, arbitrary. Yet if she does love and trust her parents, then once she has "given in to temptation," she is disposed to share their attitude toward her "misdemeanors." She will be inclined to confess her transgressions and to seek reconciliation. Rawls takes it that "in these various inclinations are manifested the feelings of (authority) guilt."[42] The process depends on her accepting the principles in her parents' instructions and seeing how to apply them to the case at hand. The strength of a principle lies in the verbal formula itself (her representation of its words and meaning) and in her associating it with the parent(s). The set of instructions yields a map of actions that are forbidden, permitted, and required. And the psychological law upon which all this depends, according to Rawls, is that the child comes to love the parents only if they manifestly love her first, by way of demonstrating and expressing concern for her welfare.[43]

Rawls emphasizes that for the morality of authority to be accepted, parents must not only enunciate clear, intelligible, and justifiable rules adapted to the child's level of comprehension, but also set out the reasons as far as they can be understood, and follow the rules insofar as the rules apply to them. He suggests that moral development fails to take place to the extent that these conditions are absent, and especially "if parental injunctions are not only harsh and unjustified, but enforced by punitive and even physical sanctions."[44] Then the child might simply obey out of fear. We can note also that the justifiable reasons the parents give and the consistent examples they set contribute to the child's knowledge of the world, so moral and empirical learning take place together. If such reasons are not given, or such examples not set, the occasion for this kind of learning is absent.[45]

Rawls's second stage of morality, the morality of association,[46] refers to standards and ideals associated with role positions within small and large groups up to the society as a whole. Let's assume that the morality of authority includes basic principles of fairness in relations with family and playmates (a point Rawls does not address). The morality of association involves the differentiation of roles required to achieve the functional ends of specialized groups. Each role is constituted by principles that can be conceived of as fair (or not) in relation to the distribution of rights and duties within the group, while the justice of the entire arrangement can be confirmed only in relation to the group's position in the broader society. Established authorities within the group, such as managers of a business or leaders on a team or in a club, explain the actions and virtues associated with a role, or at least they convey them through expressions of approval and disapproval.

Learning to play a role well involves seeing the place of the role from the perspective of other members of the cooperative scheme and in the context of the activities needed to promote the association's ends. Rawls notes that as we grow in understanding and enter new groups, this learning adds up to an understanding of society as a whole as a cooperative scheme. Assuming that a particular association has public rules known to be just, how does it come about that its members are bound by ties of friendship and mutual trust and that they rely on one another to do their part? Rawls supposes that these feelings and attitudes are generated by participation in the association. "Thus once a person's capacity for fellow feeling has been realized by his acquiring attachments in accordance with the first psychological law, then as his associates with evident intention live up to their duties and obligations, he develops friendly feelings toward them, together with feelings of trust and confidence. And this principle is a second psychological law."[47] And once these ties are established, a person experiences (association) guilt when she fails to do her part, and anger and indignation when others fail to do their share.

Under the morality of authority and the morality of association, principles play the roles in cognition that were ascribed to them above, ruling out certain interests, leading to the establishment of others (particularly under the morality of association), and sometimes leading directly to choice. Rawls holds, however, that the experience of sentiments of right under these moralities remains flawed. As long as our holding a principle is based in whole or in part on our wanting the approval of others, whether parents or associates, Rawls takes it that we do not hold it adequately or completely, so we are not yet in a position to experience the "moral emotions" (guilt, indignation) "in the strict sense."[48] According to Rawls, the feeling of guilt, for example, after a particular, possibly immoral action, is rational only when it arises from applying correct moral principles in the light of true or reasonable beliefs.[49] It is only in Rawls's third stage of morality, the morality of principles, that we properly experience sentiments of right. In the course of our experience under the morality of association, we come to understand how the successful operation of our presumptively just society is the result of a scheme of cooperation based on principles of justice. Having come to understand these principles, however, it is only when we affirm them, irrespective of the contingencies of the well-being and approval of particular individuals and groups, that we accept the morality of principles. Rawls links the authentic experience of the moral emotions with his scheme for selecting principles of justice. "Our moral sentiments [now] display an independence from the accidental circumstances of our world, the meaning of this independence being given by the description of the original position and its Kantian interpretation."[50]

Rawls explains our motivation to accept a morality of principles by a third psychological law, similar in form to the first two.

> This law states that once the attitudes of love and trust, and of friendly feelings and mutual confidence, have been generated in accordance with the two preceding psychological laws, then the recognition that we and those for whom we care are the beneficiaries of an established and enduring just institution tends to engender in us the corresponding sense of justice. We develop a desire to apply and to act upon the principles of justice once we realize how social arrangements answering to them have promoted our good and that of those with whom we are affiliated.[51]

Of course Rawls presents these laws in the course of explaining the form and stability of the well-ordered society of justice as fairness. The morality of principles explains why, for instance, relatively wealthy members of one of these societies would not try to use political power to alter the distribution of income dramatically in their favor, or if they did, why other citizens would resist them. Once this morality is established, "feelings of guilt and indignation are aroused by the injuries and deprivations of others unjustifiably brought about either by ourselves or third parties, and our sense of justice is offended in the same way."[52] Rather, citizens would find ways to promote their interests that are consistent with the principles of justice. In doing so, their self-esteem might be enhanced, but their autonomy would be expressed in their choosing to act consistently with just principles.

Rawls focuses on ideal theory because his aim is to establish a coherent account of the possibility of a just society. When principles depart from the ideal in his discussion, however, they do so in two main ways. One kind of departure from ideal theory involves failing to establish coherent moral principles, as, for example, Rawls assumes that in a less just society the force of all three psychological laws is diminished. He also suggests that a child does not develop morally when the conditions he describes as necessary for the morality of authority are absent. In this case, we can infer that the child's actions would continue to be motivated by instincts and desires, and her aims regulated (if at all) by rational self-interest (in a suitably restricted sense).[53] Anticipating Rawlsian political analysis, we should note that the child's actions would also be regulated by principles, but principles that were not justifiable and probably not very helpful for solving practical problems outside the home environment. In extreme cases, a child may develop irrational principles and become subject either to unreasonable and debilitating guilt, possibly leading to clinical personality disorders, or to angry self-assertion, possibly leading to antisocial or criminal behavior. Alternatively, a child may simply be limited in her development of moral personality, but otherwise socially competent (perhaps relying on formulae or rules of thumb that she does not fully understand).

A second way in which principles depart from the ideal is when social institutions are established on manifestly unjust principles. For example, in the introduction to *Political Liberalism*, Rawls explains how the Reformation in the sixteenth century led to intolerance and warfare. "When an authoritative, salvationist, and expansionist religion like medieval Christianity divides, this inevitably means the appearance within the same society of a rival authoritative and salvationist religion, different in some ways from the original religion from which it split off, but having for a certain period of time many of the same features."[54] For many people in this context, acquiescence in religious toleration meant acquiescence in heresy about first things and the calamity of religious disunity. If the basis of moral obligation and the nature of the highest good were taken as established in divine law, then adherents to other faiths presented a dire challenge and threat. Initially, religious toleration was accepted as a *modus vivendi* in light of the alternative prospect of unending civil war. It was only as a result of long controversy that the modern understanding of liberty of conscience and freedom of thought became possible.

As a vignette of political analysis, Rawls describes this case from our present perspective, in which religious toleration is affirmed as a basic principle of political liberalism. He identifies the cause of the injustice (in its context, the clash of principles brought about by the Reformation) and the dynamics it set in motion (war, and the eventual establishment of the principle of toleration). In the absence of toleration, the persecution of heretics, as well as all kinds of political exclusion, was justified on religious grounds.

Rawls's most extensive treatment of nonideal theory is found in *The Law of Peoples*, particularly in his discussion of relations between, on one side, liberal and what he calls "decent" peoples, and on the other, outlaw states. The distinction between a decent people and an outlaw state is based on whether it is aggressive against other peoples or follows the Law of Peoples, whether it honors and respects human rights, and whether its basic structure contains a decent consultation hierarchy. Rawls has relatively little to say about the internal structure of an outlaw state, but it would apparently be based on unjust principles. He assumes that it is ruled by regimes and elites that are prepared to use force domestically and internationally to promote their rational as opposed to their reasonable interests,[55] and that its peoples are oppressed. It is the aim of the Law of Peoples for all societies to establish either liberal or decent regimes.[56]

Principles and Honneth's Reciprocal Recognition

For Rawls, the adoption of a principle is the result of a free and conscious choice, which is consistent with his Kantian heritage. His three psychological laws rely heavily on reciprocity, as the loving and/or principled actions of others prepare the ground for the individual to choose a principle. The choice itself, however, is unconstrained. Honneth's account of recognition, by contrast, is psychologically thicker, because choice takes place in a context of response that introduces an element of necessity. In his schema, principles are as likely to be discovered and affirmed as heroically chosen. We have noted that Honneth makes little use of the concept of principles, but the dynamic of his own central concept, recognition, is not far removed from the adoption of principles. Honneth has a threefold schema based on love, rights, and solidarity, but these concepts do not represent a straightforward sequence, and each has its own unique and adequate cognitive objects.

The intersubjective normative consciousness that Honneth explores centers on our conceptualization of our self as a person like other persons.

He takes it that the core of this conceptualization, which we establish in infancy, is largely consistent through history and across cultures, but that its mature forms are historically contingent. Honneth argues that the grounds for two of three forms of self-regard that he identifies have expanded through the course of modern European history, and this expansion is linked to particular social struggles and institutional developments. The link between self-regard and principles is found in our conceptualization of our self as a person, for once we take it that we are worthy of positive regard on particular grounds, we find that we are prepared to regard others positively on these same grounds. From this point on, when we conceive of a practical situation in the relevant terms, it is likely that the principle for an action that would make this regard manifest will present itself to our consciousness.

Honneth establishes the origin of the capacity for recognition in the infant's recognition of the mother (the biological mother or the person in the role of mother).[57] In the first months of life, infant and mother remain in a state of symbiotic unity. Not only does the infant move within a "horizon of experience" in which there is no differentiation between self and environment; the mother, too, is at first incapable of demarcating herself from the infant. (Honneth wants to emphasize how infant and mother are mutually dependent; he sees recognition as a two-way operation.) The mother experiences her infant's helpless neediness as a lack of her own sensitivity, and learns to adapt her care and concern to the infant's changing requirements.[58] The infant only experiences the mother as outside her omnipotent control when the mother starts to spend more time away from the infant, and when the infant begins to find clues in sensory information to the likely satisfaction of her needs. Honneth suggests that the infant's response to the loss of omnipotence is to attack the mother's body, by hitting, biting, and kicking it. The infant discovers that the "affectively charged object" belongs to "a reality that is beyond influence, and, in that sense, 'objective,'" and so "actively place[s] himself or herself into a world in which he or she exists alongside other subjects."[59]

At the same time, the mother's ongoing care establishes a pathway for the infant's former passionate love for the mother's body and for the unbounded pleasure in the satisfaction of his or her needs to be associated with this newly discovered subject. It is, however, the mother's recognition of the infant as an independent person, along with her continuing love and approval, that allow the infant to establish a consciousness of herself as a separate and valuable person. The fruit of this consciousness is the capacity to be alone. Honneth takes the child's progress through these processes (as well as others that need not detain us) to be the basis for the development of a psychologically healthy personality and of the capacity to form healthy interpersonal relationships. The recognition of the mother as a subject, and, therefore, of the self as an "I," provides the background for the acknowledgment of the self as one among others, and for the intersubjective normative consciousness that this brings about.

The infant's original experience of symbiotic union with the mother, however, is not completely lost. The infant finds herself on an arc between a boundary-dissolving merging and a boundary-establishing recognition of self and mother as independent persons; and this becomes the model for all subsequent relationships of love and close friendship.[60] This concept of the person is not the politically charged idea of the free and equal individual, but rather that of a needy, physically embodied self. Therefore, to become engaged with another person on the basis of this cognitive framework is to establish a cognitive field in which each one's physical and emotional neediness is presumptively legitimate, a possible ground for claims that one finds oneself predisposed positively to consider.

We probably cannot satisfy all the physical and emotional needs and desires expressed by friends and loved ones, and the relationship between infant and mother contributes little to the material production upon which this satisfaction ultimately depends. Material production typically requires coordinated labor. Like Rawls, Honneth takes for granted that this is something social collectives achieve by organizing a division of labor in terms of an allocation of rights and responsibilities, "and the individual can normally ensure that these rights are adhered to by calling upon an authorized, sanctioning force."[61] Neither author offers a cognitive account of how we conceive of rights, a topic I address below. Whereas Rawls considers how such rights and responsibilities would be arranged in a just society, Honneth interprets the historical development of rights based on the western European experience.

Honneth finds a change in the form of recognition based on rights in the transition from traditional to postconventional morality, the transition from tradition to modernity, beginning around the seventeenth century. In the prior period, the rights a person could claim depended on the person's social position. Afterward, it was accepted that all persons are due a basic set of rights, although who counts as a person and the content of the set of rights remained contested.

In a traditional society, Honneth takes it that social roles are secured by the self-evident authority of ethical traditions, and that the rights and obligations associated with a role depend on the conventional view of the role-holder's contribution.[62] This leads to a norm of differential respect, and the maintenance of respect for any individual depends, in theory, on her acting in a manner consistent with her role. According to Honneth, given that the forms of our self-respect depend on the respect in which we are held, each person would consider her own status to be contingent upon her role behavior and would view others in the same light. Due to changes originating in philosophy and carried out through social struggle, the legal system came to be understood as the expression of the interests of all members of society. The state became not only an instrument for the people but also an instrument of the people. Instead of status depending on correct role behavior, legal subjects came to recognize one another as persons capable of making "reasonable, autonomous decisions regarding moral questions."[63] Since this capacity is assumed to be universal among citizens, each citizen has a presumptive basis for self-respect and a similar basis for respecting others.

Honneth emphasizes that this respect is realized only in terms of the specific set of rights in a given legal order. Its content and boundaries are fluid. In Europe, civil rights developed in the eighteenth century, political rights in the nineteenth, and social rights in the twentieth, roughly speaking. Civil rights are negative rights that protect a person's life, liberty, and property from unauthorized state interference; political rights are positive rights guaranteeing the opportunity to participate in processes of public will-formation; and social rights are positive rights that ensure that each person has a share of basic goods adequate to fulfill her role as a citizen. Self-respect derives not from the abstract knowledge that these rights are available but from the practical experience of benefiting from them, and the conviction this yields that they are deserved.

Honneth finds a historical source for the dignity we attribute to each person in the status accorded to particular roles, or estates (e.g., nobles, peasants, clergy) in traditional societies. In place of the respect due to a member of an estate by virtue of the estate's purported contribution to the established order, we consider all persons to be due respect by virtue of their purported moral capacities. This respect is underwritten and its limits are established by legal rights, which, of course, vary by society. Also, whether a particular individual actually affirms and adopts principles based on rights remains contingent.

Honneth finds traditional estates to be the historical source for a third form of recognition as well: social esteem, by which we value ourselves and others for particular acquired traits. In traditional societies, the value horizon was organized around estates, each with its roles and standards. One earned the honor due to a member of the estate by performing the role well, although one was presumptively due this honor by virtue of estate membership. When the bourgeoisie, at the threshold of modernity, took up a struggle against the nobility's notions of honor, they were not only attempting to establish new value principles, they were also initiating a confrontation over the status of this kind of value principle.

> The place that the concept of honour had previously held in the public arena gradually comes to be occupied by the categories of "standing" or "prestige," which are supposed to capture the measure of esteem that individuals are socially accorded for their individual accomplishments and abilities. Now the new organizational pattern that this form of recognition thus acquires can, of course, only refer to the narrow stratum of a person's worth which is left over from the two processes of, on the one hand, the universalization of "honour" into "dignity" and, on the other hand, the privatization of "honour" into subjectively defined "integrity."[64]

In today's postconventional morality, as a consequence of this struggle, we find traits in ourselves that can serve as the basis for social esteem (and indirectly for associated self-esteem) by performing tasks and occupying positions.

Honneth imagines an ongoing conflict in assigning cultural value, or esteem, to particular objects (traits, accomplishments, positions) being carried out in the symbolic field represented by language. He takes it that our self-esteem depends on attaining objects to which others assign value. Any small group can establish a local community of value around particular objects, even in opposition to prevailing value principles, but the demands of production and reproduction impose constraints on the range of value principles that a society can sustain overall. A counter-culture that is not engaged in the mainstream productive scheme must nevertheless find a way to subsist from it. But even within the productive scheme, maintaining a trait as an object of esteem is an ongoing task. Since the definition of such traits is constantly in flux, and the supply of cultural esteem, although highly elastic, is limited, Honneth characterizes the conduct of this task as a struggle.

Honneth's "esteem" is closely related to Rawls's "morality of associations." A group identifies an object as worthy of esteem, and, perhaps at the same time, it establishes principles of conduct in relation to this object. An individual can take steps to attain the object, and, if successful, she establishes a ground for self-esteem. Once she has conceived of an object as a basis for esteem, then to find that object in another person is to find that person worthy of esteem, and this disposes her to adopt certain principles for her conduct in relation to this person.

To share an esteem object is to share the value horizon that it establishes. Honneth argues that in a traditional society, some esteem objects are fixed for an entire status group, and each member of the group is attributed the same status by those outside the group. Therefore, each member also esteems each other member to the same degree, and this symmetrical mutual esteem can be called "solidarity." This term is appropriate because members of the group would be likely to support one another in performing their roles well, just as members of an oppressed group might support one another in opposing an oppressor. Once esteem objects become individuated, of course, the old basis for solidarity falls away. Honneth suggests, however, that to the extent that we come to see one another's distinct individual accomplishments as contributing to a joint social task, so that "every subject is free from being collectively denigrated,"[65] we can view the competition for social esteem in a positive light. Since there is no unit of measure for comparing the value of each person's contribution, we can consider our mutual esteem to be symmetrical. When this symmetrical attitude leads us normally to support one another in the joint task of social construction, we can say that we have established a completely modern and potentially universal form of solidarity.[66] Once we have reason to recognize fellow citizens as associates, we are inclined to adopt principles in order to support their projects separate from any legal obligation, even when there is no apparent benefit to ourselves.

Possible Origins of Principles in Human Prehistory

I have noted that Rawls and Honneth take for granted the capacity to conceive of principles. They simply accept that principles constrain our inclinations and our conception and pursuit of interests. In Honneth's account of forms of recognition, for example, there is a gap between the infant's recognition of herself as an independent and valued person and the medieval villager's acceptance of the rights and responsibilities associated with the traditional view of her estate's role. Since the task of this book is to establish principles alongside interests as the microfoundations of political analysis, however, it would be helpful if the origins of the distinct and separate role of principles in practical reason could be explained.

Jon Elster is probably the rational choice theorist who has most thoroughly explored the distinction between rationality and social norms. Although he acknowledges both as distinct sources of motivation, he nevertheless argues that rationality should be accorded methodological priority.

> It is logically consistent to imagine that everyone always acts rationally, but not that everyone always acts irrationally . . . Similarly, it is possible to imagine a world in which everyone always acts exclusively for his own selfish benefits, whereas a world in which everyone always acts exclusively for the sake of others is an incoherent notion. The second-order values of altruism and morality are parasitic on the existence of some first-order benefits; for instance, the second-order pleasure from giving presupposes an expected first-order pleasure of the recipient.[67]

Rawls argues that besides the reasonable and the rational representing distinct cognitive capacities, the reasonable also cannot be derived from the rational.[68] There is no need for the reverse argument. It seems unambiguous that natural desires, anyway, are prior to principles in an evolutionary sense, and that although natural desires are typically served by interests, principles often curb them.

Can we accept that natural desires, interests, and rationality are cognitively prior to principles and conceptions of right while rejecting Elster's argument that rationality should have methodological priority? It may be that if Rawls is correct that the reasonable cannot be derived from the rational, this is sufficient to reject Elster's argument. Another approach to the problem is to consider how the cognition of principles is distinct from that of interests. If the cognition of principles is substantially separate from the cognition of interests, and if choice can be centered in either form of cognition, then for the purposes of the methodology for empirical political analysis it would be arbitrary to give priority to either.

The last two decades have witnessed intense interest in the cognitive basis for morality from a variety of perspectives: evolutionary biology and psychology, behavioral economics, and medically based neuroscience, to name a few. Behavioral economists such as Ernst Fehr and Urs Fischbacher have produced strong experimental evidence that the "self-interest hypothesis" in economics needs to be supplemented with concepts such as "strong reciprocity,"[69] neurologists have identified regions of the brain that carry out specific tasks associated with moral reasoning,[70] and scholars of evolution have shown how "moral minds" can enhance evolutionary fitness.[71] It is widely accepted that morality has an evolutionary and physiological basis and that it is economically important. Given different ontological assumptions, conceptual frameworks, and methodologies, however, as well as the relative infancy of brain science, there certainly is no unified account of the cognitive basis of morality, much less of how the relationship between self-interest and morality plays out in the mind.

In the context of the present discussion and these ongoing investigations, I would like to offer three hypotheses.

1.   Interests are grounded in natural desire, but principles are grounded in our cognition of the regularity of the natural world.
2.   Sentiments we can recognize as aspects of a sense of fairness are found in other primates, but the decisive evolutionary moment for the sense of right came with the development of language.

3.   Many regions of the brain are engaged in feelings and ideas associated with the sense of right, and many of these regions also have other cognitive functions, but: (a) our warrant for conceiving of a single or unified sense of right, or moral sense, is due to our ability to mold these feelings and ideas; (b) we mold our feelings and ideas according to conceptions of right, so changing our notions of right can change the way we experience and interpret sentiments of right; and (c) our conceptions of right are established by neurons that embody a sense of fairness that has prior evolutionary roots.

I suspect that with the arrival of language, a seat of agency took shape that was rooted in the sense of fairness, manipulating neurons that are also involved in our conceptualization of the regularity of the natural world (e.g., the behavior of animals and other people, the properties of plants, the turn of the seasons, our mental maps of places), and recruiting other cognitive capacities or colonizing other brain functions that previously were largely instinctual and relatively independent.

In his book *Moral Minds: How Nature Designed Our Universal Sense of Right and Wrong*, biologist Marc Hauser explores how the "moral faculty" evolved. According to Hauser, we share a built-in "moral grammar that enables each child to grow a narrow range of moral systems,"[72] similar to the physiology that underlies our linguistic abilities and broad consistencies in human aesthetic preferences. He notes that morality is built up from many composite abilities or capacities, and he summarizes evidence from hundreds of studies of human and animal behavior to find which components of morality are shared with other animals and which are uniquely human.

> To determine what is special about the moral faculty, we need to run two critical tests. First, we must determine whether any of the mechanisms that support our moral faculty are shared with other animals. We take all of the components that enable our moral faculty to operate and we subtract the components that we share with other animals. Those components left over are unique to humans. Second, we take those components that are unique to humans and then ask whether they are unique to the moral domain or shared with other domains of knowledge.[73]

Hauser suggests that early origins of our sense of right and wrong involve the process of generating an expectation based on patterns of recurring events.[74] The individual generates a mental model of the sequence
of events, and then when the resulting expectation is violated there is
some negative emotion.[75] All social animals, such as primates, have a
sense of contingency, so one can initiate a cooperative sequence, but
continuing it is based on the other's response. This indicates that there
is a script that both in some sense understand. Examples among chimpanzees include grooming, babysitting, and food sharing.[76] Many species
have power relations with patterned actions for gaining and exercising
dominance (e.g., taking mating opportunities or food), and the knowledge of one's own status appears to be most exquisite among primates.[77]
The repertoire of roles for each nonhuman species, however, is narrow.
Cheating—especially using a signal falsely to encourage a response that
leaves an opportunity for access to resources—is also commonplace
among animals, but punishment is rare and inconsistent among nonhu-
mans. Animals may lash out, however, when another animal violates a
rule in the context of resource defense.[78]

Scientists have recently confirmed that some animals possess an incipient form of what Hauser calls a "theory of mind." This involves animals recognizing in some way that other animals also have minds, such
as by taking account not only of the other's actions but also of what the
other animal can see. Interestingly, nonhuman animals' abilities in this
area seem to be narrowly focused. Experiments find that chimpanzees
take account of what other chimpanzees can see in the context of competition for food, for example, but so far they have not found similar results
for chimpanzees in other contexts.[79]

The sense of fairness is most likely to arise in an evolutionary context
of reciprocity, and Hauser points out that the primary locus for reciprocity across a broad array of species is food exchange. Many species
cooperate to secure food, and many provide for their own children and
other close kin, but long-term food exchanges among unrelated individuals are rare and inconsistent. When animal studies do find what Hauser
calls "reciprocal altruism," it almost always involves a single commodity
within a single context over a brief span of time.[80]

The traits of human moral psychology that Hauser finds to be absent
in animals are the moral emotions, inhibitory control, other aspects of a

theory of mind, and punishment of cheaters.[81] The traits he identifies that are part of our moral faculty but not unique to it include "basic aspects of action perception, theory of mind, and some emotions."[82] But Hauser does not juxtapose the sense of right with the sense of the good. Some capacities that he takes to contribute to the sense of right—developing expectations, contingent cooperation, exercising status, using a theory of mind, and cheating—are components of behaviors that are at least as central to the pursuit of interests to satisfy natural desires as they are to the exercise of the sense of right.

It seems that in evolutionary terms the sense of the good arises from natural desires and an evolving consequentialism. This consequentialism involves delaying gratification for specific reasons—what Hauser calls inhibitory control. Nonhuman primates use tools, which indicates a form of consequentialist reasoning. But when one observes the narrow repertoires of social roles, the failure to punish cheaters, and the limited capacity for food exchanges among our primate cousins, one is struck by a general conceptual rigidity, limited conceptual time frame, and limited scope for cooperation. Similarly, the narrow focus of the theory of the mind found among nonhuman primates indicates a lack of conceptual plasticity. The forms of empirical practical reason that Kant calls "maxims of skill and of prudence" involve conceiving of an interest in order to satisfy some desire. The interest's representation of the desire supports inhibitory control and implies a sense of one's own agency. The thought of a generalized interest (e.g., the blade should be sharp) implies an understanding of consequences as well as an awareness of personal agency. I do not think we are in a position to deny that other primates can conceive of general interests, but what capacity they may have here is narrowly focused.

In the period between the point at which our human ancestors took a separate evolutionary pathway from that of their primate cousins and the point when language began to develop, it is not clear how plastic our conceptualizations of interests, status roles, theories of mind, and the sense of fairness associated with food distribution and exchange may have become. Perhaps early hominids gained some greater capacity to conceive of steps toward satisfying desires involving more complex symbolic manipulation, an increased ability to conceive of reasons and interests, and a clearer sense or conceptualization of time. If so, this would have enhanced inhibitory control, and one can imagine punishment of cheaters, for example, in the context of collective efforts to secure food.

Whatever kind of consequentialism humans may have possessed before language, it was deepened with the development of language to include an increasingly abstract and analytic conceptualization of interests. Language is the supreme symbolic medium. It increases possibilities for communication and hence for expanding vocabulary, adopting new concepts, and collective learning over generations building on these concepts. Of course, we should not think of humans acquiring language as a discrete ability, like learning to ride a bicycle. Language depends on physiological capacities that underlie speech, and it could well be that the arrival of these capacities opened the way for selective pressures based on other, preexisting capacities. What I am describing as increased capacity for symbolic manipulation would not have arisen "in general" but in specific areas such as those already identified: conceptualizing interests, defining roles (deciding who is going to do what), and working out distributional conflicts. It is likely, however, that increased conceptual plasticity in one area, such as articulating interests, facilitated plasticity in others, such applying the appreciation that others can think (theory of mind) to areas besides the visual sphere in food competition. The symbolic manipulation inherent in language would have facilitated rational self-interest and humans' conceptualization of the scope and potential of their agency in many ways.

An important, fairly recent discovery in neuroscience is that primates understand one another's behavior in part through a kind of built-in neural modeling. For example, when one macaque observes another macaque, or a human, grasping an object, the neurons activated in the observer's brain are the very same neurons that would be activated if the observer herself were grasping. Similarly, hearing peanuts breaking activates the same neurons that would be activated if she were breaking peanuts herself. Since these neurons activate both when the animal itself engages in an activity and when she perceives another engaging in the same activity, scientists have named them "mirror neurons." Scientists have also established that mirror neurons are present in humans, for example, involving feelings of disgust. When we observe someone's facial expressions indicating disgust, our mirror neurons activate as though we were experiencing disgust ourselves. The human capacity to imitate (a capacity shared with chimpanzees and other great apes but not, apparently, with monkeys) also involves mirror neurons.[83]

These findings about mirror neurons suggest that human empathy is based not only on abstract understanding of another person's situation but also, at least for some experiences, on physically feeling their feelings.[84] It seems plausible that even prior to the development of language, such empathy could have served as a basis for sympathy, particularly among immediate family members.

Let's say that at the time of the development of language, humans had some capacity for empathy and perhaps sympathy, some kind of theory of mind, and some sense of consequentialism. The possession of language would necessarily have led to a more complete theory of mind and to a richer sense of one's own agency. Through communication it would have become apparent that other people have mental powers similar to one's own, and this knowledge would have become a standard assumption. Similarly, as I have noted, the development of interests and a more analytic rationality would have led to a greater sense of one's own agency, and this would have been enhanced through communication as it was recognized by others. All of these capacities in concert, under the pressure of the normal demands of the hunting and gathering life of the community or group of extended kin, would have led to a sense of responsibility for one's actions and a routine attribution to others of responsibility for theirs. Even if there had been some incipient appreciation of agency before language, a full sense of responsibility is likely to have arisen only through communication based on language, taking agency for granted.

Hauser argues that humans are born with a physiologically built-in moral grammar; I would like to suggest that the sense of right emerges from a developmental sequence humans experienced around the time of the development of language and that is recapitulated in individual development during childhood. In particular, language gave us the capacity to make commitments. Once I agree, for example, to meet at such and such a rock at dusk, my conceptions of the world that include me at the rock at dusk are imbued with the weight of this commitment. I not only expect it, I now feel it is right, and a world in which I am not there at dusk needs to be fixed (e.g., with an explanation).

The capacity to make commitments, the sense of responsibility (and attribution of responsibility to others), and a rich consequentialism together are the ingredients for a full-bodied morality. Let me illustrate: I can see that I am a person like others, and that they are people like me. Now a situation with distributive consequences presents itself. I need to make a decision on the basis of which I may commit myself to a path of action, and I can see its likely consequences for myself and for others. Given this set of capacities, the question of fairness presents itself to me.[85] (Even quite a young child can see that other children would like what she likes,[86] and that it is fair to share or to take turns.) Given language, I can state my choice to myself and to others. The principle behind the choice may be apparent, but if asked I can state it as well.

We need to acknowledge that sometimes the question of fairness presents itself and sometimes it does not. Within the normal personality range, some individuals may have a greater disposition to regard distributive questions in terms of fairness. Also, for a variety of legitimate reasons, sometimes our take on a situation is oriented more to fairness and sometimes more to self-interest. When it is oriented to fairness, the notion of fairness can be framed in different ways. However, there could be no orientation to fairness without a reasonably fully elaborated theory of mind and a sense of consequentialism, and each of these depends on communication for its later stages. The primitive sentiments of fairness that arose in the context of securing and distributing food are embellished and integrated through this cognitive development. Now the idea of fairness extends to a full conception of the state of our world, and our conception of the world is rebalanced by our conception of fairness. It is due to this extension that I hypothesize that (a) the sense of fairness is grounded in our cognition of the regularity of the natural world and (b) it is the possibility for choice from this perspective—choice that alters the construction of our social world—that establishes a new seat of agency distinct from the seat grounded in natural desire.

Recall Rawls's definition of the reasonable as the capacity to propose fair terms for cooperation and then to abide by those terms. It obviously was not possible to propose terms for cooperation before the development of language. I argue that when we do propose terms for cooperation, or when we make any commitment, our sense of what we have committed to is cognitively grounded in our conception of the regularity of the natural world.

With language, more decisions become collective decisions, and collective deliberation deepens their collective nature. When reasons are stated, one ground that presents itself for consideration is their fairness. Reasons behind decisions that are made, and, at least implicitly, the principles on which they are based become part of our cognition of our practical world, part of the basis for our expectations, alongside our conception of the physical world. Once words are the basis for practical decisions—and, given the regularities of our social worlds, the contexts for decisions tend to recur—some principles eventually turn into norms, shared assumptions that underpin the life of the community.

Making a choice on the basis of a principle (or norm) tends to build that principle into our conception of right. Once principles are part of our social world, we realize that we and others have an established sense of right that constitutes a substantial part of our identities, and we see that it is important for the life of the community for each of us to live up to its imperatives. It is at this point, when we expect ourselves and others to have a sense of right, that moral emotions such as guilt and resentment arise. We respond with these emotions to a rupture in the social world that our principles have established—guilt when we have failed to maintain a principle ourselves, and resentment when someone else's violation remains unhealed.

The most important thesis of this discussion is that the moral point of view arises naturally with the development of language. The categorical imperative and the original position provide careful articulations of the moral point of view for particular purposes, but they both depend on the person being able to adopt and to deliberate from a perspective of fairness. It is also apparent that different principles will become embedded in the discourse of different communities, but given similarities in cognition and in contexts, the different sets of principles will tend to bear family resemblances to one another. The awareness of status preceded the development of language, but this sensibility was elaborated with principles.

To respond to Elster: The fact that the sense of right can restrict the adoption of interests is explained genealogically by the constraints one places on oneself when one makes a commitment. These constraints are implied in the scenario one wills, often drawing from the community's norms. Such a scenario always bears the cognitive weight of its potential consequences, so to work out arrangements that take account of the relevant roles is to engage in moral deliberation. It is true that deliberation from the perspective of fairness is "parasitic on the existence of some first-order benefits," that is, on the consequences for the different persons' interests, but this does not imply that the person cannot deliberate and choose from this perspective.

A person can also think through the logic of the perspective of right from the perspective of her interests. There is an incentive, therefore, to use the power of words to shape the scenario in her favor, and this can be achieved through naming and the construction of role definitions. The division of labor characteristic of the hunter-gatherer societies in which humans evolved provided concepts that could be revised, after the dawn of agriculture, to construct the slave and caste societies of antiquity and eventually the societies that Honneth calls "traditional." Once "lord" and "peasant" carried adequately strong meanings, given limitations on the peasant's practical experiences, it became impossible for her realistically to conceive of the full range of consequences arising from the role of "lord."

Principles and Political Analysis

For Rawlsian political analysis to be viable, not only must it be possible for choice to be grounded in principles, but such grounding must also be routine. This chapter has offered several demonstrations that this is the case. It has shown that principles (as well as interests) play such a fundamental role in Kant's and Rawls's philosophies that these philosophies are ruined if principles do not have the independence my project requires. Kant's ideal of autonomy involves a person acting consistently with appropriately selected principles at all times, and sometimes such actions conflict with rational self-interest. Rawls offers an extended account of a three-stage sequence by which people come to adopt principles, and he distinguishes among principles on the basis of the manner of their adoption. Just as this account suggests the ubiquity of principles, so too does Honneth's account of different forms of recognition once its link with principles is established. Honneth shows, moreover, how recognition has developed historically to encompass wider and wider sets of rights. My account of possible origins of principles in human prehistory suggests something of a cognitive structure for principles that is consistent with Rawls's and Honneth's accounts and that sustains the idea of their ubiquity.

Given the danger that principles may be associated too closely with ideal theory, it is perhaps well to establish that principles are central to our moral scaffolding regardless of whether they are consistent with the categorical imperative or would be chosen in the original position. This is apparent from the first two stages of Rawls's sequence. Principles that form the basis of moralities of authority and of association are likely to be inconsistent with ideal theory, especially in an unjust society. Rawls has little to say about outlaw states, but these must be based on some structure of principles. Similarly, in Honneth's traditional societies, one finds forms of recognition that are clearly inconsistent with freedom and equality.

If this account of practical reason is largely correct, then political analysis should proceed on the assumption that institutions are constructions of principles and interests. In order to fulfill the obligation to promote social justice, it is imperative to identify how much present institutions depart from this ideal. This account also indicates, however, that present institutions were forged through the process of solving practical problems, so they are likely to represent the present distribution of political power. Many people who are empowered by established institutions are likely to see progressive change as a threat, and established institutions do serve many interests, however imperfectly. Therefore, political analysis should articulate not only the structure and identity of established institutions, and the changes needed to secure social justice, but also plausible pathways by which power can be met with power. This is likely to involve organizing the victims of injustice and appealing to others' reason and sense of justice.

If principles play the role in cognition proposed here, the question arises as to how analyses informed by neoutilitarian assumptions have dealt with them. This question is addressed in chapter 3.

chapter three

The Analytic Limits of Rational Choice Theory

Two Kinds of Analytic Limits

From a Rawlsian perspective, rational choice theory has two kinds of analytic limits. First, it has limits as a positive theory, because it fails to account for patterns and dynamics associated with the reasonable, whereas Rawlsian analysis can provide more convincing accounts of social phenomena. Also, rational choice analyses routinely rely on motives grounded in the sense of right to account for the behavior of their subjects, regardless of the ambiguous status of these motives in their theory. Second, social and political analysis cannot be merely positive. To engage in political analysis is not only to explain but also to construct the social world; but rational choice theory's focus on interests leads it to conceive of social relations as fundamentally based on conflict. The inadequacy of rational choice theory for constructing a just society is an analytic shortcoming.

The primary task for this chapter is to demonstrate rational choice theory's limits as a positive theory. Relatively few political scientists or economists use the experimental methods of the natural sciences, but when they do, the most frequent application by far has been to a class of experiments based on the prisoner's dilemma. The results of prisoner's dilemma experiments provide, therefore, an important locus for assessing the adequacy of rational choice assumptions for a positive theory of human behavior. I argue that we can better account for these results if we assume that the person has a sense of fairness independent from her sense of her interests. Also, discussing the prisoner's dilemma provides a convenient point of entry for considering the constitutive character of a political analysis based on rational choice assumptions. Experimental results are interpreted on the basis of the so-called objective behavior of the subjects and also in terms of the concepts that frame the experimenters' perception. Rational choice theory's conceptual schema constructs an opposition between self-interest and altruism that makes it harder to think in terms of motivation grounded in the sense of justice.

Outside of experimental contexts, the particular strength of rational choice analyses lies in their articulation of structures of interests. I argue, however, that patterns of social relations grounded in consistent and conflicting interests and principles are mutually embedded. Several rational choice theorists have developed their own approaches to negotiating their accommodation of principles, particularly as the tight constructions of earlier analyses have given way to looser analytic narratives. In order to demonstrate not only the power of rational choice microfoundations but also different points at which they break down, I compare an analysis that adheres quite rigorously to patterns of interests with one that takes ample recourse to patterns grounded in principles. Robert Bates organizes his analysis of the political economy of agrarian development in Kenya largely on the basis of the economic and power interests of different categories of farmers and politicians and of people in different roles in Kenya's tribes. The core of rational choice analytics in Margaret Levi's analysis of compliance with drafts and other calls to arms in five Anglo-Saxon democracies and France, by contrast, is much more limited. Although she locates her analysis in the rational choice tradition, the model of contingent consent that she develops is not well supported by rational choice assumptions.

The secondary task for this chapter is to discuss rational choice theory's limits as a constructive theory. Rational choice theory can of course be put to constructive uses, such as identifying arrangements of interests that produce stable and productive equilibria. Economists are likely to disagree that a focus on interests leads to a view of social relations based on conflict, since competitive markets cause individuals in pursuit of personal utility (however individuals define it) to promote the general good. In competitive markets and other productive institutional arrangements, however, individuals are thought to strike the best deals they can on the basis of their resources and preferences. Someone who starts with limited resources—say, someone who is raised in a poor region and who is not very well educated—must simply hope to do the best she can. From the perspective of our interests, natural limits on the availability of resources set us at odds with one another.

From a Rawlsian perspective, the constructive imperative for theory involves two separate but related notions of construction. First is the ontological proposition that social relations are constructed from principles. When we are engaged in political and social analysis, whatever else we may be doing, we are also building conceptions of right. The principles that become embedded in our consciousness may at first be merely personal, but they are cognitively equivalent to the bonds through which relationships and organizations are built. The second notion comes from the ethical imperative that arises from this ontological proposition: that we can and should choose principles that reflect our nature as free and equal persons. Given that the primary subject of justice is the basic structure of society—its basic division of rights and duties—the imperative is to build a basic structure based on principles that reflect our free and equal nature. Although this is a political task, the theoretical and analytic imperatives are to construct a set of principles that can provide the basis for such a society, to identify the principles that form established societies, and to identify pathways and strategies for reform.

When a principle is institutionalized, when it becomes a shared basis for action in a personal or organizational relationship, its status as a fixed part of our cognitive construction of our social world is secured. Although any principle can be called into question, in cognition we rely on principles as unquestioningly as we rely on our conception of the natural world. It is possible, however, for a set of principles to constitute a world that supports all persons in their pursuit of their legitimate interests, or, one might say, in the enjoyment of the realization of their human potential. While our interests tend to set us at odds, therefore, our principles can bind us together. Given this possibility, the criteria for assessing a social theory's merits should include its constructive features.

The constructive features of rational choice microfoundations become apparent when principles arising from rational choice assumptions are adopted as the basis for a political economy. Because these assumptions were borrowed from economic theory, their constructive features are also revealed when economic principles are employed as the basis for social organization. Granted, the view of the person in neoclassical economics is narrowly crafted and not intended to provide a basis, say, for constitutional design. Nevertheless, social arrangements based on the economic view of the person have often been promoted quite forcefully. We can gain some insight into differences between the constructive features of Rawlsian and rational choice microfoundations by comparing the institutions of Rawls's property-owning democracy with those of laissez-faire capitalism proposed by Milton Friedman.

Interpreting Prisoner's Dilemma Experiments

The prisoner's dilemma describes a situation that might arise after two collaborators in an offense, say, Smith and Jones, are arrested. The police separate them and interrogate them individually, explaining the consequences if one and/or the other confesses. If they both confess to the crime, each receives a sentence of, say, three years. If Smith confesses but Jones does not, Smith is set free but Jones gets five years (and the sentence is reversed if Jones confesses but Smith does not). However, if neither Smith nor Jones confesses, both know they will receive one-year sentences. In this situation, according to the canons of rational choice theory, it is rational for both to confess. Yet the rationality of this result is paradoxical because both would obviously be better off if neither one confessed. What is individually rational may be collectively irrational, or, if one is not prepared so rashly to ascribe rationality to collectivities, then unfavorable.

Scholars began to take an interest in this scenario in the early 1950s, and a more or less steady flow of formal experiments, articles, and books based on it and its variations continues to the present. This sustained interest is due partly to this dilemma expressing something of the nature of fundamental difficulties facing any society in the provision of so-called public goods such as a clean environment or national defense. But this period coincides with that of efforts to use the economic model of the person in political analysis, efforts for which these experiments formed a foundation. The formulation of the dilemma depends on the previously established economic conception of the person and the person's rationality and the analyst's adoption of the associated analytic framework. It seems to me that part of the allure of the prisoner's dilemma is its privileging a particular form of explanation, and a perhaps less than fully conscious tension with excluded interpretations. Within the narrow confines of the experimental framework, from the perspective of the Rawlsian view of the person, the prisoner's dilemma loses much of its appeal.

Of course, most of these experiments do not use actual prisoners. Typically, the subjects have been university or high school students, or sometimes the experimenters' spouses and their friends. The prisoner's dilemma is usually reinterpreted to involve pairs of players facing binary choices—to cooperate or to defect—with points or a modest financial payoff in lieu of escaping years of confinement. It is this experimental context that we must interrogate, although the original idea of the prisoner's dilemma provides a preview of the subsequent dialogue between senses of interest and of fairness.

The sense of right, which is constructed from principles, informs our interpretation of social situations. The prisoner's dilemma has the police, who are representatives of the primary social institution for maintaining order, attempting to impose the rule of law upon two people who have apparently violated it. Depending on our view of the police, our first take is likely to be in sympathy with them. Nevertheless, we may also identify with the prisoners. Their dilemma is supposed to be decided on the basis of prospects of future freedom and incarceration, but we take it that the prisoners have been co-conspirators, and we can imagine a degree of friendship and loyalty between them. If we imagine confession as betrayal, we can find a triumph in mutual silence, even if we essentially side with the police. In the 1950s, an American introduced to the prisoner's dilemma might have wanted to ask, "Which are the Allies and which are the Nazis (or the Japanese)?" Particularly if the prisoners are the "good guys," their response to the threat to their loyalty to one another takes on a heroic dimension. But this interpretation could not have been pursued because to raise questions of loyalty, a sentiment of right, is to exceed the boundaries of the interpretive framework in which the experiment has been conceived.

We have noted that actual prisoner's dilemma experiments are often conducted with small sums of money as the payoffs. The players are told the payoff structure, and, as in the original scenario, their decisions are usually independent, with no discussion allowed. In the prisoner's dilemma portrayed in Figure 3.1, if both Smith and Jones defect, they each get nothing. If Smith cooperates and Jones defects, Smith loses ten cents and Jones gets $3 (and vice versa if Jones cooperates and Smith defects). However, if both Smith and Jones cooperate, they each get $2. In terms of the logic of game theory, under this incentive structure it is rational for Jones to defect no matter what Smith does. Jones avoids losing ten cents if Smith also defects, and if Smith cooperates, Jones gets $3 rather than $2. But Smith faces the same incentive structure, so it is always rational for him to defect too. Theory based on instrumental rationality predicts that both Smith and Jones will always defect, no matter how many times the game is played.

Figure 3.1   **The Prisoner's Dilemma**

		Jones	
		Cooperate	Defect
Smith	Cooperate	$2, $2	−$0.10, $3
	Defect	$3, −$0.10	0, 0

Scholars would not have continued for decades to carry out prisoner's dilemma experiments if the results were neatly consistent with the theory. Experimental subjects consistently cooperate much more than game theory predicts, prompting scholars to revise the instructions to the players, the structure of incentives, and eventually the framework for interpreting the results. Before considering some of their interpretations, however, let us consider these experiments from the perspective of the Rawlsian view of the person. If the person has a sense of fairness independent from her sense of her interests, we need to ask how that might influence the behavior of the experiments' subjects.

When an experiment subject is presented with the rules of the game, under Rawlsian assumptions it is plausible that she would frame the issue either as one of fairness between herself and the other player, as an occasion for pursuing her own interests, or as some combination of the two. If she frames it in terms of fairness, it seems that she will cooperate, so if the other player does as well, each gets $2. If she frames it in terms of instrumental rationality, presumably she will defect (absent certain conditions discussed below). If the game is repeated, however, it is not implausible that she would alternate between the two options, perhaps testing the other player along the way. It is also plausible that some subjects will frame the game more often in terms of fairness and others more often in terms of interests, depending on prior dispositions. These assumptions make the experiment as it stands considerably less compelling, because virtually any result could be construed as consistent with theory. The different predictions from the two theories could prompt scholars to develop hypotheses and experimental designs that test them against each other. Although this obviously has not been done, the history of prisoner's dilemma experiments seems more consistent with the Rawlsian approach.

According to early prisoner's dilemma experimenters, significant instances of cooperative behavior on the part of participants were, above all, a symptom of poor experimental design.[1] Early experimenters criticized one another for allowing too much communication between the subjects or for making division of the game's proceeds into fair portions too obvious.[2] They suggested altering the experimental design so that the path to a fair, fifty-fifty division of the profits would be less obvious, thereby to discourage such thoughtless cooperation. These scholars could not accept their subjects' seeking to achieve a fair outcome as a legitimate result, so they were inclined to interpret excess cooperation as reflecting some kind of mistake.

As more experiments were conducted, however, it became apparent that cooperative results occurred far too frequently to be reduced to error.[3] In the utilitarian framework, this could be explained if some significant proportion of subjects took a direct (and positive) interest in the payoffs to the other player. In most cases, the other player was a stranger, so such an interest could not be attributed to an ongoing relationship. Under the prevailing utilitarian framework, one subject's purported interest in the other subject's payoff came to be interpreted, instead, as altruism. As soon as the possibility that some people may have altruistic preferences is introduced into the analysis of prisoner's dilemma experiments, however, the way even purely self-interested players ought to approach the game changes. In a repeated prisoner's dilemma in which purely self-interested players believe that other players might have altruistic preferences, defecting at every move is no longer the preferred strategy; instead, to maximize her own payoffs, a purely self-interested player should adopt a strategy of either cooperating until the final round of the game (and defect only then) or of defecting only after the other player does so.[4]

Rational choice analysts can readily explain how cooperation makes sense for self-interested players who are maximizing their utility when they suspect that the other player might have altruistic preferences. But the altruists themselves, those with an apparent preference for cooperation, remain a puzzle. That some people may "care directly about the payoff of the other player" changes the dynamic of the whole game for all its players.[5] Nevertheless, those who have such preferences are still, according to game theory analysis, "irrational" or "silly."[6] Altruistic preferences seem so puzzling from the perspective of rational choice theory that a number of experimenters are genuinely stumped by the problem of how to set up a situation in which such preferences could be overridden or rendered irrelevant.

Rational choice theorists preferred to explain cooperative behavior by admitting that for some people "maximizing utility" means maximizing some combination of their payoffs and those of others rather than by describing it simply as a failure of rationality. Nevertheless, if one believes that the best way to explain why some people cooperate is by spelling out their altruistic utility functions, then one implies that merely odd tastes rather than moral perspectives or conceptions of right are what distinguish such people from others. These people "get additional utility from mutual cooperation," a satisfying but to others inexplicable "warm glow" that somehow makes up for the lower payoffs their cooperative behavior reaps for them.[7]

The trouble with altruism so conceived is that it becomes the exception that proves the self-interest rule. Even those who criticize economic explanations of altruism often define altruism so narrowly that rational choice theorists can easily maintain that the rational pursuit of self-interest is nevertheless the norm; for example, Kristen Renwick Monroe:

"action designed to benefit another, even at the risk of significant harm to the actor's well-being."[8] And if one conceives of altruism as an approach to maximizing utility, altruists appear unusual because they insist on regarding such things as others' payoffs and others' cooperation as benefits to the self when, according to the theory, there is no prima facie reason to regard these things as such. In much of rational choice theory, the concept of altruism performs the function of reinforcing the view that acting on one's self-interest, narrowly conceived, is the royal road to maximizing utility.

Should one find it intuitively plausible that many subjects in prisoner's dilemma experiments would interpret their choice in terms of fairness, one might recall that the prisoner's dilemma is an artifact of utilitarian scholarship. It is not surprising for empirical explanation to reflect theoretical assumptions. Nor is it surprising that it was a pair of sociologists, Gerald Marwell and Ruth Ames, in a discipline that takes norms as basic objects of analysis, who generated some of the strongest evidence that the sense of fairness is often regulative in these experiments. They set out to determine whether experimental results would confirm the following theoretical claim: in situations in which each individual's interest in the provision of a collective good is less than the cost of the good itself, contribution toward the purchase of the good will be essentially zero (the free-rider hypothesis of the theory of collective action). Although their results confirmed a weak version of the free-rider hypothesis (enough free-riding happens to prevent groups from being able to purchase optimal levels of collective goods with voluntary contributions), Marwell and Ames found that in numerous differently structured experiments, participants consistently contributed "between 40 and 60 percent . . . of their resources . . . to the provision of a public good."[9] The experimenters note that they did not expect these results; indeed, they believed that they had so pared down their initial experimental conditions as to "maximize [the] effect [of] the free-rider problem" and, by implication, to occlude "normative factors."[10] But once they saw that their results, even in these conditions, did not conform to a strong version of the free-rider hypothesis, they asked their participants what they considered fair contributions to the public good and how concerned they were about being fair. "The great majority of all subjects (88 percent) felt that a fair investment required 40 percent or more of their available resources[, and] more than a third of the subjects felt that investing all of one's resources in the public good was the fair thing to do."[11] Seventy-five percent of respondents stated that they were concerned with being fair in investing.[12] In sum, Marwell and Ames concluded that people's responses to these questions about their conceptions of fairness make much better sense of the levels at which they contributed to the public good than does the free-rider hypothesis.[13]

People who are economists prove to be the strongest exception to the implicitly reasonable rule suggested by Marwell and Ames's results. In a series of experiments under different conditions with different populations, Marwell and Ames generally replicated their original results—except with a group of first-year graduate students of economics. Although only two of the thirty-two students in the experiment could "specifically identify the theory on which [the] study was based," the mean percentage of private goods contributed to the provision of the public good was markedly lower among these students than among any other group (20 percent versus 40 to 60 percent).[14] The responses of a number of these students to the experimenters' questions about fairness are notable. Marwell and Ames reported: "More than one-third of the economists either refused to answer the question regarding what is fair, or gave very complex, uncodable responses. It seems that the meaning of 'fairness' in this context was somewhat alien for this group."[15]

So it appears that most people find it natural to interpret choices like those in the prisoner's dilemma in terms of fairness. Given their utilitarian frames of reference, however, most experimenters have interpreted cooperative behavior as reflecting altruism instead. Also, whether through self-selection or training, the perspective of fairness seems foreign to some economists (first-year graduate students). In the highly structured environment of these experiments, the implications of the idea of fairness seem quite straightforward. To be fair is to cooperate, so that hopefully both players can gain, or, in the case of public goods experiments, to be fair is to make a significant contribution to the public good. Outside the narrow confines of these experimental environments, however, it is often much less clear what it means to be fair. What should be done about poor public schools, global poverty, environmental degradation, or any of the host of issues informed by the idea of public goods? To divide responses to these issues into two categories—self interested or altruistic—is clearly inadequate. Rather, the application of the idea of fairness needs to be more fully analyzed in these cases, so that appropriate principles can be identified and their consequences understood. In Rawls's theory of justice, it is by applying the idea of fairness to the basic structure of society that he arrives at two principles of justice. Just as the Rawlsian moral psychology makes prisoner's dilemma experiments appear less compelling, it opens the door to the untamed analytic territory of charting principles that constitute—and might resolve—many social issues, translating them from public goods problems to problems of justice along the way.

Political Analysis under Rational Choice Assumptions

Despite our interdependence, another person's behavior, as the object of her choice, is ultimately unpredictable. Yet, in light of our interdependence, we need a secure conception of our essential relations in the same way that we need a basic understanding of our physical world. Hence, we construct maps of our social territory, social narratives that we can inhabit. Because the complexity of our social world has increased, we need more sophisticated maps to achieve a unified perspective. Alongside the division of labor in production, we find a division of labor in ideology; so now we find, as high priests to our storytellers, methodologists.

Rational choice theorists tell us that ours is a world of interests; Robert Bates is among the masters of illuminating the features of such a world. His slender volume *Beyond the Miracle of the Market: The Political Economy of Agrarian Development in Kenya* is at once a demonstration of the craft of rational choice analysis, a promotion of rational choice theory against other theories in the study of developing societies, and a contribution to rational choice methodology. In the 1980s, neoclassical economics had supplanted the traditional development economics of the '50s and '60s, replacing an emphasis on state promotion of industrialization with an emphasis on free markets. Bates criticizes neoclassical and traditional development economists, however, for lacking theories of institutions and of politics. Bates argues that economic theory is unable to account for the institutional underpinnings required to maintain competitive markets and that there is a "microeconomics of institutions" underlying political incentives.[16] By the early 1980s, Kenya had enjoyed twenty years of agricultural growth rates over twice those of sub-Saharan Africa as a whole. Bates sets out to explain the causes of Kenya's exceptionalism.[17]

He finds the key factors to be an incipient agricultural gentry's rise to political power and its members' use of the levers of state power to enhance the profitability of their farms. Given that this gentry, represented by Jomo Kenyatta, Kenya's first president, was dominated by the Kikuyu tribe, Bates begins his analysis with this tribe's economic and political structure prior to the arrival of British colonists. "Initially, land was abundant and people scarce."[18] Hence, in order to cultivate the land, and also to act on a belief in the need for descendants to care for the soul after death, there was an incentive to have large families. Moreover, the main political institutions were the tribal councils, and progression to more senior councils depended on one's children's progression through the stages of life. Polygamy was the norm, and grooms were expected to give cattle to the brides' families. "The accumulation of wealth, preferably in the form of livestock, thus formed a prelude to the accumulation of dependents, and, as a consequence, social standing and political power."[19]

In Bates's method, one starts with an economy with a particular structure of production and a society with a particular structure of institutions. The economy and society are perturbed by exogenous shocks that change the values of variables that are fundamental to economic behavior. The analyst then observes the impact of changes in these economic variables upon politics.[20] The analysis is centered midway between micro and macro levels, on the interplay among institutions, sometimes including the strategies of individual politicians. Bates makes use of concepts such as "legitimacy" and "loyalty" that are grounded in the sense of right within the mechanics of his explanations, but they are merely embedded in the narrative, and at this middle level of social analysis such use begs no questions. Given that Bates is promoting rational choice methodology, interests are of course at the core of his analysis. Conceptions of right form part of his social material, part of the yarn, so to speak, for his tapestry.

For the most part, this method serves his purposes. Within the social dynamic of the movement toward Kenyan independence, however, there is an episode in which sentiments of right loom particularly large. Bates argues that the British were driven from Kenya by the Mau Mau Rebellion, and most Mau Mau rebels were members of the Kikuyu tribe. Ironically, it was other Kikuyus, favored by the British, who emerged as the dominant class after independence. Although the rebellion was crushed and many of its partisans killed, the British allied themselves with Kikuyu elites, using a classic divide-and-rule strategy. The British-allied Kikuyus benefited from an intensive rural development program focused on growing and marketing cash crops.

This narrative raises questions, particularly from a rational choice perspective, about the motives of the rebels who took on the vastly superior military might of the British Empire. Bates explains that many of them were thrice dispossessed. Europeans in the fertile highlands initially imported Africans from areas reserved for tribes to work their farms, growing maize, coffee, pyrethrum, and the like. They allowed the Africans to bring their cattle—a significant incentive, since grazing lands were increasingly scarce in the reserves. As Nairobi and Mombassa became more populous, however, there was a growing demand for milk and milk products, and many European settler farmers began to establish herds of high-yielding exotic-breed dairy cattle. These cattle lacked resistance to local diseases, which could be spread from local cattle by ticks. Hence, the settlers began to pass resolutions in the colonial district councils restricting local livestock, and to expel Kikuyu laborers from their farms.[21]

In the reserves, in the meantime, population growth had caused land values to rise. In the context of growing opportunities for investment and trade, property owners had come to define kinship relations, and associated entitlements to land and to other economic support, more narrowly. Ownership of land became increasingly highly concentrated. Traditional tribal norms emphasized sharing and mutual obligations, but now the returning Kikuyu laborers found themselves excluded and their claims and requests denied. Bates documents that those who took oaths to join Mau Mau were disproportionately poor, hence, "Mau Mau represented a civil war, which pitted those who had established a 'rightful stake' in commercialized agriculture against those who had been disinherited of their legal entitlements."[22]

Bates's accounts of the strategies of the British settlers and of the Kikuyu elite are clearly consistent with rational choice analytics: they are accounts of the pursuit of interests. When it comes to the Mau Mau rebels, however, Bates the storyteller takes over from Bates the rational choice theorist. He describes a growing conflict based on competing conceptions of right, one based on traditional notions of obligation, the other on private property. The reader follows cattle-herding Kikuyus who were first restricted to reserves, then invited onto what were now called the "White Highlands," then expelled from the Highlands only to have their claims to land rejected by their own kinsmen. Reduced to paupers, it was their grievances that fueled the revolt.[23] The reader apprehends a growing pool of resentment, first against the Europeans, and then also against collaborating kinsmen, and this resentment explains the taking of oaths and the reckless rebellion.

This is a powerful narrative, with echoes from revolutionary struggles around the world. The motivations that it represents, however, find no place in rational choice microfoundations. Resentment, which I discuss further in chapter 5, is a sentiment of right. It results not from misfortune or loss but from the uncompensated violation of an established principle. The individual inhabits a cognitive world constructed of principles, and the violation shatters this construction, if only temporarily. Because resentment is our sentiment when we live with such a damaged construction, it is often associated with a lapse in the rational assessment of consequences, and in extreme cases, in a propensity to all-or-nothing logic. The dramatic tension that Bates builds in his narrative depends on the reader's identification with the Kikuyu laborers and sympathetic appreciation of their resentment, but he makes no attempt to reconcile the rebels' decisions with the theory of rational choice.

Margaret Levi, in *Consent, Dissent, and Patriotism*, also addresses the choice to go to war. In a study spanning two centuries of wartime history in Britain, Australia, New Zealand, Canada, France, and the United States, Levi seeks to explain why young men choose to comply or not with government requests and requirements for military service. The study is organized around an insightful model of factors entering into the choice to serve, and it is rigorously grounded in the relevant historical and philosophical literatures. Levi offers important insights into the reasons for governments' recruiting policies and their relative effectiveness, as well as into dilemmas facing young men in wartime. Like Bates, she explicitly aims to extend the rational choice tradition,[24] and her study is a fine example of comparative historical scholarship, but I would argue that her model of choice stretches the conventions of rational choice theory beyond the breaking point. By including ethical reciprocity, trust of government, and ideological consent/dissent in her model alongside the comparison of costs and benefits, Levi could be said to construct a bridge between rational choice and Rawlsian political analyses.

Recall that according to Rawls, persons are reasonable when, "among equals say, they are ready to propose principles and standards as fair terms of cooperation and to abide by them willingly, given the assurance that others will likewise do so."[25] When young men are called by their government to war, it is not a great stretch to think that reasonable men will wish to consider whether the war is just, whether the government that calls is trustworthy, and (in the case of conscription) whether his young countrymen are equally required to make a similar sacrifice. These kinds of criteria determine the legitimacy and fairness of the government's call. Indeed, based on her historical scholarship, Levi argues that these are among the criteria that can best explain rates at which men have volunteered, conscientiously objected, and deserted. Moreover, the evidence is better explained by including these criteria than by depending only on the relative importance of material rewards and official and social sanctions.

Levi develops a model in which a young man's decision whether to comply with his government's call to war (whether for volunteers or for conscripts) can be read in four ways. First, some men may conform to habit, whether of obedience or disobedience. Second, under Levi's rubric of "ideological consent," others may comply or not based on their belief "in the rightness of the policies." Compliance would be based on a supportive ideology, noncompliance on an oppositional ideology. Levi's third category, of opportunistic obedience or disobedience, refers to choice based on calculation of costs and benefits such as monetary compensation, social approval or disapproval, and the risk of punishment by the state. We might think of this category on its own as a crude rational choice model; this model is the straw man that Levi attacks throughout the book. The fourth category, contingent consent, involves the degree to which a young man trusts the government and the extent of "ethical reciprocity." Drafts that permit paid replacements, for example, are weak in terms of ethical reciprocity, since young men from wealthy families may not have to serve. A given individual may consider factors that fall into more than one category, but the model still provides a basis for interpreting the behavior both of broad populations and of individuals.[26]

The conscription crises in Canada during World Wars I and II provide useful tests of the model because in both cases, English-speaking Canadians, and in particular Canadians born in Britain, consented to military service at much higher rates than members of the French-speaking community.

During World War I, French Canada provided 4.3 percent of the volunteers while comprising 29 percent of the population; English Canada, comprising 43.9 percent of the population, provided 30.1 percent of recruits; and the British-born population, although comprising less than 12 percent of the total population, provided nearly 60 percent of the volunteers.[27] When conscription was introduced, registrants from Quebec obtained the greatest proportion of exemptions.[28] Levi argues that francophone Canadians had little interest in defending a French homeland that had first deserted them in the eighteenth century and then "tolerated a revolution that undermined religion as they understood it."[29] In the years preceding the declaration of war, the government of Ontario had passed a bill limiting the teaching of French in Ontario schools. French Canadians argued that the school laws violated the principles of confederation, but the federal government did nothing to defend Ontario's francophone minority. When war was declared, the government placed an Anglican priest in charge of Quebec's enlistment drive, often separated French recruits and assigned them to English-speaking units, and generally discriminated against francophone servicemen. On the basis of these and other factors, Levi argues that from 1914 to 1918, French Canadians tended to distrust the government. In applying the criterion of ethical reciprocity, Levi notes that most anglophone Canadians considered themselves part of the British Empire, and responsible for its defense. French Canadians, however, on the basis of the agreements surrounding confederation in 1867, viewed themselves as responsible only for Canadian—not British—interests. Incomes were lower and unemployment rates higher among French Canadians, so they had greater economic incentives to join the military, but their enlistment rates were lower. The only factor that favored a narrow cost-benefit interpretation of francophone noncompliance was the social sanctions against military service in the French Canadian community.

Levi argues that her model of contingent consent, which emphasizes differences in trust in government and in ethical reciprocity, provides a better explanation for the different rates at which francophone and anglophone Canadians consented to military service than a model based merely on costs and benefits. Moreover, the model of contingent consent also accounts for the increase in francophone consent in World War II over World War I. French Canadians served at lower rates than anglophone Canadians in World War II as well, but the difference was substantially reduced. Levi argues that this relative decline in noncompliance can be attributed to the Canadian government of World War II having established itself as more trustworthy. The Robert Borden government of World War I demonstrated indifference, if not antagonism, to francophone concerns, but the William Lyon Mackenzie King government of World War II included important francophone ministers and demonstrably sought to accommodate francophone opposition to conscription. Although economic pressure from the lingering Great Depression was also a factor, Levi argues that the reduction in the difference, for example, from 4:1 to 2:1 between enlistments from Ontario and Quebec from the First to the Second World Wars is largely attributable to the King government's efforts to retain francophone confidence.[30]

Levi's model of contingent consent provides a more compelling explanation than the crude rational choice alternative not only for Canadian conscription rates but also for patterns of conscientious objection to enlistment in the United States, Australia, and France.[31] One nevertheless may question whether the model itself should be taken, as Levi presents it, as a sophisticated application of rational choice theory, or if it is more consistent with the Rawlsian view of the person. The microeconomics of institutions that Bates proposes is based on interests such as wealth, status, and political power. Can rational choice theory equally accommodate choice based on ideology, trust, and ethical reciprocity?

Levi's analysis is consistent with rational choice theory's methodological individualism. She develops a model of individual choice and organizes her social analysis—in this case comparative historical analysis—around it. She employs "formal analytics" based on "a deductive model in which rational actors strategically interact until they reach an equilibrium outcome from which no one has an incentive to deviate."[32] Levi argues that game theory allows one systematically to evaluate counterfactuals—the analyst outlines a range of sequential choices available to the actors and then works out why the actors did not follow other possible paths. "Thus, the model generates testable hypotheses about: (1) what the beliefs of the actors had to be and what they could not have been; and (2) what the critical junctures were in the decision-making process."[33] The main difference from the standard rational choice approach is that Levi includes "incentives" based on fairness: "Recognizing fairness as an important influence on behavior helps put to rest critiques of rational choice as a model that unrealistically assumes only narrowly self-interested actors."[34]

Levi begins with the behavioral assumption that individuals "can be narrowly egoistic or ethical, but they are rational in that they act instrumentally and consistently within the limits of constraints to produce the most benefit at the least cost."[35] She suggests that many people optimize with regard to combinations of egoistic and ethical objectives. "A large proportion . . . appear to have dual utilities. They wish to contribute to the social good . . . but they also want to ensure that their individualistic interests are being satisfied as far as possible."[36] Using the deductive methodology of the economist (with the addition of the dual utility hypothesis), one assumes that individuals act as if they are maximizing utility. This allows one to hypothesize about behavior under varying constraints.[37]

Note that Levi has come quite close to the model of choice proposed in chapter 1. But Kant and Rawls do not consider pure practical reason or the reasonable to be a form of cognition that is engaged, in the first instance, in optimizing or maximizing. Rather, the reasonable assesses whether an action or a scenario conforms to a principle. Consider the influence of (dis)trust on anglophone and francophone Canadians' decisions to enlist during World War I. Presumably, Levi takes it that, given the element of trust for anglophones, despite the danger in going to war, the choice to enlist yielded utility for them, while francophone distrust either neutralized the utility or caused negative utility to be associated with enlisting. Levi does not explain the link between trust and utility. In this and her other cases involving ethical objectives, I would argue that the choice in question is decided by the relevant principle, and it is the apprehension itself of the satisfaction or violation of the principle that most affects the choice, not whatever satisfaction, pleasure, or utility may be derived from it. For the anglophone, the formula—that yields the response, "Yes, I should/will enlist" is this: "My government calls me to defend the empire of which I am a part and that is threatened." If the fundamental principle is something like, "I should defend my group when it is threatened," in the context of a far-away war, the appropriateness of this principle depends on identifying both with the empire and with the Canadian government. For the francophone, the concept "my government" is called into question by distrust, and there is also little sense of belonging to the group that has been threatened. Therefore, the francophone feels no obligation to enlist, or perhaps the thought of enlisting offends rather than affirms a sense of propriety.

There is nothing to stop Levi from asserting that satisfying a principle yields utility. It is not clear, however, what this assertion would add to her analysis. There is no reference to utility in her model of contingent consent, nor in her analysis of the Canadian conscription crises. The model is better explained by assuming that the person has two moral capacities, the reasonable and the rational, associated with distinct forms of reasoning, than by assuming that there are two forms of utility that the person maximizes individually and collectively. Also, the dual utility hypothesis wrongly attributes a schema of maximization to ethical objectives or the reasonable.

Consent, Dissent, and Patriotism serves as a bridge from rational choice theory to Rawlsian political analysis because Levi's departures from standard rational choice assumptions lead to a form of analysis that is largely consistent with a Rawlsian moral psychology. Since the rational is grounded in interests, standard rational choice analyses are organized around factors that affect specific interests, or structures of interests. Since the reasonable is grounded in principles, and Rawlsian political analysis is based on both the rational and the reasonable, large parts of Rawlsian analyses will be organized around factors that affect principles. However, structures of principles, if that is what we call them, have different dynamics and tend to have different shapes from structures of interests. In political analysis, interests typically derive from the ownership and productivity of assets, from the powers of and control over offices, and from the terms of contracts and similar agreements. It explains social relations and distributive consequences regarding external objects. Principles, by contrast, involve the claims we can make on one another, our assessments of and responses to other persons' actions based on background conceptions of right, and the terms of social relations (including efforts to construct new terms). Rawlsian political analysis is grounded in persons' judgments of the fairness, legitimacy, or justice of actions or terms. As exemplified by French Canadians' noncompliance with their government's call to arms, these judgments typically have a historical basis, so analysis of structures of principles is typically historical, often referring to foundational written or spoken agreements. It centers on right relations more than on external objects. The analyst reconstructs a sequence of factors that plausibly contribute to the person's judgment of right, and notes the consequences of this judgment.

We have seen that a range of analyses by rational choice theorists can be deepened or given greater analytic coherence when we conceive of the person as having a sense of right that is independent from the sense of the good. This indicates that compared to rational choice microfoundations, Rawlsian microfoundations provide a more secure basis for empirical social analysis. If true, this is an important result. The implications of this result do not end, however, with a different approach to empirical analysis. If Rawls's moral psychology provides a closer approximation than rational choice assumptions of the nature of practical reason, then we must also reevaluate the role and function of political analysis. In short, we find that although political analysis should certainly make use of the methods of the natural sciences, it cannot adequately be modeled on these sciences. For on one hand, if practical reason is constituted by principles as well as by interests, then political analysis is never merely empirical. When we analyze politics, we build and rebuild our political consciousness; in this sense, political analysis is always also constructive. On the other hand, if our social institutions are largely a construct of principles, then we are responsible, individually and collectively, for their design. Now we must assess microfoundations of political analysis, and of social science generally, also in terms of the kinds of social constructions that they yield. One of the great contributions of the Enlightenment was the idea that we should establish social institutions on the principle that persons are free and equal. Although there are many interpretations of this idea, we gain some insight into the constructive features of Rawlsian and rational choice microfoundations by comparing Rawls's vision for society with that of the economist Milton Friedman.

The Limits of Rational Choice Theory as a Constructive Theory

To see how political analysis is constructive in the ontological sense, as in the idea of constructing a sense of right, consider what occurs when the aspiring Mau Mau rebel takes an oath. For the Kenyan rebel, or freedom fighter, the oath is a public decision to join the fight against the colonial government. We can assume that the man has been party to a tribal and/or nationalist narrative that explains specific perceived injustices, such as perhaps the expulsion of his cattle from the White Highlands. The oath anchors, or institutionalizes, this narrative, and the narrative becomes part of the reason for all that follows from the oath. The injustice painfully tears the fabric of his conception of a right social order, but the oath in some measure redresses the tear, restoring integrity to his sense of social order. It accomplishes this, however, only by making colonial officials and those who collaborate with them into enemies, and by making other rebels into comrades. Like any promise, the oath places the man under obligation; he takes on a debt that at some time may be called. It may place him within an organization, subject to the organization's norms and hierarchy of authority.

Thus, the oath alters and builds upon the structure of the man's conception of right. The nationalist narrative is anchored and deepened, so that not only for himself, but in due course for his community as well, it becomes a significant element of the shared conception of the social order. There may be a palpable change in the man's perception of particular individuals with whom he interacts in his normal routines. When he sees a person he knows, say, James, that person is no longer just James the policeman but now also James the enemy. He may find between himself and a friend a new social distance, a consequence of his altered identity.

The oath is incomprehensible without the nationalist narrative. At the time of the oath, this narrative can be understood as part of the man's background conception of right. It provides reasons by which he finds it right to take the oath. Later on, the oath, too, is part of his background conception of right. It may provide reasons for his participating, for example, in particular military exercises.

A rebel's oath is a dramatic example of how, with decisions and actions, we build our conceptions of right, and it is similar in kind to a young Canadian's decision to enlist—and also to our decisions when we accept an offer of employment, take a position in an organization, or commit to a relationship. If the decision and the action alter the cognitive framework by which we are morally constituted, however, the content and thus the significance of the change depend on the specific narrative that explains the decision. In the case of a Mau Mau rebel, the narrative may cast some Africans as collaborators and others as coerced participants in the colonial government. In the case of a Canadian enlistee, the decision implicates him in the narratives that define the country's military program. These narratives may define particular persons as friend or foe on a field where the agent has little choice but to treat them as such. These narratives are, of course, political analyses.

I have argued above that insofar as rational choice theory understands decisions to be based on interests and maximizing utility, it misconceives of the nature of many decisions, or at least that a model with separate conceptions of the right and the good provides a closer approximation of our moral psychology. We have noted Bates's argument that rational choice theory can provide better explanations for patterns of economic development than other theories. He and other rational choice theorists have modeled political analysis on the natural sciences, as a means to enhance our understanding of particular kinds of empirical phenomena. If Rawls's account of our moral psychology is closer to the truth than that of rational choice theory, we can anticipate that Rawlsian political analysis will be empirically superior. It will offer more complete, more compelling, and ultimately more truthful accounts of political phenomena. From a Rawlsian perspective, however, this view of the function of political analysis, while not mistaken, is incomplete. For if to engage in political analysis is to construct and reconstruct our background conceptions of right, then when we are analyzing the world, we are also changing it. We are molding and embellishing the framework that will condition our perception and interpretation of future events and provide possible grounds for future actions.

In light of the constructive function of political analysis, one criterion for assessing any form of political analysis is its constructive features. What kinds of conceptions of right are likely to be built on rational choice microfoundations? I have noted that in a world of limited resources, political analysis founded on interests conceives of persons as fundamentally in conflict with one another. This may explain why, under experimental conditions, graduate students of economics contributed less than other populations to public goods. Whether due to training or self-selection, these individuals were less disposed to conceive of a public goods scenario as an occasion for applying the schema of fairness. I have noted also that scholars applying the prisoner's dilemma, a basic model in rational choice analytics, have often interpreted behavior as motivated by altruism in contexts where it is at least as plausibly motivated by fairness or a related conception of right. Since altruism is an inexplicable motive from a rational choice perspective, this analytic propensity is likely to reinforce conceptions of social relations based on interests. Hence, individuals are likely to conceive of one another in a consequentialist framework, in terms of their threat potential or what they are worth. A Rawlsian analysis, by contrast, while acknowledging the importance of interests, is likely to build and to reinforce conceptions of social relations that give a prominent place to justice and fairness.

We gain additional insight into the constructive features of rational choice and Rawlsian microfoundations by comparing more or less fully developed ideals for a political economy based on their respective moral psychologies. Based on the Kantian microfoundations of his theories, Rawls has proposed a basic institutional design for a just society, but rational choice microfoundations do not lend themselves to grand theorizing. There is no fully articulated social ideal that equally represents the rational choice tradition. Since rational choice theory borrowed the idea of the person from neoclassical economics, however, and since utilitarianism provided loose foundations for classical liberalism, for the purpose of making a few broad contrasts we can compare Rawls's social ideal with that of University of Chicago economist and self-avowed classical liberal Milton Friedman.

There are many similarities between Rawls's property-owning democracy and Friedman's free-market capitalism. Both theorists favor elections based on universal suffrage, both support private property and at least permit private ownership of the means of production, and both envision a role for the state in providing public goods and redistributing income.[38] A major distinction between their proposals, however, is that whereas Rawls considers liberty, equality, and fraternity to be equally fundamental ideals, Friedman places his main emphasis on liberty alone.

A rational, utility-maximizing agent would clearly like to have as wide as possible a range of choices. It seems that Friedman's emphasis on liberty arises directly from this desire. His concessions to public goods and to redistribution are due, respectively, to necessity (there is hardly an alternative to government providing public goods) and to humanitarian sympathy.[39] In Friedman's view, the government's primary role is to uphold rules, serving as impartial umpire to the capitalist game, and even on this subject he argues for as much decentralization as possible.

An agent who is reasonable as well as rational would also like to maximize her choices, but subject to appropriate constraints of right. Rawls's emphasis on equality arises from working out a conception of right that is based on the idea of a social contract that all could agree is fair. Thus, in a Rawlsian society, with their material needs secured and excessive concentrations of power avoided, all are to enjoy the fair value of their liberties. A sense of fraternity is generated through the application of the difference principle, part of Rawls's second principle of justice, which states that social and economic inequalities are to be arranged so that they are reasonably expected to be to everyone's advantage.[40] Since all members of this ideal society benefit from one another's natural endowments and economic accomplishments, citizens are likely to gain a sense of civic friendship and social solidarity.[41]

Rawls's and Friedman's programs both require the protection of the basic liberties—conscience, political participation, association, and equal protection under the law—presumably largely through the courts. Rawls provides stronger guarantees, however, for a social minimum income, for access to education to ensure fair equality of opportunity, and for access to health services to ensure the fair value of the liberties. Moreover, Friedman tends to view taxes as an affront to liberty, but Rawls emphasizes the need to avoid concentrations of wealth, again to secure for all the fair value of the liberties.

To implement this program, Rawls proposes four branches of government, one each for allocation, stabilization, transfers, and distribution. The allocation branch aims to keep the price system workably competitive and to prevent the formation of unreasonable market power, and the stabilization branch strives to bring about reasonably full employment. "These two branches together are to maintain the efficiency of the market economy generally."[42] The transfer branch maintains the social minimum income, perhaps through a negative income tax, and the distribution branch "preserve[s] an approximate justice in distributive shares by means of taxation and the necessary adjustments in the rights of property."[43] This last branch plays an important part in implementing the difference principle. First, in order to "continually correct the distribution of wealth and to prevent concentrations of power detrimental to the fair value of political liberty and fair equality of opportunity,"[44] it imposes inheritance and gift taxes and sets restrictions on the rights of bequest. Without measures like these it is likely that representative government would become such in appearance only. Second, it establishes a scheme of taxes, such as a proportional expenditure tax, to raise the revenues that justice requires.

I have alluded to the fact that Friedman also supports a social minimum income; he proposes a negative income tax as well, but on the grounds of reducing the distress that the sight of poverty brings to those who are better off. Friedman supports public funding of education (he prefers a voucher system to public schools) on the grounds that education is a public good. "A stable and democratic society is impossible without a minimum degree of literacy and knowledge on the part of most citizens and without widespread acceptance of some common set of values."[45] He agrees with Rawls that the advantages gained from natural talents, as from inherited wealth, are undeserved, but he argues against measures such as inheritance taxes and a graduated income tax to reduce resulting inequalities, on the grounds that they reduce long-term rates of economic growth and conflict with individual freedom.[46] Generally, he promotes what is often described as a "minimalist" or "night watchman" state.

It is not surprising that a theorist who begins with an idea of the person as a rational, utility-maximizing agent should conclude with a vision for society that is likely to lead to great inequalities of income and wealth. It is largely factors beyond individual agency, such as the accident of birth and the possibility of misfortune, that make it important for society to provide a range of social supports, and it is not clear why a merely rational agent should take much interest in the misfortunes of others beyond the boundaries of family and affection. For agents who are reasonable as well as rational, however, in a world where conceptions of right are social constructions, there is an obligation to promote social justice. Misfortune is no longer entirely arbitrary because its incidence can be reduced and its consequences systematically ameliorated. It is possible to establish social solidarity and bonds of civic friendship on the basis of a social construction that benefits everyone. Recognizing one another as free and equal, and as capable of deep moral attachments, these agents can build institutions that reflect and sustain this self-characterization.

If the Rawlsian view of the person provides a more accurate account of our moral psychology, therefore, and offers a more effective basis for empirical political analysis, then it also yields particular imperatives for political philosophy and for political analysis. Reasonable and rational agents need principles of justice to figure out what would constitute a just society. To offer such principles, of course, is the task that Rawls undertook. Reasonable and rational agents need political analysis to figure out how to build a just society.

This book offers three forms of analysis in response to this imperative: a program analysis, a political economy analysis, and a problem-based political reform analysis. Program analysis supports the normal operations of public agencies. In order to determine how public resources should be allocated, one wants to know how different program designs lead to particular impacts. Generally, one would like to maximize impacts from the allocation of available resources. The most fully articulated form of program analysis is economic cost-benefit analysis, which conceives of impacts in terms of gains in utility based on the satisfaction of interests.

A Rawlsian program analysis, by contrast, conceives of impacts not only in terms of the satisfaction of interests but also in terms of the establishment of principles that promote social justice. For example, the program analysis in chapter 4, of the Grameen Bank of Bangladesh, includes as impacts not only gains in beneficiary incomes and improvements in health but also enhancements in women's status in the family and their increased involvement in family decisions and in national politics. Most of the Grameen Bank's clients are women, and given Bangladesh's history of patriarchy, the empowerment of these women is a matter of justice.

Although program analysis assumes the perspective of a public agency, political economy analysis speaks directly to the citizen or person. Rawlsian political economy articulates the structure of principles and interests that constitutes a particular society. It aims to support the establishment of conceptions of right that provide appropriate orientations to the society in question. Note that justice involves not only the character of a society's politics but also the adequacy of its institutions for supplying primary goods. A political economy analysis normally has political and economic components that complement one another analytically and that together present the justice and injustice of the society's institutions. Moreover, in the event that the society is less than completely just, to explain a society's institutions in these terms is also to establish a basis for an agenda of social and economic reform. Chapter 5 presents a Rawlsian political economy analysis of the Indian state of Bihar. I argue that Bihar's poor economic performance and ongoing social violence are largely attributable to the way conflicts between egalitarian principles of democracy and hierarchical principles of caste have played out in this state. Caste-based resentments have displaced a pragmatic politics of interests in a variety of ways. In this case, justice demands not only the correction of old exclusions but also the establishment of institutions that can manage public infrastructure, carry out agricultural extension programs, and otherwise place the society on a trajectory for economic growth.

Political economy analysis is typically framed around a political unit or polity: a population subject to shared legislative, executive, and judicial institutions. A problem-based analysis, by contrast, may involve one polity or many, or, as in the case of climate change, discussed in chapter 6, all the countries of the world. It starts from an issue that is an affront to justice, and its shape and boundaries are determined by the principles and interests involved with the issue. Given the magnitude of its consequences and their distribution across countries and generations, climate change presents particularly serious and difficult problems of justice. In chapter 6, I argue that climate change presents an objective problem of social justice even though it is not clear how much weight should be assigned to each of the principles that is appropriate to its resolution. I use the example of the U.S. Senate and its limited ability to come to grips with these principles to illustrate how established institutions reflect the results of earlier conflicts over conceptions of right. Insofar as a problem like climate change does not fit the patterns of earlier problems, it exerts pressure on existing institutions, leading either to institutional reforms or to the establishment of new institutions.

As chapters 4 to 6 indicate, Rawlsian political analysis routinely invokes specific ideas of justice. Indeed, it is essential that it should do so; rational choice theory's limits in this regard constitute an analytic shortcoming. One could be inclined to view rational choice theory's circumspection on matters of justice as an advantage; to assert a particular idea of right may be to offend those who hold competing views. In its focus on interests, however, rational choice theory tends to legitimize the claims of established interests, if only implicitly.

I appreciate that the agenda that this book proposes, in its theoretical, analytic, and political dimensions, is an ambitious one. No doubt the proposed program, political economy, and problem-based forms of Rawlsian analysis will be found inadequate in various ways. But the Rawlsian moral psychology does indeed represent an improvement on that of rational choice theory, and the implications for the discipline of political science and for the social sciences generally are bound to be considerable. I hope that the forms of analysis presented below make some initial headway in working out these implications and that they illustrate the range of consequences that can be expected from moving from rational choice to Rawlsian microfoundations.

chapter four

Program Analysis of the Grameen Bank

Rawlsian Program Analysis

Program analysis aims to support cost-effective allocations of resources by public agencies, such as governments, international development agencies, and nonprofit organizations. From the perspective of an agent in the field, it may appear that such an organization's analytic problem would be to marshal its resources so as to reach the desired results for each individual program in order to achieve program goals. Certainly the construction of a consensus among the relevant agents on a goal and strategy is an important part of program management. For public agencies, however, at least for large ones, it is a comparative perspective that program analysis should sustain. The problem is to maximize impacts from an ongoing portfolio consisting of many diverse investments.

The first fully developed form of program analysis, economic cost-benefit analysis, is a branch of neoclassical economics, arising from the utilitarian tradition. Economic cost-benefit analysis (ECBA) assesses investments in terms of their economic rates of return (ERRs), an expression of the relation between total costs and total economic benefits, discounted over time. A project's ERR is the discount rate at which the discounted sum of benefits minus costs comes to zero. Public agencies such as the World Bank have often looked for ERRs of at least 10 percent from their projects in the economic sectors. As completed projects are found to have higher or lower ERRs, the agency learns what kinds of strategies are likely to work better in what kinds of environments.

Rawlsian program analysis differs from ECBA in its valuation and conception of program dynamics. It retains the overall analytic form of ECBA because it, too, aims to maximize impacts from a portfolio of investments. ECBA and Rawlsian analysis both provide consistent and determinate bases for assessing a program's cost-effectiveness. The proposed Rawlsian analysis, however, provides a more secure foundation for emphasizing benefits to the poor, and it includes as impacts not only the satisfaction of interests but also changes in norms, or the establishment of principles, that support social justice. Rawlsian analysis also differs from ECBA in its methodology. Although economics conceives of program dynamics (both internal to an organization and in its relations with beneficiaries) in terms of interests, Rawlsian analysis conceives of them also in terms of principles. Because it recognizes the construction of ideologies and the establishment and maintenance of obligations as potentially significant elements of program management, the Rawlsian approach is more powerful in the end.

One might think that program analysis drawing from a deontological tradition such as that of Rawls and Kant, which emphasizes conforming to the right rather than maximizing the good, would not aim to maximize benefits. I believe this view is mistaken. Program managers should be constrained from violating certain principles; for example, they should not lie or bribe to promote program objectives. In order to discharge the obligation that arises from their use of public resources, however, they should use these public resources as best they can to advance beneficiary interests and maximally to promote social justice. It is the particular role of program analysis to sustain an organizational culture oriented to this purpose, and this can be achieved when program analysis aims to maximize (appropriately defined) impacts.

This chapter explains how Rawlsian program analysis works and compares it to ECBA. This is achieved by carrying out a program analysis of the Grameen Bank, a nonprofit microfinance agency in Bangladesh. The Grameen Bank is an appropriate subject (1) because of its importance (it and its founder won the Nobel Peace Prize in 2006), (2) because its strategy lends itself to a Rawlsian analysis, and (3) because it has been well researched. There are enough materials on the Grameen Bank to support demonstrations of both economic and Rawlsian approaches. Given that, as noted below, the decade of the 1990s was the period when economic analyses of the Grameen Bank were most programmatically important, this chapter addresses the Bank of that period unless otherwise noted.

Economic Accounts of the Causes for Successful Microfinance

In 1977, Muhammad Yunus, a professor of economics at the University of Chittagong in southeast Bangladesh, began to experiment with small loans to poor women and men. "Nothing in the economic theories I taught reflected the life around me," he reported of his reaction to the Bangladesh famine of 1974. "How could I go on telling my students make-believe stories in the name of economics? . . . I needed to run away from these theories and from my text books and discover the real life economics of a poor person's existence."[1] His initial efforts to support petty trade and small productive ventures led to some success, and in 1983 he officially opened the Grameen Bank. It grew rapidly, despite lending mainly to women, who tend to be economically marginalized in Bangladesh's patriarchal Muslim society, and despite its policy of lending only to the poor. By the early 1990s, it was probably the best-known microfinance organization in the world. By the late 1990s, it had over 3 million borrowers and it regularly reported repayment rates around 98 percent.[2]

In the 1990s, the leading academic discipline in the international development community, and particularly at its leading organization, the World Bank, was neoclassical economics. Both rational choice theory and neoclassical economics are based on the same utilitarian view of the person, and both were becoming hegemonic, the former in political science, the latter in international development. Therefore, despite Yunus's protestations, economics constituted the primary perspective from which the Grameen Bank would be understood outside Bangladesh.

The most important proximate cause for the Grameen Bank's success, which set it apart from most microfinance programs for the poor, was its high repayment rate. According to the standard Grameen Bank story, its high repayment rate was due to its innovative group lending scheme, in which borrowers were required to form groups of five. If any member of the group defaulted on her loan, all were rendered ineligible for further borrowing. This kind of scheme generates so-called social collateral, since borrowers have an incentive to support one another in their economic ventures and to discourage defaulting.

Given that neoclassical economics conceives of the person as a rational, utility-maximizing agent, it conceives of the repayment decision as a matter of interests and incentives. Thus, Besley and Coate, in their game theory analysis of group lending schemes, model the borrower's repayments as based on comparing the gains from consuming the principal and interest with the consequences of defaulting. These latter include penalties imposed by the bank, and, under group lending, those stemming from "the wrath of other group members."[3] In Besley and Coate's analysis, the significant feature of group lending is the penalties the group can impose on the defaulting member, which mostly arise from the preexisting degree of "social connectedness" found in the village community.[4] It is notable that although Besley and Coate reference the Grameen Bank,[5] their mathematical model refers to group lending schemes in general. Their conclusion, for example, that at low interest rates group lending yields higher repayment rates than individual lending, relies not on data but on their analysis of the structure of incentives.

Another analysis of causes for success in microfinance based on economic assumptions is Chaves and Gonzalez-Vega's study of seven rural financial intermediaries (RFIs) in Indonesia, which collectively served over 4 million clients. They may have received one-time subsidies when they were established, but subsequently they covered their costs with profits derived from effective annual interest rates between 31.5 and 84.4 percent. The Grameen Bank, by contrast, charged interest rates around 20 percent to a poorer clientele, and in the 1990s it covered a substantial part of its operating costs with grants and subsidized loans. The Indonesian RFIs did not exclude richer clients; they held savings as well as gave loans, and their average loans ranged from $26 to $625 compared to $160 at the Grameen Bank.

While Besley and Coate focus on the borrower's repayment decision, Chaves and Gonzalez-Vega also consider the organizations that manage financial intermediation. "It is the managers of financial intermediaries who decide, for instance, to exert a low or high effort to collect loans;

while borrowers have to decide whether to repay. All these development-relevant decisions are the result of individuals maximizing their objective functions under constraints . . . That is, success—however defined—may occur only when it is in someone's best interest and when such interest may be pursued, given the existing constraints and environment."[6] The local villagers employed as branch managers received wages above local market rates, and they also received a portion of any profits from their branch. Therefore, they had incentives to work hard, avoid corrupt practices that could lead to job loss, and use their knowledge of the community to avoid lending to bad risks. Additionally, these RFIs required prospective borrowers to obtain character references from the village chief, or *lurah*. "Since the *lurah* earns, in most cases, a fee on each character reference, this function represents a personal asset, worth the present discounted value of future fees. When the *lurah* has provided a mistaken *ex ante* estimation of the probability of repayment, he would have a strong incentive for exerting pressure on the borrower, in order to recover the delinquent amount and maintain his credibility."[7] Also, since the *lurah* would normally provide character references to all local banks, he would act as a store of information about creditworthiness.

Explaining Successful Microfinance in Terms of Principles as Well as Interests

Besley and Coate view repayment rates as a function of the disincentive to default, and Chavez and Gonzalez-Vega attribute success in microfinance to the overall structure of incentives facing all the agents involved (branch managers, borrowers, local chiefs). Since these are economic analyses, they interpret behavior as a function of interests (and the associated incentives). Rawlsian program analysis, too, attributes behavior to interests, but because it takes the sense of right to be independent from the sense of the good, it also attributes behavior to principles. Thus, it assumes that the results of a microfinance program may be due in part to norms, ideology, and organizational culture.

Indeed, it seems that these factors are essential to explaining the Grameen Bank's high repayment rate (and other aspects of its success as discussed below). In a remarkable 1996 paper dissenting from the prevailing economic orthodoxy, Jain attributes this high rate not only to "strategic credit policies" but also to "credit conducive [organizational] culture."[8] Based on five weeks of fieldwork, Jain finds that the Grameen Bank did not enforce the social collateral policy that many scholars had singled out as the main reason for its high repayment rates. This policy was indeed used to encourage group members to exert peer pressure in favor of repayments (although it has since been abandoned), but when one member did default, others were not required, as stated in the policy, to cover the loan, nor were additional loans withheld from other group members.[9] Under the standard economic assumption of complete information, the policy cannot have had the incentive effect attributed to it.

Instead, Jain identifies the establishment of mutual obligations between Bank borrowers and Bank "functionaries" (personnel) to fulfill Bank norms as the central reason for its high repayment rates.[10] These were established, he argues, through the 6,000 field functionaries' complete reliability and openness in conducting fifty-two meetings a year with each thirty-member village center, and through intensive training, frequent reinforcement, and consistent leadership support for the Bank's norms.

Like Chaves and Gonzalez-Vega, Jain places major emphasis in explaining the Bank's success on the behavior of its personnel, but he does not present their behavior as merely maximizing self-interest. Their wages were in line with wages at government banks, and due to the Grameen Bank's pace of expansion, promotion was rapid. Jain emphasizes, however, how Bank employees were trained to adopt and promote the Bank's philosophy. Most new hires were recent college graduates, and their six months of training began with writing two case studies on transformations that the loan activity had brought about in the life of a poor borrower. They had some classroom work, but mostly they accompanied an experienced worker on weekly visits, on foot or on bicycle, to ten village centers. "The Grameen Bank organized its training such that for six months, the participants became so engrossed in the branch-level operations that they internalized the norms which became part of their personal value system."[11] Despite Bangladesh's scarce employment opportunities, however, "typically 50–60 percent of trainees left the service by the end of the training period."[12]

New borrowers began with a seven-day training program during which they were instructed in the Bank's by-laws, discipline, and norms, and learned to sign their names. Leadership of each group of five borrowers rotated each year, and each chairperson was expected to attend a seven-day workshop. "These . . . were backed up by three-day and one-day workshops organized at the branch level, covering a still larger number of group representatives."[13] Each week all thirty members of a center held a meeting, attended by a Bank worker, at which savings and loan installments were paid, loan approvals announced, and every single case of late payment publicly discussed. "All decisions, actions and transactions regarding the loan were thus taken up at the center meeting, under public scrutiny."[14] Group members were required to pay a regular group tax and to contribute to group savings, and the disposition of these funds was determined by the group. Members were encouraged to make weekly contributions to a children's welfare fund, and in 1990, centers were running approximately four thousand schools. "The Bank's activities were promoted as contributing to the overall development of members and rural society."[15]

It seems that the hard work of the Grameen Bank employees and the regular repayments of the Bank's borrowers should be attributed in part to a development ideology, an ideology that seems to have been carefully cultivated. The ideology was constituted in part by particular principles, such as, for employees, "I should get to meetings on time," "I should keep my loan records complete," and "I should encourage borrowers to stay current on payments"; and for borrowers, "I should always make my scheduled payments when I can," "I should give and take business advice from other members," and "I should work hard to build my business." These principles in turn were connected with a shared sense of purpose, oriented to development and to empowerment, and this sense of purpose would have been experienced in particular moments as individually uplifting and motivating, and as binding the group, both employees and borrowers, in a common task.

The Grameen Bank's hierarchical structure of offices included branches, areas, zones, and the head office. Jain writes that "one of the key tasks of the zonal manager was to bring the expectations, understanding, and actual behavior of all field functionaries in line with the philosophy and policies of Grameen Bank."[16] He similarly finds that "probably the most important role of the headquarters was . . . to uphold the original spirit and purpose of the Grameen Bank among its staff members."[17] The managing director, Yunus, spent about 100 to 150 days each year visiting field offices and talking to staff members, to ensure that they "understood the perspective and policies articulated by the top management, and top management remained sensitive to the field situation and the problems of people working in the field."[18]

At the village level, the organizational setup for borrowers helped to establish principles that supported collective decision making and solidarity in pursuit of the Bank's developmental ideology. Borrowers were required to contribute 5 percent of each loan as a group tax, and 25 percent of interest payments went not to the Bank but to the group's emergency fund. These funds served a purpose beyond being insurance for borrowers. Because the group decided how to spend them, they also supported the cultivation of what we might describe as "civic virtues." Loan payments were required on a weekly basis, and all transactions, including new loans, repayments, and disbursements from group funds, took place in public, normally in the presence of all thirty members of the center. "Centre meetings were conducted with solemnity and a sense of discipline, with members sitting in rows, each row corresponding to one group."[19] Jain asserts that loan disbursal and repayment procedures "were designed to be convenient to the borrowers, wasting little of their time or effort,"[20] but it must have taken quite a lot of time to sit through weekly meetings at which thirty borrowers make and discuss their transactions. If this is merely a transaction cost, it is quite a significant one. In addition to encouraging repayments in public and providing educational value, a Rawlsian analysis of these meetings takes them to support the cultivation of solidarity, of the Bank's developmental ideology, and of group-process skills and principles that are essential to collective will formation.[21]

The Grameen Bank's success was due partly to its effective cultivation of standard principles of good practice and hard work, and to its establishment of such principles within a somewhat self-perpetuating organizational culture. It also had official principles that could be said to constitute a formal ideology, the clearest statement of which is found in the Sixteen Decisions that borrowers were required to memorize and to recite at meetings:

1. We shall follow and advance the four principles of the Grameen Bank—Discipline, Unity, Courage and Hard Work—in all walks of our lives.
2. Prosperity we shall bring to our families.
3. We shall not live in dilapidated houses. We shall repair our houses and work towards constructing new houses at the earliest.
4. We shall grow vegetables all the year round. We shall eat plenty of them and sell the surplus.
5. During the planting seasons, we shall plant as many seedlings as possible.
6. We shall plan to keep our families small. We shall minimize our expenditures. We shall look after our health.
7. We shall educate our children and ensure that they can earn to pay for their education.
8. We shall always keep our children and the environment clean.
9. We shall build and use pit-latrines.
10. We shall drink water from tubewells. If it is not available, we shall boil water or use alum.
11. We shall not take any dowry at our sons' weddings, neither shall we give any dowry at our daughter's wedding. We shall keep our centre free from the curse of dowry. We shall not practice child marriage.
12. We shall not inflict any injustice on anyone, neither shall we allow anyone to do so.
13. We shall collectively undertake bigger investments for higher incomes.
14. We shall always be ready to help each other. If anyone is in difficulty, we shall all help him or her.
15. If we come to know of any breach of discipline in any centre, we shall all go there and help restore discipline.
16. We shall introduce physical exercise in all our centres. We shall take part in all social activities collectively.[22]

It is not to be expected, of course, that the Bank's borrowers actually followed these principles all or even most of the time. It is important, however, that some borrowers followed them some of the time, so they could anchor a broader set of principles, including the more banal ones.

We can conceive of the Sixteen Decisions as supporting the adoption and maintenance of the good practice principles, thus contributing to the Grameen Bank's high repayment rate.

The essential question for our present purpose is whether the Grameen Bank's high repayment rate, and the associated impacts (as discussed below), can be understood merely as a result of the incentive structures that the Bank established, or in terms of constructions of both interests and principles. Since the disincentives to default emphasized by Besley and Coate were not enforced, they cannot explain the borrowers' behavior. One could perhaps construct some kind of story along the lines of Chaves and Gonzalez-Vega's account of the Indonesian RFIs, in which Bank personnel and borrowers were "maximizing their objective functions," but these objective functions would not be based straightforwardly on material interests. Such a story would have to include interests that were established and sustained through the efforts of the Grameen Bank, such as promoting women's empowerment and village development. In this case, however, the account would rely at least implicitly on the Bank's promotion of principles, which in turn can be understood as loosely linked with the Bank's ideology and organizational culture.

My argument is, of course, more general than this. Based on the Kantian model of practical reason, I argue that program dynamics in general are best explained as constructions of principles and interests. The Grameen Bank presents a useful case because much of the analysis of the Grameen Bank in particular and of microfinance in general has been informed by economic assumptions, and economists have had very strong voices in development debates, but principles seem to have been quite important to the Bank's success. Jain's argument is informed by organization theory, a field of sociology, so he was predisposed to pay attention to norms.[23] Nevertheless, he engages in a debate that had been framed by economists. It is the Bank's high repayment rate that he seeks to explain, and his final argument is against the use of the Subsidy Dependence Index (SDI) as the "centerpiece to assess the efficacy of rural financial institutions." The SDI is a measure promoted by economists of an organization's dependence on external subsidies. In economic theory, subsidies are associated with potential utility losses, and some economists have argued that microfinance programs should not be subsidized. Jain concludes, however, that "subsidy for rural finance is yet an open issue."[24]

To appreciate the force of this argument, we need to consider different conceptions of the Grameen Bank's impacts.

Standards and Measures for Assessing Microfinance Programs

It is a corollary of the Rawlsian conception of the person that the discourse of any organization is grounded in principles. While such principles are not always oriented to the organization's mission, a large part of contemporary management advice aims to support this kind of orientation. The principles prevailing within a given organization are likely to become most apparent when there are conflicts over the allocation of the organization's resources; people appeal to principles to mediate competition among legitimate interests. For large development agencies, the central resource allocation problem can be conceived of as one of selecting among investments, such as in the choice between two project proposals. (Choices in hiring and in management strategies follow the same pattern.) Project analysis, then, can be conceived of as supporting this kind of choice, for example, by providing a basis for determining which proposal is likely to have the greater economic returns or the greater impact on poverty. Theory, in this context, provides the criteria for assessing project proposals (and hence for organizing their content and presentation). The judgments on which these assessments are made depend on evaluations of completed projects that are similar to the proposed projects. Theory determines both the units and the form of the analysis of impacts. Economic theory has yielded two main approaches to analyzing microfinance projects—one based on the SDI, and the other based on adding up benefits of one form or another and making a comparison with costs, which is a standard approach for all kinds of projects. Rawlsian program analysis involves a similar adding-up exercise, but while in economic theory the objects to be added up are understood to increase utility, in the Rawlsian approach they can be understood as contributing to autonomy. Hence, to adopt Rawlsian program analysis is to ground a development agency's organizational culture in autonomy.

Note that the economic and Rawlsian approaches to program analysis are both oriented in one way or another to helping an organization maximize its impacts. The two approaches conceptualize impacts differently, but they both take it that public agencies should be designed instrumentally in order to achieve appropriately defined objectives efficiently. Whether decisions within an organization, for example, should be made on a consensual or hierarchical basis should be based not on how it contributes to the happiness or satisfaction of the organization's personnel, but on which arrangement contributes more cost-effectively to achieving the organization's goals. The thought is that understanding each program's cost-effectiveness can aid in understanding how design choices differentially contribute to program impacts.

The SDI offers a straightforward mechanism for determining a financial intermediary's commercial viability. Developed by Jacob Yaron at the World Bank,[25] it reflects the proposition from mainstream economic theory that an unsubsidized service is unambiguously utility enhancing. Borrowers would not pay the interest required for a loan unless taking out the loan enhanced their utility. When a financial service is commercially viable, moreover, there is the presumption that it is supporting profitable economic activities, since most borrowers earn from their investments more than enough to cover the principal and interest. The presence of subsidies, by contrast, raises the possibility that the operation reduces utility overall, since losses to those who are taxed to pay for the subsidy may exceed utility gains to borrowers.[26]

Most development programs, of course, are subsidized. This can be justified by economic theory if gains to beneficiaries exceed costs—and this is what the economic analysis of projects is supposed to determine.[27] It adds to the attraction of the SDI that it is technically difficult to quantify the benefits from microfinance programs. Most of the benefits from road building projects, for example, are due to reductions in transportation costs, and these can be extrapolated fairly easily from traffic surveys. Benefits from microfinance, however, arise from increased control over financial resources and from the uses to which loans are put.[28] An important part of the benefits derives from economic gains to the borrower's household, but these are notoriously difficult to measure in a largely subsistence economy like that of rural Bangladesh. Also, given the impracticality of randomly assigning borrowers to credit programs, comparative data on the impacts of such programs are inevitably subject to selection bias.

A formal presentation of the economic approach is found in Pitt and Khandker's study *Household and Intrahousehold Impact of the Grameen Bank and Similar Targeted Credit Programs in Bangladesh*:

> Assume that households of size *n*, consisting of two working age adults (the male head and his wife) plus n-2 dependents, maximize a lifetime utility function containing time-specific utility functions of the form
>
> $$U_t = U(Q_1 \ldots Q_n, H_1 \ldots H_n, l_1 \ldots l_n) \qquad (1)$$
>
> where Q_i is a set of market goods consumed by household member *i*, the set of non-market household-produced goods allocated to member *i* is H_i, and l_i is leisure time consumed by household member *i*.[29]

In this formulation, utility comes from consuming goods and from having leisure time. Based on a quasi-experimental household survey conducted in eighty-seven randomly selected villages, Pitt and Khandker estimate benefits to borrowers and to their families from participating in the Grameen Bank and in two other credit programs. They estimate a wide range of impacts, including expenditures, contraceptive use, recent fertility, women's and men's labor supply and nonland assets, and boys' and girls' body mass indices (a nutritional measure) and schooling.

Pitt and Khandker conclude by listing a range of impacts from the Grameen Bank and the other credit programs, so the reader is left to consider the relative weights or importance of the different impacts and the expense they might justify. An ECBA would take additional steps, translating the noneconomic impacts into monetary terms based on the beneficiaries' willingness to pay, then incorporating them with costs, on a discounted basis, to determine each program's ERR.[30] In a standard ERR analysis, economic benefits would count the same regardless of the income of the recipient; but to incorporate a focus on poverty, the analyst might report both the ERR and the proportion of benefits going to households below the poverty line. Alternatively, in order to introduce distributional sensitivity, the analyst might increase the weight of benefits going to poorer households and decrease that of benefits to richer households, according to a weighting coefficient.[31] The higher the coefficient, the greater the emphasis would be on benefits to the poor. Economic theory can justify this kind of weighting with its doctrine of the diminishing marginal utility of income, although only by endorsing interpersonal comparisons of utility based on a single scale, which is contrary to mainstream economic principles (see note 26). Economic theory provides no basis, however, for determining the value of the weighting coefficient.

A Rawlsian scheme of values for program analysis starts from the original position, with the idea of primary goods. The argument is a little different depending on whether the discussion is about program analysis by a government or by an international development agency, but both reach much the same conclusion. Recall that in the original position we are to imagine that we do not know our natural abilities or our status in society. The conception of justice Rawls argues we would adopt under these conditions relies on the idea of primary goods—those goods it is rational for each person to want in order to pursue her plan of life, whatever that plan may be. Social (as opposed to natural) primary goods include rights, liberties and opportunities, income and wealth, and the social bases for self-respect.[32] Rawls argues that in a just society the liberties are secured first, and then only those economic and social inequalities are permitted that contribute to the long-term interests of the society's least well-off members. In an unjust society it is particularly urgent to secure the more essential primary goods for the poor. Governments may devote resources to programs that benefit the rich if these enhance the long-term prospects for the poor, but this does not diminish the urgency of ending extreme poverty. In a world where some peoples (countries) are rich and others are poor, the rich have an obligation to help the poor, again, particularly to secure the more essential primary goods.[33]

Note again that the idea is to secure the particular goods that it is rational for each person to want in order to pursue her plan of life. In contrast to maximizing utility, the goal here is to secure the bases for the individual's autonomy.[34] Granted, secure access to primary goods is not enough to achieve the full Kantian ideal of autonomy, according to which the individual acts always from principles that are consistent with the categorical imperative. But the vulnerability arising from a lack of essential primary goods is likely to increase the propensity to heteronomy, such as in choices that privilege a woman's or her family's own needs, so securing these goods can be expected to support autonomy. Although autonomy may seem to be an abstract idea, the criteria this approach yields for development programs are more deeply grounded in the person as an embodied and social being than those of ECBA. Adequate nutrition, health care, literacy, and recourse in case of misfortune, for example, manifestly contribute to autonomy.

In the context of a historically authoritarian and patriarchal society such as that of Bangladesh, this approach also counts as impacts the establishment of principles that support participation in collective will formation. This addresses the condition in which democratic rights and liberties are not fully institutionalized. For example, in Bangladesh the establishment of principles that support women's equal participation in decision making within the family and in politics also contributes to women's autonomy.

If program analysis is to support resource allocation decisions, it needs to provide a basis for program comparisons. Thus, a Rawlsian program analysis needs to apply weights to its measures of different kinds of contributions to autonomy (economic, health, principles that support participation in collective will formation, etc.). If this can be accomplished, then each program's impacts can be summed and compared to costs in some kind of cost-benefit calculation, and this determines the program's relative cost-effectiveness. It would be best if an appropriate procedure could be found to develop a weighting scheme that could be adopted by the entire development community, including bilateral and multilateral development agencies, governments, development-oriented nonprofits or nongovernmental organizations (NGOs), and foundations. This would be represented in a schedule of "prices" that donors and others are normally willing to pay to achieve a given impact. At this writing there is something of a de facto consensus in the standard weighting scheme of ECBA, where impacts are measured by their economic values and projects are compared by their ERRs.[35] A Rawlsian system, by contrast, would give greater weights to income gains for poorer beneficiaries, basic education, and health such as one expects from primary health care. An ERR analysis, of course, does not include gains in participation in collective will formation, but these are counted in a Rawlsian analysis.

Impact Analyses of the Grameen Bank and the Concept of Empowerment

The rough outline of the findings these three approaches yield for the Grameen Bank may already be apparent. Based on the SDI, the Grameen Bank of the late 1980s appeared somewhat weak. Standard economic analyses of the Bank around this period, although they did not speak with a single voice, generally found it to be quite cost-effective, and in this case a Rawlsian analysis would have found it to be even more so.

We have noted that in the 1990s, neoclassical economics was the dominant theoretical orientation within the development community. The SDI offered a closer and certainly more elegant approximation of neoclassical economic principles than the standard economic analyses of the Grameen Bank, so it is perhaps not surprising that the SDI tended to dominate the discourse on the analysis of microfinance programs. Indeed, at this writing, defenders of the SDI remain strong in the policy community that deals with microfinance programs. The discourse on microfinance programs, however, is embedded in the discourse of the broader development community. Analysts of microfinance programs had to come to terms with the concerns and priorities of this broader community, and when assessing the Grameen Bank, at least for less doctrinaire analysts, this meant that it was important to address its empowerment of women. The concept of "empowerment," however, does not fit neatly in economic theory. Different analysts have tried to subsume empowerment under a variety of economic concepts, but the results have been less than satisfactory. We will see that within a Rawlsian framework, where the adoption of principles that enhance participation in collective will formation is taken as a form of program impact, the concept of empowerment is unproblematic. A comparison of economic and Rawlsian treatments of empowerment helps to demonstrate the significance of the Rawlsian approach.

The Grameen Bank's Score on the Subsidy Dependence Index

The SDI expresses "the percentage increase in a [rural financial institution's] average on-lending interest rate required to compensate for the elimination of subsidies."[36] Like an ERR, it expresses an important relationship in a single number, in this case that between an organization's total expenses and the income from its operations. This relationship is standardized based on the increased interest rate that would make up the difference between expenses and income when applied to the present loan portfolio. Yaron finds that the Grameen Bank's index scores were 180 percent in 1987 and 130 percent in 1989, more than five times higher than those of the second most heavily dependent rural financial institution in his study. In order to break even, the Grameen Bank would have had to raise its interest rate from 16.5 percent to 46 percent in 1987 or to 38 percent in 1989, assuming it did not lose any borrowers. Other financial institutions in his study had interest rates up to 130 percent on an annualized basis.[37] On the basis of the SDI, the Grameen Bank is not found to be very successful. It is notable, however, that at this writing the Bank no longer accepts external grants, and its deposits exceed its loans.

Economic Analyses of the Grameen Bank's Impacts

The SDI emphasizes the value to clients of financial services—the opportunity to borrow and to save—without enquiring into the uses to which loans are put. If a financial intermediary can earn enough from interest charges to cover its costs, this establishes a presumption that it is utility enhancing. When a subsidy is present, the economic question is whether program impacts are sufficient to justify it. If so, the programmatic question is how the impacts were achieved and where the lessons can be applied to achieve similar impacts. Questions that may be relevant to the economic analysis, therefore, include the borrowers' degree of poverty (if we assume diminishing marginal returns in utility to increasing income) and the range of gains (and/or losses) to beneficiary well-being (utility) due to participation in Grameen Bank programs. In order to interpret the programmatic significance of these gains, it is important to understand the program's cost-effectiveness compared to other similar programs.

There is a consensus in the literature that the Grameen Bank is fairly effective at targeting its loans to poor borrowers, but that in the context of the extreme poverty found in Bangladesh these borrowers usually are not the poorest of the poor. The Bank has a policy not to lend to members of households that own more than half an acre of land or assets of an equivalent value. In a study of two villages in northern Bangladesh, Fujita finds only a quarter of Grameen Bank borrowers to own more than the limit and five borrowers to own more than two and a half acres. This could be low-quality land, or some could have been acquired since they became borrowers.[38] Amin, Rai, and Topa find that Grameen Bank borrowers are poorer than average for their villages, but that the poorest and most vulnerable are underrepresented.[39] One officer stated that he was looking for borrowers who were "not hopeless."[40] Pitt and Khandker find, similarly, that Grameen Bank borrowers are by many measures less deprived, on average, than the Bangladesh rural poor overall, apparently because officers select borrowers, and officers and borrowers select other borrowers who are better than average risks.[41]

On the basis of a large sample survey, Pitt and Khandker find that borrowers' annual household expenditures increase by $18 for each $100 disbursed.[42] McKernan finds from the same data that participation in the Grameen Bank increases average monthly profits for self-employed borrowers by about $80, from $45 to $125, or over $900 per year.[43] Given that in 1989 Bangladesh's gross national product per capita was $180, and with the average loan size about $160, this seems implausibly large. Khandker reports that in villages with established Grameen Bank programs, production per household is 55.9 percent higher, income per household is 29.4 percent higher, the rural wage is 13.5 percent higher, moderate poverty is 19.8 percent lower, and absolute poverty is 75 percent lower as compared to similar villages with no credit program.[44] Some part of these differences may be due to selection bias, but it seems plausible that the greater part is due to the Grameen Bank. Todd finds, similarly, that over a one-year period, 57.5 percent of long-term Grameen Bank borrowers were no longer poor based on the government's poverty line, compared with 18 percent of nonborrowers. Also, only 15 percent of borrowers were extremely poor, compared with 54 percent of nonborrowers.[45]

Moving beyond economic benefits, the Grameen Bank's female borrowers keep their sons in school 24.2 percent longer and their daughters 18.6 percent longer as compared to nonborrowers.[46] In a context in which childhood undernourishment is endemic, a 10 percent increase in disbursement to women leads to nutritional gains that increase the average arm circumference of daughters by 0.45 cm and of sons by 0.39 cm and increase the average height of daughters by 0.36 cm and of sons by 0.50 cm;[47] borrowers' children are found to be somewhat taller and much heavier than children in a control group and than average Bangladeshi children.[48] Grameen Bank women borrowers were more likely to implement the health aspects of the Sixteen Decisions than a control group—particularly in using sanitary latrines, growing vegetables, and immunizing children. They were likely to eat more and better because they often ate with their husbands rather than after them, and they were more likely than nonborrowers to consult private doctors.[49]

This impressive evidence of the Grameen Bank's impacts is reinforced by comparisons with other programs. Khandker reports that in 1991–92 it cost only $0.91 in subsidy for each dollar of additional consumption by female Grameen Bank borrowers compared to costs from $2.59 to $4.88 per dollar gain by borrowers from other Bangladeshi credit programs.[50] Food-for-work programs spent from $1.71 to $2.62 to get a dollar of benefits to participants, while infrastructure programs spent $1.38.[51] It appears that a dollar of subsidy leads to about a dollar of additional consumption by Grameen Bank borrowers. When we consider, in addition, the Bank's declining subsidy and expanding client base, it appears that economic returns from subsidies to the Bank have been significantly greater than the subsidies themselves. Taking into account noneconomic as well as economic impacts, the Bank appears to have been significantly more cost-effective at reducing poverty than other studied programs in Bangladesh.

Rawlsian Analysis of the Grameen Bank's Impacts

Since the Rawlsian moral psychology includes interests, any good found in an economic program analysis will normally appear in a Rawlsian program analysis. Besides gains in income, health, and education, both approaches attend to the Grameen Bank's role in reducing risk and in enhancing borrowers' (and savers') security. With its inclusion of principles, the Rawlsian approach also attends to the institutions that constitute borrowers' political and social relations, and their compatibility with principles that would be adopted in the original position. While Bangladesh is a constitutional democracy, legacies of colonialism and authoritarian rule remain strong, and social relations patriarchal, particularly in rural areas. Enhancements to the substantive equality of social and political relations in such a context can contribute importantly to autonomy and therefore also constitute impacts in a Rawlsian program analysis. In the language prevailing in the field, these impacts are typically referred to as "empowerment."

There are three main pathways by which the Grameen Bank leads women to adopt empowering principles, and these principles apply in two areas. The empowerment pathways for women are (1) management of economic enterprises, (2) participation in collective activities, and (3) adoption of principles from the Grameen Bank's ideology. The areas in which new principles are applied are (1) within and (2) outside the family and household.

In the early 1980s, the majority of poor women in rural Bangladesh had never managed an economic enterprise outside the home.[52] In succeeding in such enterprises, women would gain practical experience, self-esteem, and status in the household and in the community. Also, experience with an enterprise begins to demystify enterprises conducted by husbands and others. Generally, women become better able to participate in collective will formation with regard to the employment of productive resources. In many cases, however, women turn their loans over to their husbands. Indeed, it appears that after a woman establishes a degree of independence with a new loan, her husband often reasserts his authority over time. Hashemi, Schuler, and Riley report that in villages where the Grameen Bank was recently established, 27 percent of women had full control over loan-funded enterprises and 36 percent had significant control (usually with husbands taking care of marketing). In villages where Bank lending was well established, however, only 18 percent had full control and 9 percent had significant control. A full 64 percent had no control at all—the loan went to fund the husband's economic activities.[53] Rahman, an anthropologist, explains that women's status in rural

Bangladesh is intertwined with the concepts of honor and shame. He found Bank workers using shame and the threat of shame to encourage or coerce borrowers to attend meetings and to make payments regularly.[54] In the village where he conducted his field research, women were sometimes caught between husbands using them to get loans and Bank workers pressuring them to come to meetings and make payments.

Hashemi, Schuler, and Riley find, however, that women became more empowered according to other indicators as the duration of their membership increased. They were more likely to make small independent purchases, be involved in major family decisions, and participate in political campaigns or public protests.[55] Empowerment in these dimensions is partly due to the roles women play in bringing economic resources into the home, but it is also due to the other pathways to empowerment—participation in collective activities and adoption of principles from the Bank's ideology. Mizan finds that female Grameen borrowers' decision-making power in the family increases due to both their greater income contribution and their greater competence and motivation. As the number of years of borrowing increased, so did the women's negotiating skills, social network affiliations, and knowledge. Todd finds, too, that partnerships between husband and wife were the most common form of household decision making in Grameen Bank households and the least common among households in a control group.[56]

In a context of deep inequalities, a Rawlsian program analysis also accords an important place to solidarity. Shared principles provide the grounds for solidarity, which can be defined as a principle-specific value orientation shared among two or more persons that does not privilege the self and that provides a basis for individual and/or collective action. The Grameen Bank provides both the principles (in its ideology) and the occasions (group activities) for the development of solidarity. It also supports the development of skills and habits of collective action, such as when members decide how to spend their group funds and undertake development projects. Solidarity and these skills and habits together constitute what scholars in recent years have called "social capital," but this term identifies their merit as essentially economic. While they can indeed be economically beneficial, these kinds of relationships and the consciousness they build are profoundly political.

It is notable that although the Grameen Bank has built considerable solidarity, it has not encouraged egalitarian relations between its personnel and its borrowers. Scholars often remark on the Bank's hierarchical organization and emphasis on discipline. Borrower group operations are regimented and ritualized, with borrowers usually addressing Bank personnel (most of whom are men) as "Sir," or "the Sirs." Borrowers from the other major NGO in rural Bangladesh, the Bangladesh Rural Action Committee, by comparison, address its employees as "Brother" or "Sister."

Hierarchical relations may support financial discipline and also (and interactively) the adoption of the Bank's ideology. The Bank's ideology can be investigated in terms of its individual principles—for example, those of the Sixteen Decisions—but it should also be conceived, whole cloth, as an integrated system. The principles are significant both individually ("Should I ask for dowry?") and systematically, as the Bank's personnel and borrowers work through their implications and apply them in new ways. For example, Bank workers sometimes advise women not to give their loans to their husbands, or, if they do give them, to keep some for their own investments.[57] This advice at once subverts and accommodates the patriarchal status quo. To adopt the principles inherent in this advice enhances women's autonomy directly, as they carry it out, and also instrumentally, as they realize the fruits of their investments.

Within the household, conflicts between the established patriarchy and the Bank's ideology, along with the stresses of commercial enterprises, sometimes increase women's vulnerability. Among 120 women borrowers in Rahman's study village, where the Bank had been lending for about ten years, 57 percent reported an increase in verbal aggression and 13 percent reported increases in both verbal aggression and physical assaults in the past two years. Six women reported being beaten for refusing to give their loans to men or for challenging men's proposals for using the women's loans.[58] However, Schuler et al. found that women borrowers were much less likely to be beaten by their husbands than women who lived in non–Grameen Bank villages, and even nonborrowers in Grameen Bank villages were less likely to be beaten by their husbands.[59]

Because the Bank's ideology and its commercial interests sometimes pull in different directions, the ideology is sometimes compromised. Rahman reports, for example, that contrary to Grameen Bank policy, meetings in the loan centers he studied usually started without reciting the Sixteen Decisions, maintaining proper seating arrangements, chanting Grameen member mottos, or doing physical exercise, but Bank workers focused on collecting installments. Discipline was maintained and all rituals were practiced, however, when higher Bank officials or guests were present.[60]

Hashemi, Schuler, and Riley suggest that the Bank's founder and directors saw empowerment of women essentially as a means to poverty alleviation and social equity.[61] The Bank does not promote collective action against established political interests. It is inevitable, however, that as women's economic independence and solidarity increases, they become more likely to articulate and to promote their interests in the formal political arena. Wahid and Rahman note that Grameen Bank members sometimes elect their peers to positions in local government. "The voting pattern of the Grameen Bank members differs substantially from what it used to be. They no longer depend on the directives of the rural elite for voting. They now sit in their center and decide for whom to vote."[62]

In contrast to an economic analysis, a Rawlsian program analysis counts as impacts the various changes in principles that contribute to members' empowerment or to their participation in collective will formation. The Indonesian rural financial intermediaries discussed earlier in this chapter reinforce the political status quo, since, for example, they do not exclude borrowers who are male or better off, and they draw on the authority of village chiefs to encourage loan repayments. The Grameen Bank, by contrast, with its focus on poor women and its emphasis on collective action, has important impacts on redressing historic inequalities. In a Rawlsian analysis, these are added to economic, health, and education impacts. Just as a donor agency or a government might be willing to spend $100 to achieve a particular improvement in health, it might be willing to spend a similar sum to increase women's participation in decision making in the home or to increase their involvement in formal political processes to a certain extent. This willingness increases the subsidy that may be justified to support microfinance programs on the Grameen Bank model.

Since its empowerment of women has been a prominent idea in the popular discourse on the Grameen Bank, it is not surprising that it has entered economists' discourse on the Bank as well. In analyses organized in economic terms, however, it has proven difficult to find a convincing way to interpret this concept. Pitt and Khandker, for example, find positive and statistically significant effects on per capita household expenditures by the Bank's female borrowers, the hours they devote to production for the market, and the value of their assets (among other impacts).[63] On the basis specifically of increased expenditures, production for the market, and assets, they argue that "the Grameen Bank can 'empower' women."[64] They do not explain, however, why these criteria should be the particular requirements for or constituent elements of empowerment. Schreiner, by contrast, lists empowerment as one of several elements of user surplus,[65] and McKernan lists empowerment of women as an area in which microfinance programs provide human capital.[66]

Once we have seen the treatment of empowerment in a Rawlsian analysis, this confusion among economists should not surprise us. To explain empowerment as the adoption of principles that redress historic inequalities, enhancing participation in collective will formation, is consistent with the general use and understanding of this concept. The popular discourse on empowerment seems particularly congenial with a model of practical reason including principles as well as interests. Within an economic framework, however, empowerment must somehow be reconciled with concepts based on interests alone. Pitt and Khandker avoid this problem by stepping outside the framework, while Schreiner and McKernan subsume empowerment uncomfortably under different economic concepts.

The Contribution of Program Analysis to Organizational Culture

A distinctive feature of Kant's epistemology is that he views our knowledge as based not only on the nature of things in themselves but also on our cognition in our acts of perception. Indeed, this applies even more strongly to practical reason (about actions) than to theoretical reason (about things). For practical reason is grounded partly in principles, but principles are constructed by reason itself. Thus, our perception and interpretation of an action may be grounded in particular ideas of fairness (norms, principles), and these may differ between persons.[67] Our perception of things, by contrast, is grounded in our sense of space and of time, but these are presumably largely consistent between persons.[68]

Rawlsian program analysis differs from economic (and rational choice) analysis by attending to the establishment and maintenance of principles (as well as interests), both in interpreting program dynamics and in accounting for program impacts. As a form of analysis with programs as its subject, I have suggested that its role is to sustain an organizational culture oriented to maximizing appropriately defined impacts. Program analysis presupposes an executive or funding agency and an array of programs, let's say managed by implementing agencies, which the executive agency organizes and supports. (Of course an implementing agency such as the Grameen Bank may have several executive agencies and may not be subject to much direct external control from any one of them.) We can now see how the orienting function works. While impact analysis identifies a program's merit or worth, and analysis of the causes of the impacts explains how the impacts were achieved, the process as a whole—and the reports that are the product of the analysis—provide a potential basis for establishing and maintaining principles within both executive and implementing agencies that are oriented to maximizing impacts so defined. The reports provide an objective basis for designing new programs and for making resource allocation decisions of all kinds. When the process and the reports are used like this to allocate resources, the decision-making process itself constructs principles that cause members of executive and implementing agencies to see organizational problems and opportunities the same way, and to evaluate results in a consistent manner, insofar as their views are professionally relevant. Criteria are established that are intersubjectively recognized as valid, so if one agent makes a resource allocation decision (sincerely and correctly) on the basis of these criteria, she can reasonably anticipate that other agents will appreciate and support her decision.

Part of what it means to be professionally competent within the relevant offices of the executive agency is to be able to say (sincerely and correctly) after appropriate study: in this new environment X, a program of type Y, if reasonably well implemented, could be expected to have a range of impacts Z. We have seen, however, that a program analysis based on economic or rational choice assumptions is likely to miss, or to mistakenly assess, many of the dynamics at least of some kinds of programs. Such an analysis will not be attuned to the construction of ideologies and obligations. Also, analysts trained in economics are likely to see and to value program impacts in economic terms. Since Rawlsian analysts would see and value impacts in terms of their contributions to autonomy, they would be more attuned to whether benefits are reaching populations with more severe deficits, and they would recognize impacts in the area of empowerment that would not appear in economic analyses.

chapter five

Political Analysis of Problems in Bihar

Bihar . . . has become a byword for the worst of India:

of widespread and inescapable poverty; of corrupt

politicians indistinguishable from the mafia dons they

patronize; of a caste-ridden social order that has retained

the worst feudal cruelties; of terrorist attacks by groups of

"Naxalite" Maoists; of chronic misrule that has allowed

infrastructure to crumble, the education and health

systems to collapse, and law and order to evaporate.[1]

Rawlsian Political Analysis Compared to Other Approaches

This chapter presents Rawlsian political analysis by employing it to explain the causes of economic and social problems in the Indian state of Bihar.[2] It illustrates the distinctive character of Rawlsian political analysis as compared to neoclassical economic or rational choice approaches, including features at both micro and macro levels. At the micro level, resentment and a resentment-inspired urge to domination have contributed to social violence in Bihar's villages. At the macro level, Bihar's state politics have suffered in several ways from conflicts between egalitarian principles of democracy and hierarchical principles of caste. This chapter shows how these conflicts eventually fueled a politics of resentment and misplaced loyalties that yielded widespread corruption and inefficiency.

Just as chapter 4 demonstrates the analytic power that a program analysis gains by taking account of the reasonable, so the present chapter argues that the Rawlsian moral psychology permits a deeper and more convincing account of Bihar's economic and social problems than one would expect from neoutilitarian accounts. I argue in chapter 3 that the implications of this conception of the person for political science are not limited to gaining a stronger positive or empirical analysis. First, the Kantian model of practical reason indicates that while political analysis is empirical, it is also constructive, in that by doing political analysis we participate in building our social world. Second, in light of Kant's model, we find that the person has an imperfect obligation to promote social justice, and Rawlsian political analysis provides the means for developing an agenda and strategy to this end.[3]

Contemporary American political science has two forms of institutional analysis similar to the approach I propose. Both rational choice institutionalism and historical institutionalism, however, present themselves as merely empirical theories or approaches. Rawlsian political analysis presents itself as constructive as well as empirical, and, as long as we live in an unjust world order, it must also ultimately be a critical analysis. I propose that Rawls's moral psychology could provide microfoundations for historical institutionalism, or that Rawlsian microfoundations are implicit in the structural analyses that historical institutionalism offers. Certainly, a historical approach is necessary for explaining the development and dynamics of principles. Lacking microfoundations of their own, it seems that historical institutionalists have sometimes taken their agendas from the neoutilitarians, whom they criticize (for example, in explaining the causes of more or less successful industrialization). Nevertheless, characteristic tensions between economic rationality and social justice tend to be closer to the surface in historical institutionalists' accounts.[4] Rawlsian political analysis, however, intentionally occupies the analytic space at the intersection of ethics and power.

We should acknowledge the radical freedom and ambitious ideals that are inherent in the Rawlsian approach. Following Kant, Rawls points out that "practical reason is concerned with the production of objects according to a conception of those objects—for example, the conception of a just constitutional regime taken as the aim of political endeavor."[5] In contrast to Marx, Rawls does not see a just society resulting from an inevitable historical process or the possibility of social reform depending on the present configuration of interests. Progress toward justice depends on organized political action by autonomous individuals, possibly without regard to their material interests. Hence, a historical materialist would presumably find the Rawlsian approach excessively voluntaristic. Of course Rawls does not deny the deep roots and powerful inertia of established principles, much less the great influence of entrenched interests on politics.[6]

Rawls would count Bihar among what he calls "burdened societies," but he does not define what it means to be burdened on the basis of income or the satisfaction of any configuration of interests. Rather, burdened societies have historical, social, and economic circumstances that impede the establishment of a public conception of justice that supports the good of all citizens.[7] In Rawls's view, "the causes of the wealth of a people and the forms it takes lie in their political culture and in the religious, philosophical, and moral traditions that support the basic structure of their political and social institutions, as well as in the industriousness and cooperative talents of its members, all supported by their political virtues."[8] Furthermore, he conjectures "that there is no society anywhere in the world—except for marginal cases—with resources so scarce that it could not, were it reasonably and rationally organized and governed, become well-ordered."[9] The analyst's task for a place like Bihar is to explain why it is not reasonably and rationally organized and governed.

Neoclassical economics, like rational choice and historical institutionalism, often presents itself as merely empirical, although it is well known that it idealizes free and competitive markets. Free markets are expected to maximize utility, an expectation grounded in the theory of price formation. In short, price formation is driven by consumer choices among goods at particular prices, choices assumed to maximize the consumer's utility. Considering also the trade-offs made by workers between income and leisure, and those made by producers among production strategies to maximize profits, we have much of the motivational force in the theory of supply and demand. This leads to the ideal of a perfectly competitive market, because in such a market the interaction of supply and demand generates an efficient (Pareto optimal) allocation of society's resources. Competition drives producers to allocate resources prudently, and, if markets are undistorted so that prices reflect the opportunity cost of resources, allocations that are privately profitable are also socially efficient. Consumers, workers, and producers are as well off as they can be, given the distribution of assets. Given competitive markets and appropriate institutional supports, economic agents promote the social good merely by pursuing their private interests.

On the basis of this model, neoclassical economists at the World Bank and elsewhere have imposed an institutional formula on developing countries around the world. According to this formula, governments should keep their economies open to international trade and investment, maintain macroeconomic stability, minimize price distortions as they raise revenue, and provide public goods such as law and order, physical infrastructure, and education.[10] A neoclassical economic analysis of Bihar's increasing poverty would focus on the various ways in which Bihar diverges from the competitive market ideal.

Rational choice theory has no social ideal to parallel competitive markets for economists. Early rational choice analyses focused on how rational agents in government and politics are unlikely to promote the social good,[11] often exploring government failures not unlike those we find in Bihar.[12] More recent works have considered how institutional setups can align political and economic incentives so they both support economic growth,[13] typically by giving political and economic actors a determinate share in the fruits of particular investments. One can imagine recommendations for Bihar along these lines, but they would be highly contingent. Rational choice theorists' diverse insights into productive equilibria do not point toward any unified social model.

Why should the utilitarian idea of the person lead to a social ideal in economics but not in rational choice theory? It seems the reason can be found in characteristics of their subject matter—the production and distribution of goods and services for the former and the creation and use of power for the latter. Given the consistency of human needs, the plasticity of human abilities, and advantages of a division of labor, it just turns out that markets can play the role of the "invisible hand" identified by Adam Smith. Economists must continually remind short-sighted publics and self-interested politicians of this counterintuitive insight. Rational choice theory's philosophical pedigree includes political thinkers as diverse as Hobbes, Hume, Mill, and Sidgwick, but none of their views of the person approach the clean minimalism that lends rational choice theory its analytic power. But in a model that places interests squarely first and institutions second, and takes in its sights the full panoply of human institutions, there is no way around the fundamental fact that our interests set us apart from one another. As institutions create the context for power and power serves interests, the only way for competition to be contained is for power to balance power. Yet any balance of power is likely to be temporary because underlying economic and social conditions are inherently unstable. Rational choice theory reveals the stark realities underlying the comfortable illusions in which power clothes itself.

Rawlsian political analysis is like rational choice theory in seeking to identify the actual nature of social institutions and like economics in interpreting institutions in relation to a social ideal. Of course a Rawlsian analysis anticipates that institutions are based on principles as well as interests, and constituted by principles that frame and focus the pursuit of interests. Principles and interests develop according to distinct but interacting logics, so the analytic task is to build a narrative that is consistent with the central dynamics of both. To understand why life prospects for Bihar's people are so limited, we reconstruct the history that has led to present conditions. To reconstruct this history in terms of the principles and interests that constituted the people's central projects and conflicts is to provide a basis for social reform, because it allows us to see the causes for the distance between the reality and the ideal. At the macro level, a Rawlsian analysis is not markedly different from historical institutionalism, or from what some call "political economy"; it assumes that the reasons for Bihar's performing so much worse than India's other states are political. A Rawlsian analysis simply requires an overall, integrated account.

In particular, Bihar's government has not provided an effective vehicle for aggregating and promoting the people's interests. I argue that this is largely due to the caste system, but of course that is just one set of factors among many. Caste divisions contribute in different ways to explaining key episodes in the state's history: weak developmental impulses of state governments from India's independence in 1947 to 1967, multiple changes in government and resulting confusion from 1967 to 1972, violent intercaste conflict in villages beginning in the 1970s, and an extremely corrupt government from 1990 to 1997. Although Bihar's increasing poverty indicates a lack of normally competent governance, the analytic task is to explain the positive reasons for the governance Bihar has experienced.

We cannot possibly work out the microfoundations for all of the important relationships in such an historical account. Nevertheless, Bihar presents an appropriate subject for our purposes not only because its increasing poverty indicates extreme failure to do justice but also because of the importance of the recurring murderous violence in its villages. Although this violence defies rationality, it can be explained in terms of the dynamics of principles. Also, the Rawlsian approach may offer particular insights into the severe weaknesses of Bihar's governance in the 1990s.

Rawlsian Macro Analytics and the Politics of Caste

Although Bihar possesses excellent agricultural lands and a large part of India's mineral wealth, it is India's poorest and least developed state.[14] On the basis of India's ungenerous poverty line,[15] over half Bihar's one hundred million people live in poverty. In 1960, it was the fifth poorest of India's major states, but by 1990 it had by far the highest population share below the poverty line of any state.[16] It was also India's only state to see per capita income decline in the 1990s.[17] In 2002, forty thousand government employees in Bihar had not been paid salaries for at least ten years.[18] Bihar has India's lowest state literacy rate, with only 47 percent of its population able to read and write.[19]

Bihar has a long-standing reputation for firmly entrenched caste restrictions,[20] but it was the domination of Bihari politics from 1947 to 1967 by four upper castes that set the state's caste politics in motion. If the upper castes had been a tiny minority, as in Kerala, or if ideologically engaged political parties had already been well established, as in West Bengal, caste divisions would not have become so politically salient. As it was, four castes making up 14 percent of the state population (and owning more than half the farmland)[21] dominated the Congress Party in Bihar, and for the first two decades of independence, the Congress Party dominated the state government.

In order to understand the role of the caste system in Bihar's political history, we must first enquire into the nature of caste principles. Caste is a system of ritual hierarchy maintained through restrictions on intermarriage. Its notion of right livelihood in the fulfillment of duty is justified in terms of reincarnation and karma; high-caste individuals are thought to have earned status by dutiful action in previous lives. It divides rights and responsibilities according to notions of relative purity; thus, it assigns socially necessary tasks to specific groups. Socially significant, endogamous castes were divided from ancient times into four caste groups: brahmins, kshatriyas, vaishyas, and shudras. Brahmins were priests, kshatriyas were warriors, vaishyas were farmers or merchants, and shudras were servants or commoners. Dalits (formerly "untouchables") comprised a despised group below the shudras, virtually outside Hindu society. They were the most impure in the ritual hierarchy.[22]

Caste provides a basis for social cooperation by establishing principles of right relations among social groups. These principles are most clearly articulated in the religious realm of ritual; members of higher castes maintain their status through ritual performance. A sense of purity is established through various forms of abstinence; for example, in addition to avoiding beef, someone of a high caste may also avoid other foods, such as onions and garlic. Also, certain actions are proscribed at certain times. Of course a caste Hindu was not to touch a dalit.[23] Caste is also the primary form of social organization at the village level (except in Muslim or tribal villages). Where caste principles and social organization are strong, and where individual castes are populous enough to be politically significant, it would be surprising if caste did not become a primary basis for political mobilization.

Caste principles have several features that are politically salient. First, caste identity provides a basis for political organization that does not align neatly with divisions based on material interests. This helps the

establishment of patronage networks and hinders the political aggregation of interests. Second, caste identity not only divides society into
groups, it also identifies individuals as relatively superior or inferior. If I
am of caste Q, according to caste principles I feel myself superior to those
of caste R and below and inferior to those of caste P and above. Moreover, caste principles exclude lower groups from control over symbolic
and material production. Consequently, caste provides a basis for higher
groups to expect and demand respect and deference from lower groups.

The specific brahmin and kshatriya castes that initially dominated
Bihari politics were the Brahmins, Bhumihars, Rajputs, and Kayasthas.
None of these so-called forward castes was individually dominant, however, and senior positions tended to rotate among them. They made up 14
percent of the electorate, but members of the lower, or "backward," castes
made up 50 percent.[24] So if caste was to be the organizing principle of
political competition, the promise of democracy was to transfer power to
the lower castes. Dalits made up another 14 percent, Muslims 12 percent,
and members of Bihar's tribal populations 9 percent.[25]

The caste principles that gained political salience after 1947 were
not simply those of ancient tradition. Whatever this tradition may have
been in earlier centuries, it had been modified by British rule. The British had undermined some caste practices that they found particularly
offensive, but by acknowledging caste in the courts and the census they
strengthened the caste system, reinforcing its hierarchical features. Their
establishment of an all-India administration and improvement of communication and transportation infrastructures reduced the significance of
local borders and allowed regional caste councils to be strengthened. By
excluding native Indians from political power, they increased the residual
significance of caste's minute distinctions. Bihar was particularly subject
to the harsher extractive features of colonial domination. Unlike native
elites in Calcutta or Bombay, those in Bihar observed few of the creative
possibilities of domination. Repression and dispossession, however, such
as during and after the indigo boom of the nineteenth century, were extremely harsh in Bihar. The British also intensified intra-elite conflict by
sending Bengalis (mainly Kayasthas) to administer the region.

A Rawlsian analysis assumes that the character of upper-caste rule
would be influenced by the particular manifestation of upper-caste

principles in the earlier period. Being made to accept an inferior status and suffering the harsh restrictions and losses that the British imposed could perhaps have led to greater elite solidarity, but it appears that Bihar's fragmented local elites commonly sought compensation and tried to rebuild a sense of self through their own acts of domination. It is significant that a large percentage of upper-caste landowners "[did] not touch the plow"; that is, they interpreted caste principles to restrict them from much of the manual labor on the farm. Some of the principles associated with land ownership may be assumed to have transferred to "ownership" of office. These factors help to explain why the Bihar state government failed to develop a corporate agenda and organization, even to enhance the interests of the forward castes, in the two decades following independence.

There had been no doubt that independent India would become a democracy. Sources for this commitment lay in traditions of British parliamentarianism, Enlightenment liberalism, and anticolonial radicalism. The force of the commitment to democracy, however, was largely due to its providing an ideology for anticolonial nationalism. This is not to impugn the democratic credentials of the members of India's independence movement but to point out that in much of India, and certainly in Bihar, the ideologically engaged leadership made up only a tiny proportion of the social elite. The establishment of institutions of democratic accountability is problematic for any former colony, since domestic elites often take charge of a political infrastructure designed for colonial rule. In Bihar, due to the social dominance of the upper castes, demands for home rule effectively meant upper-caste rule.

After independence, India's central government aimed to uplift the poor primarily through government-led industrialization. It promoted land reforms, but the constitution left land policy implementation largely to the states. Since most state legislatures were, like Bihar's, dominated by high-caste landlords, it is not surprising that implementation was weak. As Kohli notes, the Indian central government "has not had the political or organizational capacity to implement [its own professed] redistributive goals."[26] Since industrialization also failed to gain the momentum that the planners expected, prospects for most Biharis would depend on developments within their own state.

Democratic governance did not lead, therefore, to any immediate improvement in material prospects for Bihar's poor majority. The significance for them of the egalitarian principles enshrined in the nation's constitution lay largely in formal equality before the law, government policies that took equal citizenship for granted, and equal voting rights. As a poorer state, Bihar has benefited from progressive allocations from some national programs, but implementation of these programs by the state bureaucracy has often left much to be desired. If India remained democratic, it was inevitable that political mobilization would eventually lead to a widespread consciousness of democratic rights; this was how democracy threatened social organization on caste principles. Democracy with universal suffrage tends to support a persistent presumption of equality, even if it may have little practical force.

To better economic conditions, the government's main task was to improve agriculture. With 92 percent of the 1960 population living in rural areas,[27] the overwhelming majority of the population depended on farming for its livelihood. The state's mining sector had something of an enclave nature; the main policy question was the formula by which the state's share of mining revenue was determined. Bihar has been home to many of India's major steel factories, with half the country's saleable steel production in 1960.[28] Ownership, however, has resided outside the state, and as with mining, these factories have not been integrated with the local economy.[29] As Prasad puts it, "Bihar was a living example of an internal colony."[30] Most Biharis' prospects for a better life, therefore, would depend on agriculture.

The government's orientation to agriculture is indicated by its approach to land reform. The Bihar Land Reform Act of 1950 and its amendments established a contest for revenue between the state government and the landlords and their middlemen. Due to the inadequacy of land records, transfer of titles from landlords to tenants was postponed.[31] The immediate effect of (limited) land reform was to transfer responsibility for the collection of rents from middlemen employed by landlords to government.[32] State legislators could justify their efforts as defending themselves and their high-caste constituents against impositions from the central government. In the meantime, many tenants were shifted off their traditional holdings or pushed into the ranks of landless laborers by landlords who were protecting against potential future land claims.[33]

Growth in agricultural output would depend on a mix of factors, including security of land tenure, credit, agricultural extension services, irrigation (and hence electricity), and access to fertilizer, insecticide, and improved seeds. The government's failure to secure these factors became particularly apparent with the advent of the Green Revolution. In 1969, Wolf Ladejinsky, a famous agricultural economist, published two articles in India's premier English-language news journal. In what has become a standard comparison, he explained that many Punjabi farmers were doubling and tripling yields with the new "miracle" seeds, and that the number of tube-wells (relatively deep wells powered by electricity or diesel fuel) in Punjab had increased from 7,500 in 1960 to 110,000 in 1968.[34] Comparable statistics were not available for Bihar, but in Purnea East, the district used as an illustration, the tube-well target for 1967–68 was 453, and even with this modest target, only 92 were actually dug. Ladejinsky explained that, for agricultural regions in need of such wells, "the fundamental obstacle is lack of resources and the difficulty of securing credit of Rs. 6,000 or so to finance the construction of one."[35] Construction targets in Punjab were regularly exceeded.

Although the causes for the government's poor performance in support of agriculture should not be oversimplified, the comparison with Punjab illustrates the importance of landowners' economic strategies. It was common for Bihari landlords to receive the greater part of their income from sharecroppers and tenants, but most farms in Punjab were owner-occupied. Bihari landlords had an objective interest in agricultural improvements, but their principles, arising from economic organization and from caste, oriented them to squeezing their tenants rather than increasing productivity. Thus, the forward castes failed to establish a political constituency for agricultural extension services.

By Ladejinsky's writing in 1969, the forward castes had lost their opportunity. In 1967, the Congress Party had lost control of the Bihar state legislature due in part to the forward castes' loss of control of backward caste votes. With the multiplicity of castes and political parties in Bihar, however, the result was an extended period of political confusion. Corruption was already entrenched under Congress Party rule, but the immediate result of the displacement of the Congress Party was political chaos. The opposition parties failed to form a stable coalition. There were thirteen changes in government between 1967 and 1972 as Socialist,

Communist, and Hindu nationalist parties, several smaller parties, and in 1972 a splinter Congress Party maneuvered for advantage.[36] This frequent turnover created an extremely inhospitable environment for any incipient effort to develop a legislative agenda. Indira Gandhi's strong national victory in 1972 gave her greater influence over state governments, leading to an increase in political appointments to the civil service in Bihar, where the Congress Party had retaken the legislature. In the absence of sustained programmatic politics, legislators were perhaps well advised to promote the narrow interests of individual constituents or small groups. As rational choice theory explains, however, this pattern of political exchange degenerates easily into corruption.

Political conflict between forward and backward castes intensified after 1967, and open violence and intimidation became a major factor in the conduct of elections. This can also be seen as a continuation of the pre-independence pattern of political violence. Politicians began to commonly employ armed thugs to "capture" voting booths, frightening away opposition voters and allowing multiple votes from supporters, and "unfettered and undisciplined political competition brought criminals into the political system."[37]

The 1977 Janata Party victory established Karpoori Thakur, from a backward caste, as Bihar's chief minister. He attempted to build a political constituency and to promote a pro-poor, loosely socialist agenda by reserving seats (establishing quotas) in government jobs and in educational institutions for members of the backward castes. This action can be viewed as having been an alternative to (politically unattainable) land reform. Two features of Thakur's program are significant for my argument. First, his mobilization along caste lines was a tactical move informed by socialist principles. Second, he aimed to divide the benefits of government employment more fairly, not to use government programs to improve conditions for his constituency. His strategy was distributive, not productive. Perhaps the machinery of government was already too weak to sustain a programmatic agenda, or Thakur may have thought that developing such an agenda would take too long. In any case, the forward castes saw Thakur's reservations as an immediate threat to their interests, as well as to the competence of government. They took to the streets, pushing political riots in Bihar to a new peak, and Thakur fell to a vote of no confidence in the state assembly.[38] The Janata Party failed to hold its coalition together, and in 1980 the Congress Party once more won the assembly.

That the Congress Party held the state assembly for the decade of the 1980s reflected the lack of attractive alternatives and the strength of the party at the national level, where it held the prime ministership.[39] Political appointments to the lower ranks of government service, campaigning by caste, and the criminalization of politics continued unabated and probably increased. The backward castes, having failed to use the strength of their numbers to form a polity that could promote their interests, had neither strong political representation nor effective government. As the state remained mired in poverty, social conflicts in the villages continued to smolder and occasionally to burst into flames. The failure of interest aggregation at the state level intensified the pressures of poverty in the villages and towns.

The Micro Analytics of Principles and Social Violence in Bihar's Villages

This analysis has attributed Bihar's increasing number of poor in the decades following independence to weak corporate coherence among the elite. The political configuration was absolutely inhospitable to social justice, but dalits and other poor Biharis might have seen their economic conditions improved if landlords and large farmers had increased their agricultural productivity. But the ways in which caste principles structured political and economic incentives undermined even this possibility. Turning now to caste-based violence in the villages, I first consider patterns of cognition associated with principles, then discuss the dynamics of individual principles and the effects arising from our cognition of principles, *tout court.*

As discussed in chapter 2, our cognition of principles rests on the role of intersubjective recognition in normal social relations. In the earliest years of childhood, we come to recognize the claims we make on others as those of one person on another. As our desires exceed our possibilities, we find that not all claims can be satisfied. Through instruction and autonomous insight we develop a sense of fairness, reflecting the idea that claims should be justified by reasons that are valid generally, and that what is right for one is right for another. We come to conceive of our relations with others according to principles, the very grammar of which expresses our mutual dependence. Although principles do not construct all relationships as ones of equality, we tend to presume equality. Caste principles, for example, indicate that this presumption should apply among members of the same caste, and they explain why it does not apply between castes. In this way, we construct a background order of principles that defines a domain of claims that we can legitimately make on others and they on us.

When someone violates our order of principles such that we cannot immediately restore it, resentment is our response. Neither economics nor rational choice theory can account for resentment because it depends on the prior conception of an order of principles. Because caste assigns rights and duties based on criteria fixed by birth, Rawlsian analysis takes it to be oppressive. To the extent that they accept the justifications, dalits and persons of low caste may not experience caste principles as oppressive, but, as I have noted, the establishment of democracy did lead to an awareness of rights of citizenship. The incidence of resentment, therefore, was bound to increase.

Principles tend to reproduce themselves such that established principles are available in the culture when a situation with a structural configuration similar to that of their origin arises. For example, Bihar had a long tradition of political violence prior to independence. The fact that many people had been victims and perpetrators of political violence, or had grown up with stories of it, increased the likelihood that they would find it appropriate when apparently similar conditions arose. Much of the harshest repression of dalits came from newly enriched lower-caste farmers. Finding themselves empowered by their new wealth, these farmers adopted, from the caste model, expectations for tenants' and sharecroppers' subservience. As the latter agricultural workers became increasingly aware of their democratic rights, the conflict of principles grew potentially explosive.

Often in situations of asymmetrical power, we should expect principles of the weaker party to be established in response to those that inform the behavior of the stronger. Kohli notes, for example, that from the early 1970s, Bihar saw an increase in appointments to the civil service and police based on loyalty rather than merit.[40] This undermined the quality of governance not only because of the appointment of less-qualified personnel but also because appointees established obligations to their benefactors rather than to professional performance.

Social violence often reflects a startling disregard for interests, tending to impose heavy and fairly predictable costs on many if not all parties. It is intelligible, however, in the context of our overall order of principles. Our principles are interrelated, framing our conception of our interests and collectively constituting the framework for our engagement with the social world. When a central principle is violated apparently irrevocably, therefore, it is as though our cognitive world is punctured. Our conceptions of both our principles and our interests may need to be reconstructed, leading not only to a temporary suspension of the calculus of interests but also to a perceived threat to our system of principles itself, our identity. Because this system constitutes the framework for our conception of our interests, we cannot evaluate the threat on our interests' terms. We are therefore more susceptible to all-or-nothing logic at a time when we may be caught up in extreme and unfamiliar emotions.

The significance of systems of principles is also evident in the effects of colonialism on caste principles. When a group is systematically excluded from political power, the normal range of its employment of principles is greatly restricted. This restriction can cause principles to be given new, narrower significations, and, ironically, to be affirmed with increasing rigidity. I propose that this narrowing and entrenchment of principles, along with the weakness of competing ideologies, helps to explain the particularly strong adherence to caste principles in Bihar.

The background condition for intercaste violence in Bihar's villages was the decline in rural incomes that began in the late 1960s: "Those who own[ed] land and dominate[d] the social structure . . . sought to improve their incomes primarily by squeezing those below them. . . . [This led to] an increasing use of force to maintain subservience of labor. . . . [Altogether, this] indicates surplus-appropriating strategy that in other historical circumstances has been labeled the 'second serfdom.'"[41] Mitra describes prevailing conditions for predominantly dalit poor peasants and landless laborers in Bihar:

> Enforcement of statutory wages has in no way benefited the labourers as the wages which are paid to them in kind is [sic] far below the statutory minimum, hardly enabling them to meet even half of their basic needs. There are no fixed working hours for labourers, as they are forced to work according to the whims of the masters. They are severely punished and humiliated even for minor errors, the modesty of their women-folk hurt time and again. There are various other ways also by which they are tortured. In a word, their misery and degradation knows no limit.[42]

As their oppression became more forceful, groups of landless laborers and sharecroppers increasingly organized protests aiming to draw attention to the denial of these rights. They also engaged in acts of violence that shared this aim, but, by stepping further and further outside the law, also undermined it. One would rationally anticipate that the upper and lower castes would respond to dalit violence with more terrible repression, and this is indeed what happened. Rather than considering dalit violence as simply irrational, however, or as partially rational but with mistaken calculations, Rawlsian analysis takes it as a response to the puncturing of their social order and as a partially successful attempt to reclaim a dignity denied them by their oppressors.[43]

The impetus for protest did not come from external political forces, but external forces gave the protest a more highly organized expression. In the late 1960s, a Maoist movement of peasant organization and resistance was established in several villages, including Naxalbari, in the neighboring state of West Bengal. In the early 1970s, with the support of left-wing political parties, the "Land-Grab Movement" spread to Bihar.[44] Kohli shows that the Naxalites, as the Maoist rebels came to be called, found their best reception in the less poor districts of central Bihar, where backward castes were the up-and-coming social power. Resenting their long domination by the forward castes, backward castes, upon achieving similar economic status through increased land ownership, sought to establish a similar social status by imitating forward domination of castes considered inferior to their own. (Absolute poverty was more severe and widespread in the northern region, where, in contrast to the less poor central region, long-established forward castes intensified their oppression.) Newly wealthy backward caste landlords treated dalits particularly violently and harshly, and the dalits found this harsher oppression by upstarts to be particularly illegitimate and enraging. The highest incidence of intercaste violence was in Patna Division, around the state's capital city, suggesting that increased political awareness was also a contributing factor. First with the support of Naxalites, and later often without this support, many dalits of central Bihar began to protest against their oppression.[45]

The early 1970s was a period of increasing social unrest in Bihar's rural areas. This unrest took many forms, including forcible mass harvesting of offending landlords' crops, illegal dalit encroachments on government lands, public rallies and demonstrations, and assassinations. The Naxalites and other left-wing parties supported and organized actions to avenge oppression and helped to establish paramilitary forces of dalits and other poor peasants, which began to take control of small territories within the state. The government, however, having already demonstrated its inability or unwillingness to carry out land reform, now showed itself able neither to respond to peasant demands by addressing their grievances nor to contain the "Naxalite menace." The line between local government and police on one side and local landowning families on the other was often not a clear one. The government acquiesced to and/or supported local elites in their organizing and arming themselves to put down peasant discontent.[46] Since local society was typically organized on the basis of caste, this took the form of the establishment of several private caste armies. Although the hypocrisy of this selective application of the law should not escape us, the government's denial of its own principle of equality was costly. It could be accomplished only by simultaneously abdicating its monopoly on the legitimate exercise of violence.

Bihar therefore saw a breakdown of law and order and an increase not only in intercaste violence but also and inevitably in relatively random criminal violence. This social violence interacted with political violence, such as capturing voting booths, and with an increasing entry of criminals into electoral politics. It is inevitable in such a context that most victims would be dalits. That the landowning castes aimed to crush the violence of the serving castes and to let them know that their appeals to democratic principles were hopeless explains the landlords' adoption of terror tactics. It is commonly estimated that dalit deaths due to caste conflict outnumber forward and backward caste deaths by a factor of ten to one. In the 1980s and 1990s, Bihar became infamous for news reports of groups of middle- and upper-caste villagers attacking nearby dalit settlements, hacking men, women, and children to pieces, burning them in their homes, and tossing them into bonfires or down wells.[47]

A government paper estimated that by May 1982, 10.28 percent of Bihar's villages, 8.23 percent of the population, 9.46 percent of the net sown area, and 11.98 percent of the gross sown area had been affected by the "Communist extremist" movement.[48] The *New York Times* estimated that more than 3,300 people were killed in 1986 in Bihar's caste conflicts.[49] Also in 1986, the newspaper *India Today* reported, "[Bihar] has notched up one deadly milestone after another with sickening regularity. Among the major [recent] massacres have been Parasbigha [February 2, 1980; 11 killed], Pipra [February 25, 1980; 14 killed], Gaini [June 26, 1982; 6 killed], Kaithibigha [May 1, 1985; 10 killed], Arwal [April 19, 1986; 23 killed], Kansara [July 8, 1986; 11 killed], and Darmia [October 10, 1986; 11 killed]. Roughly one caste-cum-class carnage has been perpetrated here every four months over the last nine years."[50] Thakur states that there were twice as many fatalities from caste conflicts in Bihar in the 1990s as in the 1980s,[51] and in 1999, Human Rights Watch made Bihar a centerpiece of its major report on India's caste violence.

In a state with a population of one hundred million, only a tiny fraction would be directly involved in caste killings, that number annually in the tens or hundreds. All would be affected, however, by the general sense of lawlessness and by the deep distrust that comes with it. All dalits knew that local government and police have more often sided with high-caste killers than with their victims, and hundreds of dalits have been massacred by police, as well. The failure to maintain law and order is a most fundamental failure of government. It means that millions must live by their wits and strength, and live in fear. It undermines social and economic activities of many kinds. For example, according to some estimates, nearly a quarter of Bihar's available land was not cultivated in 1985–86 due to agrarian conflict.[52]

Laloo Yadav's Bihar

As poor as Bihar's economic performance was prior to 1990, it was even worse in the following decade. In 1990, the Congress Party lost national and state elections, and Laloo Prasad Yadav and his Janata Dal Party took over in Bihar. Laloo (as he is commonly called) presided over a steep decline in the effectiveness of the already weak state government. The present analysis makes three basic assertions: (1) the state's economic problems were politically determined, (2) the political problems that arose in the 1990s were conditioned by the politics of the earlier period, (3) the specific nature of Bihar's political problems in this period are clearly intelligible from a Rawlsian perspective.

Laloo managed to mobilize broad dalit and backward caste resentment of the upper castes, thus gaining an unprecedented personal political following. I have noted that analysis based on the idea of the person as a rational, utility-maximizing agent cannot account for resentment, but that resentment tends to displace and to make demands of the rational cognition of interests. Elements of the suspension of rationality can be found in the resentment Laloo mobilized. Also, the enthusiasm he generated based on the idea of settling old scores gave him the opportunity to ignore and override the dispassionate attention to administrative details so essential to routine governance. Political enthusiasm overrode political rationality.

As we consider the conditions for the possibility of Laloo's particular form of governance, we return to the macroanalytic themes discussed above. A polity requires some form of institutionalized programmatic accountability to support economic growth, but this was virtually absent from the political culture that had arisen in Bihar. Given also a lack of new programmatic initiatives, one set of principles displaces another: the disorganization and petty corruption resulting from the state's fragmented politics had created conditions inimical to accountability. Democracy means "government by the people," but Bihar's history had given its people little experience with the processes this involves. The people were therefore particularly susceptible to Laloo's considerable charms.

In the 1980s, although there were several private armies roaming Bihar's countryside, the machinery of government was only indirectly

affected. Integrated rural development schemes, old-age pensions, school
subsidies, nutrition programs, drinking water schemes, and maternal and
child health programs proceeded in much the same way as in other states.
There was perhaps greater personalized loyalty and clientelistic service,
and more caste-based clientelism in particular,[53] but normal activities
continued. Professionalism based on specialized knowledge and training,
and basic trust in the fair delivery of services eroded gradually. The elitist
government of the 1950s, the confusion of the 1960s, the national and
state crises of the 1970s, and the return to familiar if uninspired Congress
Party rule of the 1980s together created a general cynicism toward government and low expectations.

Laloo won his first seat in the legislature with assistance from Karpoori Thakur, and his rise in the Janata Dal Party was largely due to as-
siduous political service to his superiors at the state and national levels.[54]
When he became chief minister, it had been ten years since his party had
held that post, so he had little experience legislating as the ruling party.
More importantly, the state assembly that he entered had little tradition
of programmatically effective governance. His legislative experience was
mainly of opposition to a Congress Party that was continuing to degen-
erate into clientelism and corruption. Laloo also had no administrative
experience to speak of, and he cannot entirely have escaped the casual
cynicism that pervaded state government.

Laloo initially appropriated Gandhian symbols of leadership: living
in his brother's two-room apartment at the Patna Veterinary College,
holding cabinet meetings out of doors under a tree, standing in a public
queue to have his son's fever treated at the Patna Medical College. The
distinguishing feature of his reformist efforts, however, was their personal
and symbolic nature. He took a megaphone to personally clear traffic at
a busy intersection. He would show up at government offices and police
stations to punish corrupt officials himself.[55]

A member of the backward Yadav caste, Laloo was familiar with
caste discrimination from his own childhood. When the prime minister decided to implement a commission's recommendation to reserve
27 percent of central government jobs for members of the backward
castes, Laloo vocally supported the policy. This gave him the opportunity to develop his rhetoric of caste liberation. Thakur had appealed to

backward caste interests, but Laloo presented himself as a man of the people who would right the historic injustices perpetrated by the upper castes. Hence, his slogan was to "wipe out the upper castes." The irony of the enthusiastic and widespread support that he received from the backward castes and from dalits was that many of the very actions he took to promote their interests actually had the effect of undermining the competence of government, on which strategies to improve their interests would depend.

Laloo soon became a master of the politics of symbolism, but sometimes this politics was practically effective. In 1991, Lal Krishna Advani, president of the Hindu nationalist Bharatiya Janta Party, led a procession through Bihar on the way to Ayodhya, in the neighboring state of Uttar Pradesh, where there is a mosque built over a Hindu temple.[56] Members of the Bharatiya Janta Party were calling for tearing down the mosque to rebuild the temple. Laloo took the procession to be an incitement to violence between Hindus and Muslims and had Advani arrested and his procession turned back. This and Laloo's vocal promise to protect Muslims from Hindu violence won him enthusiastic support among the Muslims, who made up 12 percent of Bihar's electorate; indeed, Muslims were safe from Hindus under Laloo's rule.[57]

In 1991, Laloo's party won the Lok Sabha (national parliament) elections in Bihar, demonstrating the effectiveness of his approach, and Laloo became accustomed to entertaining enthusiastic crowds. We can imagine that he conceived of himself in something of the manner of a benevolent fairy-tale king.[58] When he saw a problem, he would rush to set it right. He would command his ministers, and they would obey. Laloo's very popularity, however, gave him license to ignore the general implementation of government programs. As a senior official recounted,

> Laloo Yadav was a headache for officers, a nuisance and a nightmare. He would stop at the roadside and order a set of dwellings for the poor to be built without caring whether the land was the government's or where the money would come from. He would dismiss officials and not wonder about replacements. He would make announcements and expect the administration to implement them without providing the means. Laloo Yadav had no idea how the

administration ran, and he did not care to learn either. . . . He just gave orders and expected them to be implemented, anyhow.[59]

The first years of Laloo's rule saw flurries of government activity around the state—rural vocational schools established for shepherd boys, housing blocks established in slums, roads built to select villages. At the same time, he increased political appointments to the civil service and other clientelistic practices.

As a consequence of Laloo's mismanagement, the administration of government deteriorated. From 1992 to 1996, the state spent only 20 percent of Bihar's allocation from the central government's eighth five-year plan while hundreds of government employees were left unpaid and the public debt mounted.[60] State-run services in education, health, electricity, and housing collapsed.[61] Audits of the fifty-some state treasuries declined from more than twenty in 1989–90 to none at all in 1994–95, while indications of corruption and fraud increased. In the irrigation department, expenditures on works declined by 58 percent from 1991 to 1994, while expenditures on salaries increased by 42 percent. Joseph wrote in 1997 that "the system of financial control through legislative scrutiny of budgets and accounts no longer exists in Bihar."[62]

In 1995, Laloo stunned the nation when his Janata Dal Party won an absolute majority in Bihar's legislative assembly. Janata Dal won only 28 percent of the vote, but with six other national parties and many local parties dividing the remaining votes, this was enough to win 52 percent of the seats.[63] Two backward castes defected from Janata Dal to form their own party, but Laloo received strong support from Muslims and even stronger support from dalits and from lower castes. Rational choice theory can account for Laloo's political strategies as serving his interests, but it can hardly account for the enthusiasm of the backward castes and particularly for the dalit response. It might offer the notion of "bounded rationality" to account for dalit support for a program that in fact undermined their material well-being. The present analysis, however, gives credence to resentment arising from centuries of oppression. Laloo spoke to the backward castes and even to dalits as one of them. He was with them against the forward-caste authorities, and they identified with him.[64] The crowds that gave him their adulation saw him as moving to set old injustices right, a view for which the categories of "rationality" and "irrationality" are simply inadequate.

Laloo's sustained popularity is intelligible in the context of the history of caste oppression, but its intelligibility is contingent on his supporters not understanding the consequences of his governance for their objective interests. We need to be cautious here because Laloo's government did deliver additional services to some dalits and members of backward castes. The quality of government services overall continued to decline, but the support of these groups was not entirely irrational. The political dynamic that their support set in motion, however, was a perversion of the notion of democratic accountability. Since caste politics had displaced programmatic politics, and since a cynical accommodation of personal deals had become so routine as to be part of the fabric of political life, people were vulnerable to Laloo's appeals. These appeals took the form of a logic of resentment, and this logic resonated with many listeners. Yet the regal manner with which he conducted the affairs of government (while simultaneously plundering it for patronage) inevitably corroded the bureaucratic arms of the state.

After his victory in the 1995 elections, Laloo made tentative moves to encourage foreign investment in Bihar. These were showing little sign of success, however, when he became embroiled in the corruption scandal that in 1997 drove him from office. A racket based on fraudulent invoicing had been established in the Animal Husbandry Department in the 1980s, and its scale of operations increased dramatically under Laloo. Withdrawals from the state treasury in excess of the department's total budget increased from 17 percent in 1988–89 to 53 percent in 1990–91, 169 percent in 1993–94 and 229 percent in 1994–95.[65] Press reports suggested that there might have been as much as 9.5 billion rupees (about $200 million) stolen.[66] After the central government's investigative bureau charged him with several offenses and was preparing to have him arrested, Laloo resigned (leaving his wife, however, as chief minister).

There would be plenty of good neoclassical economic reasons for Bihar's poor economic performance involving failures to provide conditions for competitive markets, but they would not capture the causes for this poor performance. I have shown that these are political. Also, both Laloo's specific political strategies and the responses to them from various groups in Bihar were influenced by the politics of earlier periods; they can be more deeply understood in terms of this earlier politics. Compared to neoclassical economics or rational choice theory, Rawlsian analysis, with its sensitivity to the historical development of principles and to dynamics of sentiments of right (such as resentment), is uniquely equipped to come to grips with the political reasons for Bihar's economic problems.

Reform Agendas: Analytic and Practical

How should we understand the causes for Bihar's unhappy economic and social conditions? They should be seen in the context of the failure to establish a public conception of justice that supports the good of all the state's citizens, and they should be investigated in terms of the specific principles and interests that have constituted the state's political and economic life. In conducting this investigation, we would bring to it a certain set of norms—basic expectations as to what a government ought to do—from many of which the government of Bihar obviously departs. The orientation provided by these norms is useful, but a Rawlsian analysis needs to provide a more focused standard. Since practical reason permits the production of an object in terms of a conception of that object, it is imperative for a Rawlsian analysis to construct a practical conception of a just Bihar.

Neoclassical economists would be likely to analyze Bihar's conditions in terms of various ways in which the state's economy departs from the free market ideal. Sachs, Bajpai, and Ramiah, for example, argue that Bihar needs investments in physical infrastructure such as roads, railways, airports, and communication services, and in human capital, mainly education and health care.[67] Rational choice theorists would be likely to focus on the configurations of interests in key institutions, possibly the same institutions I have emphasized: the state legislature, the economic bureaucracies, and the institutions governing control of land and labor in rural areas. They would analyze these institutions in terms of a game theory logic in which the desire for wealth and power are the main motivational forces, explaining Bihar's suboptimal outcomes as the result of the players' maximizing strategies.

In presenting the history that has led to the current configuration of principles, the present analysis has found the hierarchical principles of caste to play a significant role. Due partly to its colonial experience, Bihar had a stronger and more ossified caste system than other states, and a governing class more oriented to extractive than to productive economic strategies. While dominating government from 1947 to 1967, the forward castes missed the boat to the Green Revolution, and in establishing patterns of political mobilization based on caste, they created conditions for the political confusion that followed the inevitable end of their hegemony.

Caste and economic failure are even more tightly intertwined in the rural violence that took so much land out of production in the 1980s and thereafter. I have argued that the particularly extreme violence in Bihar's central region, which is not the site of the state's most severe poverty, is due largely to the particularly harsh repression imposed by middle-caste farmers trying to climb the caste ladder. The organized intercaste violence that began in the 1970s had roots as far back as the nineteenth-century dispossessions associated with the rise and fall of indigo markets. Principles of domination, subjugation, and violent resistance have cycled through Bihar's history, so when local elites are enraged by dalit demands for equal respect, they are more prone to resort to violence. But the frequent massacres of dalits are attributable as much to the government's failure to contain them as to the passions that incite them.

To understand Bihar's declining productivity in the 1990s, we need to explain the principles of Laloo Yadav's political project. This takes us in many directions: to the way caste politics had undermined the programmatic competence of the legislatures in which he received his political education; to Bihar's history of oppression and consequent pools of resentment—resentment deepened by democratic politics and governance based nominally on citizens' equality; to Laloo's personal experience of oppression, which gave him the resources to channel popular resentment and make it a political force; and to the political history that blinded people to the consequences of Laloo's politics for government competence. Once this stage is set, rational choice theory may well be able to analyze the increasing clientelism in Bihar's state government and specific weaknesses of institutions of democratic accountability in this period.

These explanations are predicated, however, on Laloo's considerable popularity and consequent political power.

From the perspective of interests, a poor agricultural society like Bihar's needs a government that can carry out certain kinds of investments. From the perspective of principles, the ways in which Bihar's upper castes have been accustomed to treating dalits, particularly the manner of their incorporation into the agricultural workforce, are inconsistent with dalits' rights as citizens of a democracy. Since India won its independence, if Bihar was to establish a public conception of justice that would support the good of all its citizens, such a conception would have to address these two problems. The landed elites who initially governed Bihar, however, did not appreciate the need for government to promote a productive agenda, nor were they prepared to undermine their own caste status. The agendas of incumbents in subsequent governments tended to focus on their own narrow and short-term advantage rather than on encompassing, productive projects. Lacking statespeople promoting a unifying framework, politicians mined the civil service. As government failed to support agricultural improvements and as rural poverty increased, oppression rooted in the caste system increased as well. Dalits and other laborers, recognizing the oppression as a violation of their rights but getting little support from government, sometimes struck out in violence, and the upper castes responded with even more violent repression. At the state level, the debased political culture established the opportunity for Laloo's politics of resentment, which in turn engendered further declines in government competence. Thus, Bihar lacked the reasonable and rational organization and governance that it would need to become, as Rawls says, well ordered. The two problems that it has faced since independence still remain to be overcome.

Thus, our analytic reform leads us naturally to a political reform agenda, and the first point on this agenda is that Bihar's legacy of oppression must be halted. In order to establish a politics based on notions of common interest, backward- and forward-caste landowners must accept the equal humanity of their laborers. This is a long-term project; initially, in order to establish peace in the countryside, the democratic rights of dalits and of other laborers and sharecroppers must be protected—a goal that involves enforcing laws on workers' rights and probably some land tenure reform. Proponents of the rights of the poor should recognize that violent resistance leads to violent repression. It is the duty of government to protect citizens' rights; the reformer's task is to help the government to acknowledge this duty and to carry out its obligations. In defending the rights of workers, there are roles for central and state governments, social reformers, enlightened landlords, and the lower castes themselves.

The second item on this political reform agenda for Bihar is to increase the state's economic growth. This involves enhancing industrial and agricultural productivity. The greatest opportunities for rapid growth lie in industry, and even if the ownership of Bihar's mines and industries lies outside the state, the government could still promote selected investments and increased linkages with local firms. Given the state's extreme poverty, however, broad-based improvements in economic and social conditions require improvements in agriculture. This requires more effective management of agricultural extension and credit services, electricity generation and distribution, flood control, and other government activities in support of agriculture. It is clear, however, that development specialists have known for decades that Bihar needs these improvements. Reforming government so it can provide them is a political problem. What stands out throughout Bihar's post-independence history is the failure to build an administration that is competent to carry out development investments. We can imagine that strengthening government's administrative machinery, and particularly government management of support for agriculture and industry, could be the task of a Rawlsian political party. If it is the declining quality of Bihar's political discourse that has led to the recent economic stagnation, it is reasonable that a discourse better grounded in actual interests and in just principles should be part of the solution. A Rawlsian party would seek votes by defending peasants' rights and by promoting a programmatic agenda that could improve voters' economic and social conditions.

chapter six

The Ethics and the Politics of Climate Change

Approaches to Analyzing Climate Change

To explain the causes for a region's poverty, as chapter 5 attempts for Bihar, Rawlsian analysis inevitably turns to political history. To address the ethics of an emerging social problem not contained within national borders, by contrast, Rawlsian analysis returns to the original position. In both cases, Rawlsian analysis offers an orientation grounded in the perspective of justice. To act in the world, we need a conception of our world; initially, such conceptions are likely to be grounded in our own interests and/or those of groups of which we are a part. Each person's cognition of social relations consists in part of an orientation to fairness, and this is the seat of the orientation to justice as well. To speak of social justice, however, implies a social analysis with competing factors appropriately balanced. Otherwise, views of fairness are likely to be narrow and stilted. The original position serves as a device of representation for achieving this kind of balance; by working through a problem such as climate change from this perspective, one fairly juxtaposes competing interests in order to reach a well-grounded general perspective.

Neoclassical economics is presently the dominant form of social analysis in the Anglo-American world, so it is not surprising that the most prominent analyses of responses to climate change arise from this perspective. At this writing, the most influential analysis is *The Economics of Climate Change: The Stern Review* by Sir Nicholas Stern, head of the

British Government Economic Service and formerly chief economist for the World Bank.[1] Another influential analysis, one that adheres more rigorously to neoclassical economic theory and on which the *Stern Review* builds, is by Yale University's William Nordhaus; in its most recent (2008) iteration Nordhaus critiques the *Stern Review*.[2] To clarify the distinguishing features of a Rawlsian analysis, and to indicate its significance, I contrast it with these analyses.

Before the industrial revolution, there were about 280 parts per million (ppm) of carbon dioxide (CO_2) in the earth's atmosphere. By 2009 this had risen to over 380 ppm,[3] mainly due to CO_2 releases associated with industrialization. The scientific consensus holds that, along with rising levels of other greenhouse gasses, this has been the main cause of the observed rise in average global temperatures of about 0.74 degrees Celsius.[4] Rising temperatures are changing global weather patterns, increasing droughts and floods, and raising water levels in the oceans. In the last few million years, atmospheric CO_2 concentrations have cycled between 180 ppm and 280 ppm in rhythm with the sequence of ice ages and warmer interglacial periods; the last time they stood at 400 ppm was about fourteen million years ago.[5] Based on current trends, atmospheric concentrations will reach about 700 ppm by 2100,[6] but the science of the effects of such a rise is in its infancy. The evidence increasingly indicates, however, that the effects would likely be quite drastic.

In economic terms, the effects of CO_2 emissions (and other drivers of climate change) are understood as externalities. Those who benefit from activities that lead to CO_2 emissions impose costs on those who suffer harms from climate change.[7] Analysis based on rational utility maximization, and hence on the satisfaction of interests, takes efficiency as its primary criterion. The analysis of externalities is well developed in economic (as well as rational choice) theory: efforts should be made to reduce greenhouse gas emissions up to the point where the marginal cost is equal to the marginal benefit, with benefits understood in this case as reductions in damages.[8] Stern and Nordhaus agree on this model but disagree on how to apply it—among other points, on how to account for costs and benefits that occur in future years (that is, on the discount rate), what damages to include, and how to assign values to damages.

Industrialized nations have contributed most to causing climate change, but poor people in less developed countries are harmed the most by it. The poor are more vulnerable and less able to adapt, and most poor countries, given that they lie closer to the equator, are already hotter than most rich countries. In fact, it appears that absolute rises in temperature will be greater in some areas of the tropics and subtropics than in temperate zones (although they may be greatest around the North Pole). Harms caused by one group and imposed on another are matters of justice, but neoclassical economic theory includes no concept of social justice, and the proposals for responding to climate change by Stern and Nordhaus also lack such an idea. For Rawlsian analysis, by contrast, justice is the starting point. We are to ask what principles would be adopted for responding to climate change by agents who do not know where they live, in which time period, or whether they are rich or poor. These agents wish to continue social improvements toward greater justice, so they are interested in economic efficiency and growth, but they also aim to defend everyone's basic livelihood. Climate change threatens livelihoods for many, so protecting these people takes on particular urgency in Rawlsian analysis.

We noted in earlier chapters that Rawlsian analysis takes institutions to consist largely of principles (formal and informal rules) established as solutions to past problems. We can expect that established institutions are not equipped to solve new problems on the scale of climate change. Whereas neoclassical economics generally takes established institutions for granted and indicates efficient outcomes as targets, Rawlsian analysis explores the rough outlines of institutions needed for a just solution and how their principles differ from those of established institutions. This is a first step in analyzing the politics of climate change. Political history offers insight into the principles of established institutions. Given that the main victims of climate change are predominantly poor or not yet born, we cannot expect existing incentives to be sufficient to underwrite the reforms needed to establish just institutions. Rawlsian analysis depends instead on changing consciousness, as more people come to grips with the demands of justice in this context. No single pathway toward a just resolution can be identified, but outlines of some promising pathways can be articulated.

The institutional context for responding to climate change is the anarchic global system of nation-states. Having no central power with legitimate authority over all states impedes systematic responses. From the outset, we can observe that the rigorous demands of fairness in relation to climate change will require new and stronger international institutions representing the collective welfare. Challenges include establishing a just regime of emission controls, technology transfers, monitoring of emissions, and implementation of measures to avert and redress harms from climate change. The international state system is based on a mutual presumption of autonomy and legitimacy among national governments, but governments are often fragile and inconsistent representatives of their citizens' interests. The rights and obligations that arise from the material facts of climate change, however, apply largely to individuals. When cold political realities are at particular variance with governments' obligations, the international community will sometimes need to take corrective measures.

Economic Analyses of the Response to Climate Change

Neoclassical economics offers well-developed methodologies for analyzing streams of costs of benefits, and, in the case of climate change, for indicating how reductions in greenhouse gas emissions could be managed to minimize their costs. It provides no basis, however, for assessing obligations that arise from climate change, or institutional challenges that such obligations present. Forecasting climate changes that are expected to follow from particular concentrations of greenhouse gasses, and identifying the direct harms likely to be caused by such changes, are, of course, matters for science. With the science of climate change still in its infancy, judgments have to be made about how to address the substantial uncertainties that still remain, and these include an ethical component. As we contrast economic and Rawlsian approaches, therefore, we first accept the economists' accounts of costs and benefits and then reconsider their assessments of the harms from climate change.

The biggest differences between Stern's and Nordhaus's proposals for responding to climate change lie in how rapidly they seek to reduce it and how far they aim to let it progress. While Stern advocates aggressive action immediately, Nordhaus recommends a more gradual approach, and while Stern suggests keeping greenhouse gas concentrations within the range of 450–550 ppm of CO_2 equivalents (CO_2e),[9] Nordhaus recommends an eventual peak of about 680 ppm CO_2 around 2180. This CO_2 target implies CO_2 equivalents over 750 ppm.[10] While Nordhaus presents a specific economically optimal proposal (based on his model and assumptions) for taxes and carbon emissions, Stern emphasizes the need for immediate action but does not propose specific numeric targets.[11] Nordhaus, however, offers a numeric model "in the spirit of the *Stern Review*"[12] that employs some of Stern's key parameters. It has atmospheric CO_2 concentrations peaking at around 420 ppm around 2070 and then falling,[13] implying CO_2e concentrations in the right range.

Nordhaus proposes that average global temperatures rise 2.61°C from 1900 levels by 2100 and 3.45°C by 2200, while his model in the *Stern Review*'s spirit has rises of 1.52°C and 1.27°C, respectively (peaking before 2100). Anticipating that future generations will be much wealthier than the present, Nordhaus takes it that they will be able to cope with the harms that result from a hotter world at less cost to their utility. Stern, by contrast, counts the utility loss from a given harm to a future generation as equal to that loss if it fell on the present generation.[14] As a consequence, Nordhaus recommends a worldwide tax of $34 per ton of carbon emissions in 2010 (in 2005 dollars) rising gradually to $202 in 2100, compared to taxes of $305 in 2010 and $949 in 2100 for the Stern model.[15] Nordhaus views Stern's approach as taxing the poor to support the rich.[16]

The specific basis for Nordhaus's incorporation of time in his valuation of costs and benefits is a 4 percent discount rate based on his estimate of the market return on capital.[17] Stern, by contrast, uses a discount rate of only 0.1 percent, based on his estimate of the likelihood that humanity will be brought to an end in a given year, such as by a large meteorite striking the earth.[18] Since the returns we observe on capital reflect people's actual choices between current and future consumption, Nordhaus's approach is the more deeply grounded in economic theory. However, Nordhaus does not justify his adoption of economic growth theory as a basis for guiding policy on climate change. He asserts, for example, that "in choosing among alternative trajectories for emissions reductions, the key economic variable is the real return on capital, r, which measures the net yield on investments in capital, education and technology."[19] But this is the key variable only when growth economics is taken as the theoretical framework.

Neoclassical economics assesses economic values based on what consumers are willing to pay, but willingness to pay depends on ability to pay. Consumers "vote" with their income on how resources should be allocated; but the rich have many times more votes than the poor. Also, the worth of many of the "goods" that are harmed by climate change is not captured by their economic values, such as when death rates rise, ways of life are rendered unviable, local ecosystems are wiped out, and species are driven to extinction. It is not self-evident that growth economics provides an adequate framework in this context.

Nordhaus argues compellingly that emission reductions can generally be achieved most efficiently by way of a global system of carbon taxes (or their equivalents for other drivers of climate change). Compared to quantitative restrictions, such as emission allowances or a cap and trade system, a consistent carbon tax would be administratively easier and more flexible; it would also avoid price volatility, allow for reducing inefficiencies[20] from other taxes that could be lowered, and create fewer incentives for corruption.[21] Nordhaus suggests that it might be "reasonable" for poor countries to be exempt until their incomes reached a threshold such as $10,000 per capita,[22] tipping his hat to justice if not coming to grips with it.

Nordhaus points out that the *Stern Review*, as a British government policy study, "should be read primarily as a document that is political in nature and has advocacy as its purpose."[23] Stern's analysis is broader in its assessment of the causes and consequences of climate change, it is methodologically more eclectic, and it is largely devoted to summarizing findings from other studies. Its core analysis follows mainstream economics and has a methodology similar to Nordhaus's, but Stern draws many extensions from and contrasts with views from other perspectives.[24] Nevertheless, he sees economics and science as sufficient bases for informing climate change policy.[25] Stern offers the richer ethical discussion of climate change and, unlike Nordhaus, he acknowledges wealthy countries' responsibility to provide the major resources for adjusting. He interprets this responsibility largely in terms of beneficence and enlightened self-interest, however, and he offers no discussion of the extent of rich country obligations.[26]

Given his near-zero discount rate, Stern expects his recommended emission reductions to cost about 1 percent of world GDP compared to damages averted that sum to 5 percent of world GDP if no action were taken, with both costs and benefits on an ongoing basis ("now and forever").[27] He includes both mitigation costs, for reducing greenhouse gas emissions, and adaptation costs, but he does not disaggregate these costs. Also, it is not clear what harms remain from climate change after adaptation efforts, such as how much increased mortality. Stern uses market prices to calculate costs and benefits, so $100 in losses count the same whether they fall on a family with an income of $200 or $200,000.[28] After completing his core economic analysis, Stern considers how it would be affected if one also counted (a) harms from additional deaths, (b) harms to the environment, and (c) additional weight for harms to the poor. He estimates that keeping the rise of CO_2e limited to the 450 to 550 ppm range compared to his baseline, or "business as usual," scenario averts harms in these areas on the order of 15 percent of world GDP on an ongoing basis, but again he does not show his calculations.[29]

Nordhaus and Stern recommend low and high carbon taxes, respectively, and Stern recommends a substantial program of adaptation. Stern notes that although developing countries are responsible for less than a quarter of cumulative greenhouse gas emissions, they bear the brunt of their harms.[30] Neither author has much to say, however, about obligations for the rich that might arise from causing these harms.

The Construction of the Original Position for Climate Change

I observed in chapter 2 that the original position reformulates Kant's categorical imperative from the perspective of social justice. The original position provides a coherent way to orient the sense of right for selecting principles for organizing the basic structure of society. This is not the only appropriate application of the original position, however, and once selected from the original position, Rawls's two principles of justice may not offer appropriate guidance for other problems.

On this first point, in *The Law of Peoples* Rawls introduces a "second original position," in which representatives of a liberal people work out agreements with other liberal peoples, and also with nonliberal but decent (Rawls's term) peoples (i.e., peoples who respect human rights, use some kind of representative consultation procedure for government decision making, and are not aggressive in their international relations).[31] Note that the first original position includes representatives of individuals while the second includes representatives of peoples. The question of the basic structure of society, with its rights and obligations, is a question for citizens to work out with one another. You and I can take the perspective of the original position to justify arguments for social reforms within our own society, for example, that we might make in public discourse. International law, however, can be established only by representative of states. You and I can advocate for reforms in another society where we are not citizens, but we do so with a different status. We expect others to respect our national autonomy, and we aim to respect theirs. As much as we might want another people to adopt a freer press or to recognize women's rights, for example, and though we might support some of their national advocates, it is up to their society to do it. Hence, the original position for the Law of Peoples is populated by representatives of peoples, not of individual persons. It provides an orientation for selecting principles to guide relations among peoples via their legitimate leaders and representatives.

Nordhaus argues that from a Rawlsian perspective, "societies should maximize the economic well-being of the poorest generation. The ethical implication of this policy would be that current consumption should increase sharply to reflect the projected future improvements in productivity."[32] In fact, Rawls's second principle of justice states (in part) that "social and economic inequalities are to be arranged so that they are . . . to the greatest benefit of the least advantaged, consistent with the just savings principle."[33] The just savings principle in turn involves securing progress toward the establishment of just institutions and preserving their material base.[34] Contrary to Nordhaus's assertion, there is no idea of maximizing the well-being of the poorest generation. However, even if Nordhaus were interpreting Rawls's second principle of justice correctly, it would not necessarily apply to climate change because climate change exceeds the boundaries of the problem that Rawls's two principles of justice are designed to address.

To establish principles for climate change, we need to return to the original position, in this case populated by representatives of individual persons from around the world and from this and future generations. Why should this third original position not be populated by representatives of peoples, as was that for the Law of Peoples? Recall that Rawls excludes peoples who are neither liberal nor decent from his second original position. Once a government violates the human rights of persons within its national territory, for example, other countries individually or collectively may be obligated to intervene. Human rights (in some cases) supersede national sovereignty. Rawls's Law of Peoples aims to contain and eventually to transform outlaw states; they are not party to the hypothetical agreement in the original position.

Climate change involves sometimes dire harms to persons caused by other persons, mostly from other countries, and by earlier generations. We will see that this and other features of climate change generate several rights and duties for persons. If states reliably represented the persons within their national territories with respect to these rights and duties—if the state's commitment were sufficient to secure fulfillment of the rights and compliance with the duties—then the original position for the Law of Peoples would suffice. But this is not the case. Given the enormous and often locally unpredictable harms expected from climate change, many present-day governments, probably including many that Rawls would have considered liberal or decent states, cannot be expected to represent the rights of all of their national residents reliably and fairly.

Rawls opposes the application of his second principle of justice to justify redistributive transfers among countries for similar reasons to those for populating his second original position with representatives of peoples rather than of persons. The effective unit of cooperation for most questions of social justice is the nation-state precisely because it is the primary legal and political sphere in which such questions are addressed. And in the context of the nation-state, the rich have stronger obligations of justice to poor fellow citizens than to poor citizens of other countries. In the context of climate change, however, the rich inflict harms on the distant poor and owe their wealth in part to actions of earlier generations that now inflict such harms. Since greenhouse gasses do not respect national borders and impose harms on individuals, fair responses to climate change need to take into account the perspectives of individuals.

Addressing Climate Change from the Original Position

The original position is a device of representation for selecting fair principles for addressing problems of social justice. Rawls's *A Theory of Justice* balances the needs of the poor for primary goods with the need to maintain incentives for a thriving economy, but the material facts of climate change yield a powerful redistributive imperative. The great harms that climate change threatens to the poor are mainly caused by the rich, and from the original position it is clear that this yields responsibilities that need to be shouldered. Rawlsian analysis will place a sharper focus on relief, development, and technology transfers than analyses grounded in economic efficiency will. Also, given that it emphasizes the well-being of the poor (now and future) it will give greater weight to low-likelihood nightmare scenarios and call for more rapid reductions in greenhouse gas emissions.

In the original position, approaches for responding to climate change are to be selected by agents who do not know which specific persons they represent among the world's present or future populations. The constraints on the information available to them are to ensure that the decision procedure is fair. Whomever they represent, the agents aim to promote this person's interests as effectively as possible. Hence, they aim to maximize the supply of primary goods available to this person and, in particular, to ensure that she gains an adequate supply of primary goods to carry out her life plan, whatever it turns out to be.

Agents in the original position for climate change have two kinds of (interconnected) tasks to accomplish. First, they must map out a schedule for reducing greenhouse gas emissions over time. Based on the information currently available from science, this will imply a certain probability distribution of changes in average world temperatures, associated climate changes, and downstream effects. It will also imply a range of magnitudes and/or mixes of interventions to reduce greenhouse gas emissions or otherwise counter their effects. Deliberations in the original position are always constrained by existing knowledge; certainly in the original position for climate change, new information could significantly change the conclusions.

Second, these agents must devise systems and allocate rights and duties for achieving the specified emissions schedule (emissions mitigation) and for adapting to the effects of associated climate changes, or devise schemes for their allocation. Adaptation involves preventing harms (such as from rising sea levels), enhancing the capacity to cope with harms (such as with drought-tolerant seeds), and addressing and sometimes compensating for harms (such as with relocation schemes and income support when habitats are rendered unviable). Clearly, these categories are not mutually exclusive.

Justice between Generations

Given that the agents aim to promote the interests of future generations, they agree with economists that allocating resources to climate change (mitigation and adaptation) must be considered in the context of the trade-off with investing in economic growth. The agents in the original position, however, insist on defending the poor in their access to primary goods. Recall that Nordhaus assumes diminishing marginal utility from increasing income. Stern's central analysis is not distributionally sensitive, but when he adds the effects of increasing the weight of income losses incurred by poor people, one of the two papers he references is by Nordhaus and Boyer (2000). In this paper, global costs of climate change for 5°C warming increase from 6 percent to 8 percent of world GDP when more weight is given to impacts in poor regions (not to poor persons),[35] implying that losses to the poor count for perhaps as much as twice the value of equivalent losses to the rich.[36] Stern does note that in all scenarios the highest impacts are in Africa, the Middle East, India, and South-East Asia.[37] The overwhelming majority of the world's poor, say with incomes below $2 a day, are in Africa and India (and in this context we should also include Bangladesh).

While economists sum the value of losses to the poor and count them (weighted or unweighted) against mitigation costs, agents in the original position aim to defend the lives and livelihoods of poor people. The latter appears to lead to substantially higher costs, and it is institutionally more demanding. (Greater institutional accomplishments, however, lead to lower costs.) Costs from climate change arise from things like crop losses, investments in strategies for coping with lower water supplies and rising sea levels, health care treatments and home and infrastructure repairs due to extreme weather events, health care treatments and reduced productivity due to hotter climates and more diseases, and increasing death rates from various causes. In low-income economies, the economic values of many of the goods affected by climate change—such as homes, lost productivity, and health care—tend to be low simply because incomes are low. Adaptation, however, including protection and restoration, tends to be more costly. The cost of helping a farm family to relocate and reestablish a livelihood once they can no longer make a living on their land, for example, is likely to be many times greater than the value of their lost crops. The cost of improving and maintaining a health care system to support good health is likely to be greater than the value of lost productivity due to ill health from climate change. Agents in the original position insist on major investments in disaster management to minimize the human costs of extreme weather events. Also, once a significant proportion of extreme weather events are attributable to climate change, there is no way to identify the ones that would have happened anyway. Those who have contributed most to causing climate change (or benefited most from its causes) become responsible for mitigating the effects of extreme weather events wherever they occur; they bear a significant part (but not all) of the responsibility.

Since agents in the original position do not know to which generation they belong, they aim to promote the well-being of each generation, present and future, equally. They can agree with Stern to discount for the possibility that humanity will come to an end. Stern arrives at a target for the maximum atmospheric concentration of greenhouse gasses of 450 to 550 ppm CO_2e even before taking account of increasing deaths and other noneconomic factors and increasing the weight of losses to the poor, so the target from the original position must be lower than this. Given that total harms averted by limiting climate change are accorded a higher value in the original position than in economic analysis, based on

Stern's assumptions about the science and the related economic values, Rawlsian analysis yields a lower target for CO_2e. From the perspective of the original position, Nordhaus's targets of 680 ppm CO_2 and 3.45°C appear reckless. At this temperature there is a substantial risk of catastrophic effects, such as sea levels rising several meters, 30 to 50 percent of species becoming extinct, and hundreds of millions of deaths from malnutrition, malaria, and floods.[38] Nordhaus's economic growth assumptions do not demonstrate that the number of absolutely vulnerable persons would be reduced in the future. While the secular trend has seen a decline in worldwide proportions and numbers of persons malnourished, climate change intensifies many causes of vulnerability.

Stern's 450 to 550 ppm CO_2e target for greenhouse gas concentrations implies a rise in temperatures of about 2°C to 2.8°C relative to preindustrial levels according to his own data[39] (although this is higher than the model attributed to him by Nordhaus). At 450 ppm there is a 50 percent chance of average temperature gains exceeding 2°C (95 percent probability distribution from 0.9°C to 3.7°C).[40] If concentrations could be stabilized today at 430 ppm, temperatures would still be expected to rise at least about another 1°C over the next several decades due to feedback effects.[41] But in practical terms, stabilizing emissions today is virtually impossible. Worldwide emissions are on an upward trajectory with powerful momentum, particularly in newly industrializing countries such as China, so even the 450 ppm target is extremely ambitious. This suggests that the target temperature rise from the original position would be about 2°C, with greenhouse gas concentrations around 450 ppm CO_2e.

A few points need to be noted about this conclusion. First, according to Stern's data, the 450 ppm target already implies a significant chance of average temperatures rising more than 3°C. Second, the reason for not selecting a lower target is institutional, not ethical or technical. Agents in the original position would prefer a lower target, and there is no technical reason that greenhouse gas emissions could not begin to decline tomorrow. But this would require governments around the world—particularly governments of middle-income industrializing countries where emissions are rising fastest—to sharply rein in their programs for economic development. As I argue below, this is unlikely. Third, scientific findings since the publication of the *Stern Review* indicate that the dangers from atmospheric concentrations of 450 ppm CO_2e are greater than previously understood.

I should re-emphasize that our understanding of many aspects of the causes and consequences of climate change will improve greatly in coming decades as the science progresses. In just the three years following the initial release of the *Stern Review*, new information indicated that impacts and human costs of climate change are significantly greater than Stern expected. Stern reported that climate change was already responsible for 150,000 deaths each year,[42] but in 2009 such deaths were estimated to exceed 300,000 a year.[43] Stern reports a projected rise in sea levels of 0.09 to 0.88 meters by 2100,[44] but more recent studies indicate a likely rise of up to 1.4 meters by 2100.[45] Stern reports that the number of people at risk of hunger could rise by thirty million to two hundred million along with temperature rises of 2°C to 3°C,[46] and that with no effort to reduce emissions, average temperatures are not expected to exceed 2°C over pre-industrial levels until after 2050.[47] Subsequent studies, however, projected that seventy-five million people will go hungry due to climate change by 2030.[48] The 2009 assessment from the state of California's Climate Action Team finds greater vulnerabilities to climate change than they found in 2007, with up to $3 billion in annual revenue losses due to changes in water availability and $2 billion in annual home losses from wildfires by 2050.[49] The costs of climate change are greater than Stern estimated, and in the original position they are weighted more heavily, so a greater effort is called for to reduce greenhouse gas emissions and limit the extent of climate change. To retain a 50 percent chance of keeping global warming below 2°C, however, emissions would need to peak by 2018 and then decline at 4 percent a year, or peak by 2020 and then decline at 5 percent a year; cutting emissions by more than 5 percent a year probably is not feasible.[50]

The schedule that agents in the original position map for reductions in greenhouse gas emissions, therefore, appears to be as follows. In 2010, annual worldwide CO_2e emissions were equivalent to about fifty-five billion tonnes of CO_2. To keep atmospheric concentrations below 450 ppm and global warming below 2°C, emissions will need to peak by 2020 and then decline to below thirty billion tonnes by 2050,[51] with gradual reductions in the following centuries to reach the earth's absorptive capacity of about five billion tons per year. Notably, a 2°C target is also the closest we had to a global consensus as evidenced by the results of the 2009 United Nations Climate Conference in Copenhagen.

Justice between the Rich and the Poor

How, then, should greenhouse gas emissions be cut in half by 2050, and what should be done about the mounting harms from climate change? To address these questions, we need to come to grips with the role of fossil fuels in generating past and present prosperity and obligations that arise from the harms caused by climate change. We need to appreciate the powerful but hard-to-predict role of technology, including new discoveries, particularly in reducing emissions, and the similarly ambiguous question of what is institutionally feasible. Questions of institutional feasibility arise not only in regard to emissions reductions but also in regard to adaptation and rehabilitation. Also, at the end of the day all these issues are interrelated, and they all need to be worked out through the anarchic system of nation-states. Hard decisions need to be made; their results are far away in space and time. But although the wealthy bear the greatest obligations, they also possess the preponderance of political power. Again we should note that movement toward a just solution will strengthen institutions for international cooperation (but inadequate movement could weaken them).

Reducing total greenhouse gas emissions, agents in the original position would aim to equalize per capita emissions for each country. Today, national per capita emissions are loosely correlated with per capita income, which is also loosely correlated with cumulative historic per capita emissions. Citizens of wealthy countries are not culpable for historic emissions, but we now know that the industries that made them rich also set climate change in motion. The longer they persist with above-average emissions, the more harm they cause. For poor countries, however, energy-intensive industry remains the standard route to greater income. To deny poor countries the opportunity to industrialize is tantamount to denying them the chance to secure national autonomy and the well-being of their citizens. From the original position this appears doubly unjust, since poor countries suffer the most from climate changes to which they contributed little and they would also be denied the opportunity to catch up with the wealthy. Equal proportionate reductions, therefore, where all countries reduce emissions by half, are out of the question. Agents in the original position would require the rich to assist the poor with technology and education to help them develop their economies along low-emission pathways, but the agents would see no reason to give poor countries permanent advantages. Hence, they would require all countries to move to equal per capita emissions, say around 2050. By 2050, however, 2012's world population of 7 billion will have risen to about 9.2 billion persons.[52] At a first approximation, therefore, the agents would require all countries to move to three tonnes per capita annual greenhouse gas emissions by 2050.[53]

Following in the utilitarian tradition, neoclassical economists typically promote some idea of maximizing total utility. Hence, Stern adopts what he calls the "social welfare function" approach in which "the objective is to work out the policies that would be set by a decision-maker acting on behalf of the community and whose role it is to improve, or maximise, overall social welfare."[54] He rejects a policy whereby "all individuals in the world should either converge to a common (low) level [of emissions] or pay for the excess (and those below that level could sell rights),"[55] arguing that the right to equal emissions "is essentially asserted." "It is not clear why a common humanity in a shared world automatically implies that there are equal rights to emit GHGs [greenhouse gasses] (however low)."[56] Deliberating from the original position, however, we aim to develop a view based on the perspective of fairness. Converging on equal per capita emissions recognizes the atmosphere as a commons and each person's equal right to benefit from the earth's limited capacity to absorb greenhouse gasses given the importance to well-being of activities that generate such gasses. From the original position it appears that Stern does not take seriously enough the harms that the rich impose on the poor through climate change or the aspirations of the poor to enhance their well-being.[57]

From the original position, emissions should be equalized on a national per capita rather than an individual basis because today, and for the foreseeable future, the nation-state is normally the effective basic unit of social cooperation. Each country should move toward social justice, and the international community bears some responsibility for harms to individuals from climate change. An individual, however, cannot industrialize or move toward social justice on her own. Hence, the right to equal emissions is held on a per capita basis by countries, but it implies government obligations that if unfulfilled can justify external intervention.

The three tonne per capita target for 2050 has different implications depending on current emission levels. In 2005, for instance, total per capita CO_2e emissions were twenty-two tonnes for the United States, six tonnes for Sweden, five tonnes each for China and Mexico, and two tonnes for Egypt.[58] Many sub-Saharan African countries had less than one tonne annual per capita emissions. While the United States needs to cut its 2005 emissions by 86 percent, Sweden needs to reduce its emissions only by half, China and Mexico by two-fifths, and Egypt can increase its 2005 emissions by half (all adjusted for population growth).

Before addressing what it will take to reduce emissions, let us consider the effects of climate change. I have noted that there are already over 300,000 deaths a year due to climate change, and this number will increase as average temperatures rise and the effects intensify. To note some of the main effects: hurricanes, typhoons, and floods will cause deaths, injuries, and property damage; declining rainfall, melting glaciers, thawing permafrost, and rising sea levels will render habitats unviable; and declining crop yields, increasing malaria, and increasing heat and humidity will cause malnutrition and disease. According to agents in the original position, since deaths and other harms from climate change are caused by greenhouse gas emissions, whoever is responsible for these emissions bears responsibility for the deaths and harms. Whoever is well-off today because of past (historic) emissions bears some responsibility, as does each citizen of a country with above-average emissions.

Agents in the original position would insist that those who are responsible for climate change, if they can, should take steps to avert its main harms and to ameliorate and redress the harms that remain. Now that we know there are over 300,000 deaths a year from climate change, the agents would require the responsible parties to take steps to avert these deaths. The responsible parties do not bear this responsibility alone; national governments, compatriots, and the likely victims themselves should also take steps to avert and ameliorate the harms and to restore the victims. Particularly in poorer countries, however, where more of the harms occur, national and local governments and civil societies often lack the resources, the capacities, and/or the will to avert, ameliorate, and restore effectively. In these cases, responsibility reverts to the original responsible parties.

In 2009, the Global Humanitarian Forum estimated current annual economic losses from climate change at $125 billion (with over 90 percent of the losses falling on developing countries), and costs to avert the worst outcomes of climate change at about $50 billion to $100 billion a year.[59] Stern argues that development itself is key to adaptation, such as in promoting economic growth and diversification, investing in health and education, enhancing resilience to disasters and improving disaster management, and promoting risk pooling and social safety nets for the poorest.[60] Both Stern and the Global Humanitarian Forum, however, seem to predict rising death rates from climate change despite adaptation efforts. Yet it is clear that most of these deaths are preventable. This suggests that at least $100 billion a year is needed to avert, ameliorate, and redress harms, not including funds to support energy efficiency and industrialization along low-emission pathways. In recent years, wealthy countries have provided about 0.3 percent of their average national incomes, about $100 billion a year collectively, for official development assistance.[61] It appears that justice requires more than another $100 billion to address climate change in developing countries, and more again as the impacts of climate change intensify. In financial terms this represents a significant change, but not one that would greatly harm the wealthy countries' economies. Responding to obligations due to climate change requires important and challenging new efforts, but not unmanageable efforts in the context of other imperatives of social justice.

Implementation and the Politics of Responding to Climate Change

Thus far my analysis indicates that each country's annual greenhouse gas emissions should converge on three tonnes per capita in 2050 and wealthy countries should allocate at least $100 billion a year to avert, ameliorate, and redress harms from climate change. Wealthy countries should also help poor countries to adopt energy-efficient technologies, both to reduce emissions and to help them find low emission pathways as they industrialize (or otherwise come to base their economies on advanced technologies). We have not addressed deforestation, another important contributor to climate change, but if we can work out approaches to the central problems, secondary problems like this can probably be worked out along similar lines.

Of course, this gives us no more than a broad idea of a set of fair responses to climate change. Rawlsian analysis aims to encourage more people to adopt a view of climate change based on social justice and to support reforms. Hence, it may be helpful to discuss some aspects of implementation and associated politics. Given our anarchic system of sovereign nation-states, national governments need first to agree on plans for (a) cutting emissions, and (b) raising resources to support adaptation. Second, institutions need to be established to facilitate adaptation programs. But cutting emissions by 2050 and raising the needed funds are costly, and they involve significant lifestyle changes. Establishing institutions for adaptation involves establishing systems to monitor and evaluate implementation and to correct shortcomings, and some might see these as compromising national sovereignty. A government must impose on its citizens any obligations it accepts—with taxes, regulations, and programs, many of which may be painful and unpopular. Some emission reductions can be achieved by improving energy efficiency in ways that lower costs, new technologies may often yield net gains, and every new program creates opportunities. We have noted, however, that if total greenhouse gas emissions do not start to decline by 2020, it will be extremely difficult to keep the expected temperature gain to 2°C. Upward trajectories are associated with economic growth, and investments tend to have long-term emission consequences. Hence, many governments need to impose new and unpopular burdens.

Within constraints from total greenhouse gas emissions peaking by 2020 and from our 2050 target for national emission reductions, there is considerable scope for variations in national emission pathways. Targets for 2020 and 2050 are driven by the need to keep global CO_2e concentrations below 450 ppm, but when agents in the original position consider how to reach them, they also consider individual countries' cumulative emissions, levels of economic development, and technological capabilities. They would require countries with greater responsibility (for climate change) and capacity—that is, those with higher per capita cumulative and current emissions, higher incomes, and greater technological capabilities—to reduce emissions faster and to do more to support developing countries in their transitions. Agents in the original position identify these factors as morally relevant, but they have little basis for assigning them specific weights. Numeric agreements specifying national emissions pathways and financial contributions have to be worked out in actual negotiations, as do detailed plans for international institutions to support adaptation.

Governments engaged in these negotiations would aim to promote their national interests while also seeking an effective overall plan (although they may not define "effective" as I have). They would also evaluate proposals in terms of their domestic political consequences—what support and opposition they can expect from interest groups at home and how a proposal might affect the government's political future and those of its members. An effective overall plan will impose significant burdens particularly on richer countries with greater cumulative and current emissions, but a government may not believe it can secure agreement at home to shoulder such burdens. On one hand, a government would be prepared to make greater so-called concessions depending on the positions of other governments. On the other hand, it may view certain concessions, for one reason or another, as impossible in the domestic arena. Hence, we may see a few limited and inadequate agreements before a satisfactory one can be reached.

Domestic constraints in rich countries involve committing to emission reductions and to funding adaptation. Since poor countries suffer more harms from climate change, they would push for lower global emission targets and for greater funds for transitions and adaptation.[62] The more interesting practical and analytic issues for poor countries, however, arise in regard to implementing adaptation programs. In most rich countries, as long as political constituencies for particular emission and funding targets are strong enough, implementation is in a certain sense relatively straightforward. Most rich country governments possess adequate bureaucratic capacity. Within poor countries, however, harms from climate change tend to fall most heavily on poor people, who tend not to be adequately represented in their national political arenas. Nor can established national or international organizations be relied upon adequately to represent these people's interests. Climate change presents challenges of institutional design and construction for supporting the interests of its poor victims, and these may be thought to challenge poor countries' national sovereignty.

Recall that for Rawlsian analysis, institutions consist of principles for solving past problems, so efforts to establish new institutions disturb the prior equilibrium (however inadequate or unstable it may have been). As the institution that claims the unique right to employ coercion within its national territory, the state is the central arena for an ongoing contest among principles and interests held by citizens. Hence, we may assume that institutional demands from climate change imply conflicts with established principles and interests. Conflicts of principles and interests, however, are not always expressed as such. They may appear as disagreements about facts—for example, denials that observed climate changes are anthropogenic, or attacks on other parties for failing to do their part. Conflicts of principle are seen in disagreements about particular agencies' authority and mandate for addressing climate change, and conflicts of interest are seen when authorities cite harm to economic growth as the reason not to pursue reforms.

The Politics of the Response in the United States

There is no simple metric for social change, but the changes needed for a just response to climate change, particularly in some countries, are quite significant. Nordhaus finds a worldwide tax of $60 per tonne of carbon emissions in 2010, rising to $863 in 2100, sufficient to achieve the emission reductions needed to limit the rise in average temperatures to 2°C.[63] This equates to a 2010 tax of $16 per tonne of CO_2 emissions,[64] or $356 per person in the United States based on 2005 emissions of twenty-two tonnes per capita. The agents in the original position, however, require faster than average emission reductions in the United States due to the country's high cumulative and per capita emissions and high incomes. Assuming that this would involve tripling the U.S. tax from 2010, the tax would be $180 per tonne of carbon ($49 per tonne of CO_2) or $1,069 per person. Total U.S. federal government revenues averaged about $7,004 per person in 2010,[65] so carbon taxes would equal about 15 percent of federal revenue. In practice, taxes would not be the only instrument for reducing emissions, but this indicates something of the scale of effort needed.

At this writing, neither the U.S. government nor public opinion is prepared for such an effort.[66] It often happens that a crisis provides the impetus for reforms, and no doubt this pattern will be seen in the climate change arena. But this "reform mechanism" is fraught with danger, given the long lead times for reforms, the deep momentum of greenhouse gas emissions, and the less than fully understood feedback effects from climate changes. Rather, we have to hope that many American leaders and citizens will change their minds and adopt responding to climate change as a goal. Americans' views may be influenced by crises and by international politics, but the needed changes will require autonomous choices based on reasonable and rational deliberations.

In the United States, the ideology of the Democratic Party is more favorably oriented than that of the Republicans to responding to climate change. The Democratic Party is home to environmentalists and labor, while the Republican Party is home to business; also, the Democrats have the stronger internationalist orientation. Since the founding of the United States, American culture, with roots in classical (pro-business) liberalism, libertarianism, Tocquevillian localism, and the myth of the pioneer, has had a strong streak of skepticism regarding central government. More recently, it has also developed a populist, low-church anti-intellectualism. These ideologies have tended to find homes in the Republican Party, and they provide infertile ground for responding to climate change. When the program associated with a set of ideas offends someone's principles and interests, she may reject it out of hand, placing it in categories she dislikes and suspending further consideration. Then, although the human mind is naturally curious and receptive, her first response when someone promotes these ideas is likely to be negative. Also, climate change and its consequences are complicated phenomena, and many people are not accustomed to assessing the associated forms of evidence. Even fully grasping the evidence, from a rationally self-interested perspective, individual

Americans might expect that they, personally, can avoid serious harms. Given the increasing weight of evidence confirming anthropogenic climate change and increasing knowledge of its consequences, these factors help to explain why Republican governments have generally failed to take significant steps to respond to climate change.

It was a Democratic-majority Congress that in 1978 enacted the National Climate Program Act requiring investigation of climate change, and Democratic president Jimmy Carter who asked the National Research Council to investigate the matter. The Council responded that "if carbon dioxide continues to increase . . . [we find] no reason to doubt that climate changes will result and no reason to believe that these climate changes will be negligible. . . . A wait-and-see policy may mean waiting until it is too late."[67] In 1987, it was again a Democratic Congress that directed the Environmental Protection Agency to develop a national policy on climate change and directed the Secretary of State to coordinate diplomatic efforts to combat global warming.[68]

The Intergovernmental Panel on Climate Change was established in 1988 by the World Meteorological Organization and the United Nations Environment Programme, and in 1990 it published its first report confirming human-induced global warming. The 1992 United Nations Framework Convention on Climate Change was "a nonbinding agreement among 154 nations to reduce atmospheric concentrations of carbon dioxide and other greenhouse gasses," and it was signed by Republican president George H. W. Bush and ratified unanimously by the U.S. Senate. In 1997, the Framework Convention signatories met in Kyoto, Japan, and adopted a protocol that assigns mandatory targets for industrialized nations to reduce greenhouse gas emissions. It assigned the United States an emissions target for 2012 that was 7 percent below the U.S. level in 1990.[69] Democratic president Bill Clinton signed it, but the Senate unanimously passed a resolution stating that the United States should not enter into a treaty that did not include binding commitments from developing countries or that would cause harm to the U.S. economy. Since U.S. treaties come into force only when supported by two-thirds of the Senate, Clinton did not send the Kyoto Protocol for ratification.[70]

Republican presidential candidate George W. Bush promised to regulate CO_2 emissions, but as president, citing lack of participation from developing countries and possible harm to the U.S. economy, he repudiated the Kyoto Protocol and chose not to regulate CO_2. In 2002, Bush announced a climate change policy centered on a plan to reduce the greenhouse gas intensity of the U.S. economy by 18 percent by 2012. The goal, to be met by voluntary action, was to reduce emissions from 183 tonnes per million dollars of GDP to 151 over ten years.[71] Given that GDP was projected to grow more than 18 percent during the same period, this amounted only to a reduction in the rate of increase of total U.S. emissions.[72]

Despite the general Republican intransigence, the first significant government action in the United States to respond to climate change was by Republican governor Arnold Schwarzenegger, although in often liberal and environmentally progressive California. In 2005, in a move that appears to have helped his subsequent reelection, Schwarzenegger ordered that the state's total greenhouse gas emissions should be reduced to 2000 levels by 2010, 1990 levels by 2020, and 80 percent below 1990 levels by 2050.[73] These correspond to per capita emissions of about 12.5 tonnes of CO_2e in 2010, 10 tonnes in 2020, and 1.5 tonnes in 2050.[74] With 1,100 miles of valuable coastal real estate and natural habitats, and significant dependence on water from Sierra mountain snowpacks, California is particularly vulnerable to the impacts of climate change.[75] But California's actions alone, of course, can have little impact on climate change.

In 2009, the Democratic majority in the U.S. House of Representatives narrowly passed an important climate change bill, although one that fell short of the targets I have identified. Sponsored by California representative Henry Waxman and Massachusetts representative Edward Markley, the bill proposed a cap and trade system for greenhouse gases from covered sources, yielding an estimated price of about $13 in 2012 to emit a tonne of CO_2, although most permits would be given for free in the early years. It aimed to reduce U.S. greenhouse gas emissions to 17 percent below 2005 levels (about eighteen tonnes per capita) by 2020 and 83 percent (four tonnes per capita) by 2050,[76] and it had several provisions that would have reduced emissions directly, outside the cap and trade system.[77] In the Senate, however, despite initial support from several senators and from Democratic president Barack Obama, the bill first stalled and then died.[78] In late 2009, Hillary Clinton, President

Obama's secretary of state, promised that the United States would help to raise $100 billion annually by 2020 to help poor counties cope with climate change, but only if fast-growing countries like China and India accept binding commitments that are open to international inspection and verification.[79]

If countries like China and India do not reduce the growth rates of their greenhouse gas emissions soon, and if China does not start to reduce its total emissions by 2020, it will be extremely difficult to keep CO_2e concentrations below 450 ppm.[80] The United States itself, however, has hardly begun to implement measures to reduce emissions except in a few states such as California. Given America's high cumulative and current emissions and its wealth and technological competence, there is no country with a greater obligation to reduce emissions. There is little indication, however, that its government acknowledges this obligation. Even the relatively ambitous measures proposed by Hillary Clinton and Waxman-Markley impose few costs on American people or businesses for several years, If the United States is still emitting eighteen tonnes of CO_2e per capita, and if global funding for poorer countries' adaptation is only $100 billion by 2020, global society will probably be on the way to catastrophes. The economic recession in the United States in 2008–9 appears to have dampened public interest in climate change. Between April 2008 and October 2009, the proportion of Americans who said there is solid evidence of global warming due to human activities declined from 47 percent to 36 percent, while the proportion who thought it a very serious problem declined from 44 percent to 35 percent.[81]

Given this evidence of public opinion, if Congress and the president were to promote costly measures to respond to climate change, it could reduce their popularity, each politician's chances of reelection, and their ability to secure other political goals. But until the United States commits to significant measures, it is hard to see how an industrializing country like China, with a per capita income of $6,000 compared to $47,000 in the United States,[82] would commit to slowing its emission increases and to subsequent reductions. As economic theory suggests, the deep changes in investment patterns and the technological advances needed for substantial emission reductions will be made only if there is a secure incentive environment that makes them appear profitable. Nordhaus and

Stern recommend global carbon taxes because they offer economically efficient means to lower emissions, and also because carbon taxes could also be used to raise revenues for adaptation in poor countries.

Given problems of social justice, existing incentives generally are not sufficient to secure the needed reforms. Even in California, Schwarzenegger could not have known that committing the state to significant reforms would aid his reelection, although his reforms, too, postpone high costs to citizens. Politicians will need to take greater risks to initiate the costlier programs. There is a critical need for public education to raise awareness and understanding and for activists to promote reforms. Even 2°C warming carries risks of enormous loss of human life, widespread extinctions, and dramatic ecological changes. Since existing greenhouse gas accumulations already commit the planet to another 1°C warming, the inevitable rise in the number of extreme weather events will provide more evidence for skeptics. It may be that striking a deal with China or other countries will clinch American reforms, but Americans will need to better acknowledge their obligations due to high cumulative and current emissions before they are prepared to strike an adequate deal. A more ambitious target, such as reducing greenhouse gases to 350 ppm, would require much more rapid emission reductions by the United States as well as immediate reductions in countries like China and India. It is hard to imagine in institutional terms how this might come about.

Institutions for Adaptation in Low-Income Countries

In climate change negotiations, poor countries—unlike the United States and China, for example, which are wealthy and mutually dependent—can do little more than demand compensation and support on a moral basis. The $100 billion a year by 2020 proposed by Hillary Clinton is too little too late, but these countries have little recourse. It is the rich and industrialized countries that have largely caused the harms, so it is up to people in the more powerful countries to ensure that an overall deal includes meeting the victims' needs. If the poor countries were to become hosts to high-emission industries, it would undermine any deal, so they also need to be helped to develop their economies along low-emission pathways.

The more than 300,000 deaths a year already due to climate change are mostly from diseases associated with declining environmental quality, such as reductions in arable land, desertification, and rising sea levels. In addition, over 200 million people each year need immediate assistance or find their livelihoods significantly compromised, many due to disasters—such as hurricanes, floods, heat waves, and droughts—which have increased from around two hundred recorded in a year (on average) before 1990 to over four hundred a year in 2009.[83] Of course, with harms from weather there is no way to identify the specific victims who would have been spared in the absence of global warming. All victims of extreme weather events (as well as of environmental degradation) that could have been caused by climate change, therefore, should be considered equally as victims of climate change.

As financial resources become available for adaptation, how can the harms from climate change be averted, ameliorated, and redressed effectively? There are two immediate difficulties. First, these are technically challenging tasks to be carried out in institutionally challenging environments. Second, most of the likely victims of climate change are poor citizens, often of the world's poorest countries. Their interests generally are not well represented in the political economies in which they find themselves, many of which, to use Rawls's terminology, are burdened or outlaw states. They generally are not in a position to hold their governments or local powers effectively to account, while the powerful are often adept at gaining control over any resources that enter their system.

The international organizations that one might expect to address these problems, however, cannot be relied upon to do so effectively. Whether official development agencies such as the World Bank, the United Nations Development Programme, and the U.S. Agency for International Development, or international NGOs such as Oxfam, CARE International, and Doctors Without Borders, they have their own organizational interests. None has demonstrated that it consistently and cost-effectively represents the interests of the poor or of intended beneficiaries in developing countries.[84] From the start, therefore, it is likely that many of the resources for adaptation will be used ineffectively or to serve other, often bureaucratic, interests, although usually in the victims' names.

In the context of limited and probably inadequate resources, agents in the original position would find the primary goal to be averting, ameliorating, and redressing the harms from climate change cost effectively. Other goals, such as respecting poor countries' national sovereignty, empowering likely victims, and strengthening the poor countries' institutions would not be without weight, but they would be secondary.[85] The challenges, therefore, are to identify good strategies and to hold implementing agencies accountable. Tasks include developing drought-resistant crop strains, improving agricultural extension systems, building better roads and water management infrastructure, strengthening primary health care systems, helping poor families gain additional productive assets, improving disaster management systems for extreme weather events, strengthening and sometimes subsidizing insurance markets, and, when their habitats become unviable, helping individuals and communities move and rebuild their livelihoods.

Agents in the original position would place particular weight on averting the worst harms, and they would aim to avert as much harm as possible, securing adequate primary goods for as many likely victims as possible, given available resources. This requires developing metrics for quantifying and comparing the various harms that climate change causes and developing systems for estimating the likely reduction in harms (or improvements in well-being) from a given expenditure. It involves choices such as between investing in roads or in water catchment and distribution systems in Kenya or in Somalia. The analysis involves identifying technically superior approaches in terms of both their internal technical characteristics and the practical constraints and demands imposed by alternative environments.[86]

In practice, estimating the likely impacts and cost-effectiveness of proposed projects depends on estimating the likely impacts and cost-effectiveness of completed projects. Also, such estimates for completed projects provide a basis for holding implementing agencies accountable. Prior to about the year 2000, the World Bank used to estimate economic rates of return for most of its projects. Economic returns do not capture all improvements in well-being, nor do they weight gains appropriately according to Rawlsian principles. But the World Bank's evaluation system is a useful point of reference because it provides a basis for comparing benefits to costs in consistent units and for ranking projects in terms of their cost-effectiveness. Evaluation of World Bank projects, however, was controlled and organized by the World Bank itself. This produced perverse incentives, and rate of return estimates were often technically weak, inconsistent with one another, and upwardly biased.[87]

To build organizational cultures oriented to maximizing appropriately defined impacts and cost-effectiveness, it is necessary (although not sufficient) for routine evaluations to demonstrate certain characteristics. First, evaluations should be grounded in estimates of impacts and cost-effectiveness, and these estimates should be consistent in their units and evaluative judgments across evaluations. Second, evaluations should be explicitly comparative, locating the program under consideration within the range of similar programs in terms of their estimated cost-effectiveness, and explaining the program's relative strengths and weaknesses. Third, evaluations should be strategically engaged in terms of the factors that influence program design. For example, should there be questions about the division of responsibilities among national governments, official development agencies, and international NGOs for the kind of program under consideration, such questions should be addressed by routine evaluations. Fourth, evaluators should be independent of the agencies they evaluate, and they should be held accountable for the quality of their evaluations.

Given the importance of evaluation, it would be reasonable to devote at least 2 percent of funds for adaptation to such an independent function. Programs should empower the likely victims of climate change, but the victims are often not in a position to hold implementing agencies responsible for taking their interests appropriately into account. Instead, professionalism among evaluators should be cultivated so it rests on effectively representing the interests of likely victims, such as through a professional association with written standards and peer review. If cost-effectiveness is the criterion for allocating resources, however, other criteria will be compromised, including equity between countries. Governments of recipient countries would receive only those funds that they could use more cost effectively than others, and their programs would be subject to the same independent evaluation. Note that this results from the agents in the original position representing individuals rather than countries.

Since it is the interests of expected victims that are to be protected, their governments should not be privileged in implementation arrangements. When resource allocation is based on cost-effectiveness, neither donor nor recipient governments can allocate resources as they like, but this protects the interests of expected victims of climate change.

Resource allocation to help countries adopt low-emission pathways to industrialization, by contrast, should be based on equity between countries and on need, as well as on effectiveness. Here, the aim is largely to compensate poor countries for foregoing development strategies based on high-emission technologies, so support should be channeled through governments in exchange for enacting and enforcing appropriate controls. Implementing agencies should be held accountable for delivering support that is appropriate to the needs and is also of high quality, but governments should not be penalized if they fail to achieve high economic growth rates with the technologies and support provided.

Rawlsian vs. Economic Analysis of Climate Change

Both Rawlsian and economic approaches offer overall orientations for responding to climate change. Starting from the idea of rational utility maximization, economists aim to minimize the aggregate loss in utility due to climate change. This is to be done by reducing greenhouse gas emissions to the point where the marginal cost of an additional tonne of reductions is equal to the value of the marginal unit of harm avoided. The solution, then, depends on how costs and benefits (harms avoided) are calculated. We have seen that a major factor is how the analyst chooses to incorporate the time dimension. Since Nordhaus bases his discount rate on the real returns to capital, the weight he attributes to harms that occur far in the future is greatly diminished. Hence, he recommends permitting almost 3.5°C of global warming, even though this would have catastrophic effects for millions of people. It also permits greater investments, yielding economic growth that balances out the harms.

Stern, by contrast, discounts only for the small chance that humanity will come to an end in a given year. With a core analysis based on standard economic measures of costs and benefits similar to Nordhaus's, his proposal would see a rise in temperatures of about 2°C to 2.8°C. However, Stern notes that taking account of deaths and harms to the environment and giving greater weight to harms to the poor would substantially raise the total value of harms for a given degree of warming. This would lower the targeted temperature rise.

The Rawlsian approach is to ask what policies would be chosen by agents who do not know the income, country of residence, or place in time of the person they represent but who aim to advance this person's interests. The thought is that this procedure yields a fair conclusion. Such agents would be particularly concerned to protect the lives and livelihoods of those most vulnerable to climate change, so they would call for greater efforts to avoid deaths and give greater weight to harms to the poor than in the economists' models. The Rawlsian approach would lower the target for the rise in average global temperatures to below 2°C if it were institutionally feasible, but it appears this is unlikely to be the case.

Although utilitarian philosophy includes the concept of obligation, economic theory does not,[88] and Nordhaus does not address support for the victims of climate change. Stern does argue that developed countries should help developing countries to adapt, and he includes as reasons the developed countries' high cumulative and current greenhouse gas emissions. When he addresses adaptation costs, however, he argues only that developed countries should honor existing commitments to increase their development assistance budgets. Agents in the original position, however, would find people who contribute more to the causes of climate change, or who benefit disproportionately from earlier contributions, to bear responsibility for the harms that climate change causes. Industrialized countries are obligated to support adaptation, particularly given that the costs of doing so are manageable, while harms from failing to do so are enormous.

Nordhaus and Stern support emissions taxes as economically efficient means to emissions reductions. An equal global emissions tax, however, would not address the great differences in per capita emissions between countries and associated differences in responsibility for climate change and in levels of and prospects for economic development. Taking these factors into account, agents in the original position would select a global target for equal per capita emissions, with emissions taxes as one tool to reach it. They would have wealthy industrialized countries move quickly toward significant emissions reductions, allowing poorer industrializing countries to make more gradual transitions with less compromise to their industrialization processes. They would also direct rich countries to help poor preindustrial countries with technology and education so they can pursue economic development along low-emission pathways. Stern, too, argues that rich countries should provide these kinds of help to poor countries, but without a clear idea of obligation or a target for equal per capita emissions.

In economic analyses, once a target is identified on the basis of economic efficiency, the framework for reaching it is typically articulated in terms of appropriate tools (e.g., taxes), perhaps with some discussion of constraints to be overcome. This framework could be said to naturalize or to objectify the social world. The Rawlsian approach, by contrast, takes institutions to consist largely of constructions of principles. In order for significant social reforms to be enacted, new principles must displace old ones. The reform challenge can be articulated by describing the existing structure of principles, the new ones to be established, and how the change could be carried out. I demonstrate two variants of this approach—a historical analysis of the politics of the response to climate change in the United States and an institutional analysis of requirements for cost-effective adaptation in poor countries.

The former analysis emphasizes interactions among structural and ideological factors. It finds that not enough Americans have yet come to grips with the full weight of the consequences of their country's high historic and ongoing greenhouse gas emissions, so there is not yet the political will for the deep reforms required. And it presents some of the main structural prisms through which the politics will play out. The analysis of requirements for cost-effective adaptation identifies structural challenges due to the limited capacity of poor people in developing countries (the main victims of climate change) to hold their governments or international development agencies accountable. It finds that it would be possible to generate an appropriate incentive environment for agencies implementing adaptation programs by professionalizing the evaluation function along particular lines. Stern, by contrast, offers detailed discussions of policies for reducing greenhouse gas emissions and for developed and developing countries to adapt to climate change, but he does not systematically address constraints to their implementation. Nordhaus mainly presents what he finds to be an efficient overall approach and he compares it to some of the prominent alternatives.

Rawlsian analysis reveals the substantial institutional distance that needs to be covered to respond adequately to climate change in the areas addressed. Ways of life in the contemporary world are deeply dependent on energy from fossil fuels, the main driver of climate change. The principles that people have adopted to regulate their behavior involving energy use, however, do not and could not have taken account of all the consequences of this use. Now we know that the unforeseen costs are great, and that accommodating them takes hard changes. It is not surprising that it should take time for our systems of principles to accommodate this knowledge, but the longer it takes, the greater the costs become. Also, in its social essence, climate change is a mechanism by which the present generation imposes harms on future generations and the wealthy impose harms on the poor. These harms were not intended, but they still establish significant obligations. Rawlsian analysis aims to help people reasonably and rationally to adopt orientations that serve as grounds for doing justice.

chapter seven

Kantian Ontology of Practical Reason and Social Science

If our social world is constructed substantially from principles, it follows that social analysis cannot be merely empirical. The social world remains part of our natural world, and we cannot conceive of it otherwise, so all the tools of the natural scientist are available to the social scientist. Our naturalistic conception of the social world, however, is embedded in our principles. As social scientists and as readers of social science, we cannot avoid an ethical take on our conceptions of social relations, and as humans in society we need principles and analyses that help us to live justly with one another. Additionally, in our naturalistic conception of the social world, we need to take account, as an empirical matter, of the condition that social relations are grounded in principles. Human autonomy, or simply the fact that principles can change, imbues causation in human relations with different dynamics than causation for stars, plants, or fish.

Given that heretofore utilitarianism has provided the only available microfoundations for social analysis, many of the regularities in human relations based on interests are pretty well understood. Neoclassical economics provides a powerful framework for explaining changes in prices that we observe in the market based on supply and demand, even if our interpretation of these changes may be influenced by our concept of social justice. We have noted that the economic concept of "externalities" is important for an understanding of climate change, and my analysis of the Grameen Bank depends on an economic understanding of interest rates.

By the same token, we probably have a lot to learn about patterns of behavior based on principles, and on interactions between principles and interests. I noted in chapter 3 that rational choice theorists often employ explanations based on principles either without theorizing them or by attempting to found principles on interests. Once the places of principles and interests in practical reason are better understood, we can expect social analysis to improve. Chapter 4 shows how economists seriously misunderstood the causes for the Grameen Bank's success, which suggests that much of the advice given to other microfinance organizations has probably been misguided. Resentment has played an important part in caste conflicts in Bihar's villages and in its state politics, as well as in Kenya's Mau Mau Rebellion (see Bates's account, discussed in chapter 3). A rigorous comparative analytics of resentment that is both theoretically and empirically grounded, however, has yet to be developed.

While neoclassical economics and rational choice theory have been constructed from theoretical foundations based on rationality, the mainstream of comparative politics engages routinely with dynamics based on principles as well as interests at the macro level. Comparative institutional analysis and mainstream, historically grounded political economy routinely address topics that rely on both, such as the bases for a state's claims to legitimacy, the characteristics and capabilities of bureaucracies, and the structure of relations among social classes.

For the most part, we cannot directly observe the dynamics or mechanisms that drive the organizations and states that make up our social world. Nevertheless, as citizens, colleagues, clients, and officials we construct mental models of these institutions. We make agreements and commit them to text, and the words take on a life of their own; actual events, near and far, ground our interpretations. When we are members of a collectivity that bears our interests, our views will be shaped in part by how these interests are served. We appreciate that outsiders have their own views, however, and that we need the words that establish a general perspective. Here, the social scientist has become the specialist, trying to develop perspectives on organizations and states that are adequate to the events for interested persons and that can add up to a coherent view of the social world.

Natural language already expresses the basic dynamics of principles and interests. However, when social analysis is theorized based on patterns of interests alone, patterns of principles will be neglected. The resulting perspectives will privilege established interests, and the discourse of justice will be neglected. Political economy has built upon natural language and used systematic comparison of social institutions in its attempt to take account of the various affected interests. The comparative method has been elaborated (a) through nuanced comparisons of units that vary in relevant dimensions with respect to one another and/or that represent relevant positions within the relevant universe, and (b) through statistical analysis, often of large numbers of units based on criteria and measures that the units share. Sources of principles are often explored de facto through historical analysis. Accomplished practitioners of comparative political economy often use neoutilitarians' findings but consider their methods too restrictive. They often do not bemoan their own lack of microfoundations, finding the comparative method adequate to itself.

It is too soon to tell how empirical findings from Rawlsian analysis might enrich political economy. Political economy has been limited in some respects by having often been conceived of merely as an empirical science and by its critical orientation to neoclassical economics. For instance, since about the 1980s neoclassical economists and political economists have offered conflicting explanations for differences in economic growth rates among developing countries, with the former attributing the highest rates to free markets and economic incentives and the latter attributing them to government support for industrialization.[1] When political economists approached this as merely an empirical question, however, it led to tensions and inconsistencies in their accounts. Neoclassical economists analyzed causes of economic growth rates within a relatively narrow and highly quantitative utility-maximizing framework, but political economists used concepts and methods that tended to shed light on coercion and manipulation. Given that our conceptions of the natural world are embedded in our principles, and assuming that a person has given serious thought to problems of social justice and adopted particular views on them, once she addresses an overall national policy framework, she will respond to it in terms of these views. When political economists adopted the neoclassical economists' question about growth rates, however, coercion and manipulation seemed to arise merely as by-products to the analysis. Although some scholars offer insights into cruel choices between civil and political rights and economic growth,[2] their analyses do not give coercion and manipulation their full moral weight. To do so they would need to do more to articulate the ideological and institutional constraints to social justice.

A leading work in the political economy tradition is Robert Wade's *Governing the Market: Economic Theory and the Role of Government in East Asian Industrialization.* Wade shows how, between 1955 and 1985, having been driven from China by Mao's communists, Taiwan's nationalist Kuomintang government transformed the country from an agrarian backwater into a thriving industrial economy. Through most of the book, and particularly in the conclusion, Wade celebrates the government's economic accomplishments, and he urges other governments to follow Taiwan's example. He also explains how the Kuomintang operated as a Leninist state, maintaining authoritarian rule and martial law based on the fiction that it was the legitimate government for all of China.[3] To dominate the native Taiwanese majority, the Kuomintang pursued strategies to prevent dissent from being heard, to prevent it from being acted on, and, chillingly, to check the desire to question.[4] Wade discusses a "brilliant control system," "mass cooptation," and "ideological molding," including indefinite imprisonment without trial, government ownership of the media, ongoing censorship, and gatherings of three or more persons requiring police registration.[5]

Wade asserts that he cherishes civil and political freedoms, but he argues that "in societies . . . where freedom is . . . restrained by fear of the assassin's bullet and fear of being thrown off one's land by trumped-up suits and corrupt judges . . . the priority is to institutionalize a system of order before it is democratized—to move from a system where the press is controlled by people with wealth and private armies to one where it is controlled by the state, before reaching one where it is controlled by people with wealth but without private armies."[6] Although Wade critiques economic accounts of East Asian economic growth based on limitations of economic theory, he explains his own analytic approach in terms of the logic of an inductive explanation of this growth. His political economy framework directs him to the political analysis I have discussed, but he does not theorize this analysis. Hence, he arrives at a functional account of political processes that can lead to rapid economic growth, assuming that political leaders are benign.[7] He offers a disquieting analysis of the Kuomintang's methods but accepts their necessity.

From the present vantage point, we can see that Taiwan's economic growth created conditions that subsequently supported democratization, and Taiwan's democratization may well turn out to support democracy in China. Nevertheless, if a regime today adopted authoritarian and repressive practices like those of the Kuomintang in the 1950s and 1960s we should not support it, and it is not clear if Wade would.[8] His methods lead him to analyze economic and political strategies as mutually embedded, but the way he frames his question leads to political conclusions that are weakly founded.

In his book *State-Directed Development: Political Power and Industrialization in the Global Periphery*, Atul Kohli develops a more systematic view of the role of coercion in economic development. Kohli's methodology is rigorously comparative; he investigates the histories of South Korea, Brazil, India, and Nigeria to explain their divergent experiences with industrialization. A key factor, he finds, is whether a given state develops "a well-established public arena that is both normatively and organizationally distinguishable from private interests and pursuits."[9] If it does not, then patrimonial forms of authority generally found in traditional societies are likely to be reproduced within the institutional shell of a modern state, and "public officeholders tend to treat public resources as their personal patrimony. . . . Whether organized as a nominal democracy or as a dictatorship, state-led development under the auspices of neopatrimonial states has often resulted in disaster, mainly because both public goals and capacities to pursue specific tasks in these settings have repeatedly been undermined by personal and narrow group interests."[10] Among states that do develop a public arena, the next key factor is whether the state devotes itself wholeheartedly to rapid economic growth via an exclusive ruling alliance with private capitalists. If so, in order to sustain the focus on growth, the resulting "cohesive-capitalist state" typically has to repress and subjugate other social groups, labor in particular. If it does not, it is likely to become a "fragmented-multiclass state" that dissipates its energy by trying to pursue multiple goals.[11]

Kohli explicitly distinguishes his empirical conclusion that cohesive-capitalist states are the most successful at industrialization from a normative assessment. Like Wade, when Kohli describes a state's repressive practices, his disapproval is clear, but unlike Wade, Kohli repeatedly expresses misgivings about the cohesive-capitalist pathway to economic development. If anything, Kohli is more insistent that the political economist's task is an empirical one, as he seeks to identify the most appropriate concepts for characterizing the process of "late-late development," and the most concise yet powerful set of factors to explain divergent outcomes.

It seems, however, that Kohli came to be convinced that political economy is not or should not be conceived of as merely empirical. He notes that at a seminar he attended, Susanne Rudolph (another leading political economist) "pointedly remarked" that he must take moral responsibility for his argument, and he states that he would try his best to do so.[12] Hence, he argues that economic successes in cases such as South Korea, Taiwan, military-ruled Brazil, and contemporary China "must be weighed against the serious political costs paid by the citizens of these countries," and he suggests that the "preferred agents of change" may be "disciplined and inclusionary political parties, such as well-organized social democratic parties."[13]

Since the social world is part of our empirical world, any systematic investigation of it can add to our understanding. An investigation based on neoutilitarian microfoundations, however, would be unlikely to identify and articulate the role of a public arena as a prerequisite for economic development. A public arena consists, in part, of a discourse grounded in normative ideas of the public good, where agents systematically promote these ideas, temporarily setting aside personal and sectional interests. Such promotion flies in the face of the idea of the person as a rationally self-interested, utility-maximizing agent, except when agents adopt the public good as their interest. By developing this idea of a public arena, Kohli makes an important contribution to political economy. With differential success at industrialization as the object of his investigation, however, Kohli does not have to go very far in deconstructing the public nature of these arenas. His analysis demonstrates that the public whose interests are included may not be very wide, excluding, for example, the Brazilian majority of indigenous and African heritage; the interests of workers may be represented ambiguously at best.

The Rawlsian approach to justice, of course, seeks to identify principles that promote the interests of all members of society and to build a public arena based on these. It is important to recognize that for low-income, neopatrimonial societies, this requires very deep social change. Justice seems to require both increased investment to promote economic growth and better distribution to address basic needs, but these societies are likely to lack technical competencies in both strategic arenas. Building a political constituency that supports both is a real challenge. Yet, social analysis is as inherently ethical as it is empirical, and the touchstone for its ethical dimension is social justice. For a social analyst properly to take moral responsibility for her arguments, she must ground them in this understanding. It often happens that a configuration of institutions and incentives offers no straightforward pathway to social justice. The persons involved are likely to privilege their own interests in their conceptions of the situation, but social analysts should offer conceptions that, if often only loosely, represent all affected interests fairly. When we incorporate such conceptions in our worldviews, we stand on the side of justice. To go even further—developing a conception of a just solution—is, of course, still a long way from implementing it, and imagined solutions should be taken as provisional. But once imagined solutions do take account of the actual structure of established principles, they provide an essential ideological basis for just social reform.

I tried in chapter 6 to offer the beginnings of such an analyses of the politics of climate change in the United States and of requirements for cost-effective adaptation to climate change in poor countries. Like establishing equitable economic growth in societies with neopatrimonial states, building a constituency in America that can promote a just response to climate change is a real challenge. Yet, surely this is the kind of task to which political science ought to be able to contribute. It is important to convince people that climate change is real, and it is helpful for individuals to reduce their personal carbon footprints. Principles that support America's generation of greenhouse gases, however, help to constitute the identities of many Americans, and they are expressed in much American law. For the United States to adopt a just response is for many of these principles to change. Surely, political science should include concepts and methods for articulating such a strategic landscape.

On the empirical side, Kantian ontology demands a slight reframing of our interpretation of statistical findings in the social sciences. If principles and interests are the basic structural components of our social world, then they underlie our responses to changes in empirical phenomena. But since principles in particular must be assumed in the long run to be fluid, relations among empirical variables that involve behavioral regularities among humans must also be fluid. Our social world is part of our empirical world, and statistical and econometric studies can identify causal relationships among social phenomena. Such studies normally explore how a variable of interest, the dependent variable, is affected by changes in other variables, which are framed as independent. The thought is that even though the dependent variable behavior of any two individuals may be affected by many factors that the study does not include, over large numbers of persons the general strength of the relationship between independent and dependent variables can often be determined well enough to have predictive value.

This is all well and good. The nature and magnitude of the dependent variable response to changes in independent variables, however, depends to some extent on the construction of principles and interests in terms of which each individual perceives and interprets these changes (or mediating factors). Random selection across the universe of individuals addresses this source of variance, but in comparative politics, statistical and econometric techniques are often used without random selection. There seems to be no reason to think that the strength of these deep correlations would be consistent over time, or between study and nonstudy populations. Whereas in the natural sciences empirical regularities reflect physical properties that may be taken as constant, this is not the case in the social sciences. Differences in these correlations outside the study population may often be small, but we should appreciate that predicting human behavior is not the same as predicting other relationships in the natural world.

In Kant's ontology, practical reason guides choice, and theoretical reason is the basis for our knowledge of external objects. Kant holds that both practical reason (and its maxims) and theoretical reason (and its knowledge) depend on characteristics of the mind as much as on sense impressions from the external world, including most famously our sense of space and of time. Practical reason precedes theoretical reason in that although theoretical reason is transparent to practical reason and practical reason can invoke its fruits at any time, theoretical reason can only reflect upon the features of practical reason as though it were one more object in the world. Practical reason depends on theoretical reason for its knowledge of external objects, and to view a situation in terms of theoretical reason is to take a naturalistic view. Such a view is always available to practical reason, but when it comes time to choose and to act, a framework grounded in principles and interests will be restored.

If practical reason has the senses of right and the good as its two basic capacities, it follows that principles and interests are the fundamental building blocks of the social world. This is not to say that passions and emotions do not enter fundamentally into practical decisions; their influence can certainly be profound.[14] Emotions can color and displace reason, but they are not building blocks of reason, and at the end of the day, reason can trump emotions, even if often in practice it does not. Hence, every organization and every long-standing relationship among persons can be understood as a construction of principles and interests. A relationship may also include powerful aesthetic elements, and our principles and interests may take these into account. Like emotions, aesthetic judgments can inform principles and interests, but they are not building blocks of reason.

In the long run, we bear responsibility for the principles and interests that constitute our social world, and in this responsibility we find freedom in the internal sense. Neoclassical economics and rational choice theory have framed social analysis as a merely empirical science based on the dynamics of interests, and the interaction of these features yields a deep conservative bias. Failing to articulate structures of principles, these disciplines place principles in the analytic background, implicitly endorsing the status quo; neglecting the ethical dimension of social analysis lends this background normative weight. Insofar as political economy has articulated macro-level social dynamics based on both principles and interests, Rawlsian political analysis offers to work out its implicit microfoundations. While this can be expected to strengthen political economy as an empirical discipline, it also reframes political economy as inherently ethical and grounds it in a conception of social justice.

Rawls argues, as noted in chapter 2, that we do not experience complete autonomy until we live in a just society, and that we have an imperfect obligation to promote social justice. Political scientists bear a particular responsibility to provide the ideological means to satisfy this obligation, and Rawlsian analysis offers a basis for doing so, but it is important to understand the limits of this responsibility. On one hand, the obligation to promote social justice is only imperfect, and many people exercise their freedom mainly in arenas in which the political dimension is secondary. The politically engaged life can be deeply meaningful and fulfilling, but I cannot endorse the view that it is superior to other ways of life or that it represents the highest degree of excellence.[15] On the other hand, promoting social justice depends on action, and as an arena for action, the ideological dimension is necessary but not sufficient.

When we do social and political analysis, we are constructing our social world, but possibly only provisionally. For a naturalistic view to be integrated with one's established cognitive construction of principles and interests, one must accept or affirm it, and it may not be fully integrated until one acts upon it. One may carry out a social analysis and find that it incorporates normative elements (implicitly or explicitly) that are inconsistent with one's established views. Then one may reject it in principle and treat it as merely naturalistic, noting its normative features, or accept it provisionally but with reservations.

Given that the social world of all persons consists of the principles and interests of all persons (and of the narratives in which they are embedded), there is a certain structural/conceptual problem or challenge. Social collectivities greatly exceed the number of persons who can have face-to-face relationships, and such collectivities have great influence on one another, but the individual's conception of her own group and of other groups inevitably involves a high degree of abstraction. Under contemporary conditions, she has conceptions of many relationships in which her group is engaged that are not grounded in her personal experience. The group's internal and external management, however, which is highly consequential, is grounded one way or another in the sum of the conceptions of its members. Any conceptual structure differentially privileges the various interests of members and nonmembers in terms of their roles, so the conceptual structure itself will be subject to competitive pressures. Given its abstraction, however, many members of the group may have limited grounds for assessing the structure's propositions. Political science should offer conceptions that serve members' interests while also supporting social justice.

It seems to me that our contemporary social world is one of many and deep injustices. There is no necessary or inevitable historical movement toward greater social justice, and humanity may be on its way to ecological catastrophe. Neoutilitarian forms of social analysis have contributed to our present predicament, and I offer Rawlsian analysis as an alternative. My hope is that it can support deeper understandings of the nature and form of our social world and richer expressions of human freedom.

notes

chapter one. **Introduction**

1. Here I refer to the sense of the good as it has been understood in these branches of the utilitarian tradition. This conception of the good makes up a large part of the good as Rawls understands it, that is, as the satisfaction of rational desire, and Rawls attributes this view of the good to Kant (as well as to Henry Sidgwick, the primary utilitarian philosopher whom Rawls cites). However, Kant's idea of the supreme good centers on virtue and the worthiness to be happy. Rawls, *A Theory of Justice*, 79–80; Kant, *Critique of Practical Reason*, 141.

2. Hauser has been found responsible for scientific misconduct and has resigned from Harvard, but the accusations against him do not undermine the arguments—mainly logical in form—that I draw on. See N. Wade, "Scientist under Inquiry Resigns from Harvard."

3. For instance, Rawls notes that for the purpose of developing a political conception of justice he gives "the reasonable" a more restricted sense than Kant gives to the categorical imperative and to pure practical reason. Rawls, *Political Liberalism*, 48–49 including note 1.

4. Kant, *Groundwork for the Metaphysics of Morals*.

5. Ibid., 31.

6. Ibid., 33.

7. Rawls, *Political Liberalism*, 49.

8. Ibid., 54.

9. Elsewhere, Rawls summarizes the reasonable as the capacity for a sense of justice, for example, Rawls, *Political Liberalism*, 413.

10. This and four other formulations are listed in Kant, *Groundwork for a Metaphysics of Morals*, xviii.

11. Rawls, *Lectures on the History of Moral Philosophy*, 151.

12. Note that the model of choice in rational choice theory and neoclassical economics is much narrower than that in classical utilitarianism as represented, for example, by John Stuart Mill or Sidgwick. I present Rawlsian analysis only as an alternative to these established forms, not to any analysis that could be developed from utilitarian foundations.

13. Rawls, "Kantian Constructivism in Moral Theory," esp. 308 (originally from Rawls's 1980 Dewey Lectures). In some cases the interests attributed to actors by scholars using rational choice models may be more consistent with categorical imperatives, such as when scholars of the courts assume that justices wish to promote a particular judicial philosophy.

14. Kant, *Groundwork for the Metaphysics of Morals*, 30n.

15. According to Kant, the consciousness of righteousness can instill a virtuous attitude or respect for the moral law that then serves as an incentive, or interest of sorts, to make choices consistent with this law. The key point here is that some choices are made from principles of pure practical reason directly, without being subjected to maximizing calculations involving inclinations, or hypothetical imperatives of empirical practical reason. Kant, *Critique of Practical Reason*, 147, 186, 189.

16. Several applications of this model are found in chapters 4 and 5.

17. Kant, *Groundwork for the Metaphysics of Morals*, 36.

18. Kant, *Critique of Practical Reason*, 44.

19. March, *A Primer on Decision Making*, 57.

20. Elster, *The Cement of Society*, 15.

21. Ibid., 97.

22. Ibid. Elster also refers to the demands of rationality as hypothetical imperatives. Ibid., 98.

23. Ostrom, *Governing the Commons*, 37.

24. Ibid., 142.

25. Knight, *Institutions and Social Conflict*, Cambridge: Cambridge University Press, 4–9.

26. Ibid., 14.

27. Ibid.

28. Ibid., 128.

29. Rawls, *A Theory of Justice*, 109.

30. Knight, *Institutions and Social Conflict*, 125.

31. Ibid., 126.

32. Ibid., 129, emphasis original.

33. A term I borrow from Peter Evans, *Embedded Autonomy*. See 21–28.

34. See, for example, Shaw, "A World Bank Intervention in the Sri Lankan Welfare Sector."

35. In 2001, Bihar was split into two states, Bihar and Jharkhand. All references in this book, except the quote from Long at the beginning of chapter 5, are to pre-2001 Bihar.

36. Rawls, *The Law of Peoples*, 5, 90. See also Rawls, *A Theory of Justice*, 4.

37. In contrast, say, to disappointment.

38. This is probably because, despite its population exceeding those of all but eleven countries in the world, Bihar is a state rather than a country.

39. Additionally, I conducted research on Gandhian village development organizations in Bihar in 1982–83 and wrote a paper on the political economy of Bihar during my graduate studies.

chapter two.   **The Cognition of Principles and the Role of Rawlsian Political Analysis**

1. Rawls, *Political Liberalism*, 100.
2. Kant, *Groundwork for the Metaphysics of Morals*, 57.
3. "Justice is the first virtue of social institutions, as truth is of systems of thought." Rawls, *A Theory of Justice*, 3.
4. Ibid., preface to the 1971 edition, xviii.
5. Ibid., 171–76.
6. Kant, *Critique of Practical Reason*, 111–13.
7. Rawls, *Political Liberalism*, 93.
8. A third central idea, freedom, which we do not consider in the present discussion, is also based on this distinction, as is a fourth, dignity, which I mention briefly. Kant, *Groundwork for the Metaphysics of Morals*, 63–65.
9. Ibid., 31.
10. Ibid., 33.
11. Ibid., 37, emphasis original.
12. Ibid., 58.
13. Ibid., 59. However, "*considered in themselves* natural inclinations are *good*, i.e. not reprehensible, and to want to extirpate them would not only be futile but harmful and blameworthy as well; we must rather only curb them, so that they will not wear each other out but will instead be harmonized into a whole called happiness. Now the reason that accomplishes this is called *prudence*." Kant, *Religion within the Boundaries of Mere Reason and Other Writings*, 78, emphasis original.
14. Kant, *Groundwork for the Metaphysics of Morals*, 62.
15. Rawls points out that Kant uses the term *vernünftig*, often translated as "rational," to express a full conception of reason that covers the terms "reasonable" and "rational" as they are often used in English. *Lectures on the History of Moral Philosophy*, 164.
16. Kant, *The Metaphysics of Morals*.
17. Rawls, *A Theory of Justice*, xviii.
18. Ibid., 3.
19. For example, Rawls, *Political Liberalism*, 285.

20. This is, as Kant would say, analytic, since the concept of a just law or institution implies that it is based on just principles.

21. Rawls, *A Theory of Justice*, 118–19. The agents also do not know the society's level of civilization or the generation of the person they represent, which is important for securing justice between generations (as discussed in chapter 6).

22. Ibid., 54–56.

23. Ibid., 266.

24. Rawls, *Political Liberalism*, 72.

25. Ibid., 77.

26. Ibid., 78.

27. Ibid., 77–78.

28. Ibid., 78.

29. Ibid.

30. Ibid., 72.

31. Ibid., 79.

32. Sen, *The Idea of Justice*.

33. Ibid., 56–57; see also 109, 198.

34. Ibid., 91–96, 106.

35. Ibid., 57, 90.

36. Ibid., 101–2.

37. Ibid., 90, 143.

38. Ibid., 205.

39. People in other countries may be affected by policies based on principles in *Theory*, such as those that promote the interests of the least well-off in a given country, but the principles governing relations between countries are addressed elsewhere (particularly in *The Law of Peoples*).

40. Sen, *The Idea of Justice*, 138–52.

41. Rawls, *A Theory of Justice*, 402. By the time he wrote *Political Liberalism*, Rawls might no longer have called this "rationalist."

42. Ibid., 407.

43. Ibid., 406.

44. Ibid., 408.

45. Learning still takes place, but about different principles and a harsher social world.

46. Ibid., 409–13.

47. Ibid., 411.

48. Ibid., 415.

49. Ibid., 416.

50. Ibid. This is the basis for ethical autonomy, which Rawls excludes in his later account of political liberalism. Here we see clearly that Rawls's original position is a reformulation of the categorical imperative.

51. Ibid., 414–15.

52. Ibid., 417.

53. Ibid., 406.

54. Rawls, *Political Liberalism*, xxv.

55. Rawls, *The Law of Peoples*, 91.

56. Ibid., 5.

57. Honneth draws his account of the infant and the mother coming to recognize one another as independent persons largely from Winnicott, *The Maturational Process and the Facilitating Environment*, and Winnicott, *Playing and Reality*.

58. Honneth, *The Struggle for Recognition*, 99.

59. Ibid., 101.

60. Ibid., 105.

61. Ibid., 109.

62. Ibid., 110.

63. Ibid., 114.

64. Ibid., 126.

65. Ibid., 130.

66. Rawls argues, however, that we rightly take this view of one another only in a just society, particularly one with a just distribution of income. *A Theory of Justice*, 90.

67. Elster, *The Cement of Society*, 36.

68. Rawls, *Political Liberalism*, 51–52.

69. Fehr and Fischbacher, "The Economics of Strong Reciprocity." "Strong reciprocity means that individuals behave as if their positive or negative valuation of the reference agent's payoff depends on the actions of the reference agent. If the actions of the agent are perceived as kind, a strong reciprocator values the payoffs of the reference agent positively. If the actions are perceived as hostile, the payoff of the reference agent is valued negatively" (151).

70. Verplaetse, *The Moral Brain*.

71. Hauser, *Moral Minds*.

72. Hauser, *Moral Minds*, 419–20.

73. Ibid., 358.

74. Ibid., 167. Note that this is a very primitive cognitive capacity shared by many species.

75. Ibid., 168.

76. Ibid., 318.

77. Ibid., 375.

78. Ibid., 408, 413.

79. Ibid., 336–41.

80. Ibid., 391.

81. Ibid., 413.

82. Ibid., 358.

83. Fogassi, "The Mirror Neuron System: How Cognitive Functions Emerge from Motor Organization."

84. Ibid., 72–73.

85. It is my understanding that psychopaths perceive the question of fairness but are not moved by it. Exploring the basis for this abnormality may shed light on the cognitive basis for the normal sense of right.

86. Ibid., 207–8.

chapter three. **The Analytic Limits of Rational Choice Theory**

1. The following arguments in this section draw substantially from portions by Emily Hauptmann in Clements and Hauptmann, "The Reasonable and the Rational Capacities in Political Analysis."

2. Flood, "Some Experimental Games," 16; Kalisch, et al., "Some Experimental N-Person Games," 326–27.

3. Ledyard, "Public Goods," 143.

4. Andreoni and Miller, "Rational Cooperation in the Finitely Repeated Prisoner's Dilemma," 572.

5. Ibid.

6. Andreoni and Miller, "Rational Cooperation," 572; Marwell and Ames, "Economists Free Ride, Does Anyone Else?," 299.

7. Andreoni and Miller, "Rational Cooperation," 582.

8. Monroe, *The Heart of Altruism*, 4.

9. Marwell and Ames, "Economists Free Ride, Does Anyone Else?" 307–8; see Table 2 on page 307 for a summary of experimental conditions. Public goods provision experiments resemble prisoner's dilemma experiments because of the way the payoffs are structured. If few participants contribute to the public good, those who do receive a "sucker's payoff," while those who choose not to contribute keep the resources allocated to them at the outset and still stand to reap the possible dividends of others' contributions (the "temptation payoff").

10. Marwell and Ames, "Experiments in the Provision of Public Goods I," 1359. The passage cited continues: "Despite isolation, instructions which emphasized the monetary importance of the situation and minimized social factors, and the chance to develop full information regarding the parameters of the situation, normative factors such as fairness seem to have strongly influenced economic decisions."

11. Ibid., 1357.

12. Ibid., 1358.

13. Ibid., 1358–59.

14. Marwell and Ames, "Economists Free Ride, Does Anyone Else?" 306–7.

15. Ibid., 309. Further on this point, "Those who did respond were much more likely to say that little or no contribution was 'fair'. In addition, the economics graduate students were about half as likely as other subjects to indicate that they were 'concerned with fairness in making their investment decisions" (309).

16. Bates, *Beyond the Miracle of the Market*, 6.

17. Ibid., 1.

18. Ibid., 14.

19. Ibid., 16–17.

20. Ibid., 9–10.

21. Ibid., 18–27.

22. Ibid., 33.

23. Ibid., 12.

24. Both books are part of a Cambridge series explicity oriented to rational choice approaches, Political Economy of Institutions and Decisions, edited by James E. Alt and Douglass C. North.

25. Rawls, *Political Liberalism*, 49.

26. Levi, *Consent, Dissent, and Patriotism*, 18–19.

27. Ibid., 140.

28. Ibid., 142–44.

29. Ibid., 141.

30. Ibid., 157–61.

31. Ibid., 165–99.

32. Ibid., 7.

33. Ibid., 8.

34. Ibid., 2–3.

35. Ibid., 9.

36. Ibid., 10.

37. Ibid., 11.

38. I draw on Milton Friedman, *Capitalism and Freedom*.

39. Ibid., 23, 191. Friedman argues that some redistribution is justified because people find the sight of poverty distressing.

40. Rawls, *A Theory of Justice*, 53.

41. Ibid., 90–91.

42. Ibid., 244.

43. Ibid., 245.

44. Ibid.

45. Friedman, *Capitalism and Freedom*, 86.

46. Ibid., 161–76.

chapter four.   **Program Analysis of the Grameen Bank**

1. Yunus, *Banker to the Poor,* viii.

2. However, the Grameen Bank uses a different method to calculate repayment rates from that of commercial banks. Morduch finds the percent of current loans outstanding not repaid after more than two years to have averaged 5.87 percent from 1985 through 1994. This is still a very favorable repayment rate compared to most rural microfinance programs in that period. Morduch, "The Role of Subsidies in Microfinance," 233.

3. Besley and Coate, "Group Lending, Repayment Incentives and Social Collateral," 2, 4.

4. Ibid., 10.

5. They point out that the Grameen Bank had caused a surge of interest in group lending schemes.

6. Chaves and Gonzalez-Vega, "The Design of Successful Rural Financial Intermediaries," 76.

7. Ibid., 75.

8. Jain, "Managing Credit for the Rural Poor," 80.

9. "In no case were group members required to make good on behalf of defaulting members, and even new loans to regular members were not denied when other members continuously defaulted. Our study was not designed to cover a statistically representative sample. . . . [W]e repeatedly questioned the Grameen Bank field officers on this issue. We found that the Bank did not normally make group members pay loan/saving installments of defaulting members." Ibid., 83.

10. Ibid., 85.

11. Ibid., 87.

12. Ibid.

13. Ibid., 82.

14. Ibid., 83.

15. Ibid., 81.

16. Ibid., 85.

17. Ibid., 86.

18. Ibid. One of the Bank's original objectives was to "bring the disadvantaged, mostly the women from the poorest households, within the fold of an organizational format which they can understand and manage by themselves." Grameen Bank, "History," http://www.grameen-info.org/index.php?option=com_content&task=view&id=19&Itemid=114.

19. Ibid., 83.

20. Ibid., 81.

21. "Women consistently report a preference for the group structure—they repeatedly mentioned the access to advice, support, and assistance it facilitates,

as well as the sense of legitimacy it gives them. . . . Many also expressed the belief that they would not have been as successful in an individual lending program as in the group lending program. Mutual support and cooperation were identified as additional contributors to women's success in their loan activities and to the successful repayment of their loans." Bernasek, "Banking on Social Change," 378.

22. Grameen Bank, "Sixteen Principles," http://www.grameen-info.org/index.php?option=com_content&task=view&id=22&Itemid=109.

23. He argues that "the Bank followed classical methods of a scientific/bureaucratic approach to management for obtaining performance from its front-line functionaries as per organizational norms," noting that traditions arising from the views of Frederick Taylor and Max Weber recognize the powerful role of routinization and standardization. Jain, "Managing Credit for the Rural Poor," 85, 89n2.

24. Ibid., 88.

25. Yaron, *Successful Rural Financial Institutions*.

26. At issue here is the proposition from welfare economics that there is diminishing marginal utility to increasing income and that valid interpersonal comparisons of marginal utility can be made based on levels of income. Although this proposition can justify taxing the rich to aid the poor, it is inconsistent with the SDI and with most of mainstream economic theory. See Robbins, *An Essay on the Nature and Significance of Economic Science*.

27. A project is seen as justified if its economic rate of return exceeds the cost of capital, as represented, for example, in prevailing interest rates.

28. Gains also arise from increased security and from interest payments when the service includes savings.

29. Pitt and Khandker, *Household and Intrahousehold Impact of the Grameen Bank and Similar Targeted Credit Programs in Bangladesh*, 6–7.

30. In this context there is a tension between taking the relevant impacts into account and avoiding double-counting. An improvement in child nutrition, for example, may be in part a downstream impact due to an increase in household income and in part due to the bank's educational efforts and encouragement of vegetable gardening. Gains due simply to increased income should be taken into account in the weight attributed to the income gain.

31. Clements, "A Poverty-Oriented Cost-Benefit Approach to the Analysis of Development Projects"; Squire and Van Der Tak, *Economic Analysis of Projects*.

32. Rawls, *A Theory of Justice*, 54.

33. Rawls, *The Law of Peoples*, 105–20.

34. Sen argues that judgments of distributional equity are better based on his concept of capabilities—that is, a person's capability to do things she has reason to value—than on Rawls's concept of primary goods. A given allotment of primary goods can yield substantially different sets of capabilities, for example, for persons with disabilities. In Rawls's theory of justice, the needs of persons

with disabilities are addressed at the legislative stage rather than in the selection of first principles; following this general approach, Rawlsian program analysis can assign greater weights to benefits that reach persons with special needs. *The Idea of Justice*, 231, 234.

35. This consensus has been undermined by the Human Development Index—developed by the United Nations Development Programme to measure a country's progress in development and incorporating measures of health, education, and income—as this index has been applied in analyzing development programs.

36. Yaron, *Successful Rural Financial Institutions*, 16.

37. Ibid., 83.

38. Fujita, "Credit Flowing from the Poor to the Rich," 359–60.

39. Amin, Rai, and Topa, "Does Microcredit Reach the Poor and Vulnerable?"

40. Ibid., 79.

41. Pitt and Khandker, *Household and Intrahousehold Impact of the Grameen Bank and Similar Targeted Credit Programs in Bangladesh*.

42. Pitt and Khandker, "The Impact of Group-Based Credit Programs on Poor Households in Bangladesh," 980.

43. McKernan, "The Impact of Microcredit Programs on Self-Employment Profits," 106.

44. Khandker, "Grameen Bank: Impact, Costs, and Program Sustainability," 118.

45. Quoted in Bernasek, "Banking on Social Change," 375.

46. Khandker, "Grameen Bank: Impact, Costs, and Program Sustainability," 117.

47. Schreiner, "A Cost-Effectiveness Analysis of the Grameen Bank of Bangladesh," 370.

48. Todd, *Women at the Center*, 184, 239–40.

49. Bernasek, "Banking on Social Change," 377.

50. Khandker, *Fighting Poverty with Microcredit*, 136. Some of these other programs may, however, have included services in addition to credit that the Grameen Bank does not provide.

51. Ibid., 139, 141.

52. They did, of course, provide labor in the fields.

53. Hashemi, Schuler, and Riley, "Rural Credit Programs and Women's Empowerment in Bangladesh," 647.

54. Rahman, *Women and Microcredit in Rural Bangladesh*, 74–77.

55. Hashemi, Schuler, and Riley, "Rural Credit Programs and Women's Empowerment in Bangladesh," 641.

56. Quoted in Bernasek, "Banking on Social Change," 377.

57. Hashemi, Schuler, and Riley, "Rural Credit Programs and Women's Empowerment in Bangladesh," 650.

58. Rahman, *Women and Microcredit in Rural Bangladesh*, 27, 121.

59. Quoted in Bernasek, "Banking on Social Change," 379.

60. Rahman, *Women and Microcredit in Rural Bangladesh*, 91.

61. Hashemi, Schuler, and Riley, "Rural Credit Programs and Women's Empowerment in Bangladesh," 650.

62. Wahid and Rahman, "The Grameen Bank and the Power of Rural Administrative Elite in Bangladesh," 170.

63. Pitt and Khandker, *Household and Intrahousehold Impact of the Grameen Bank and Similar Targeted Credit Programs in Bangladesh*, 42, 52.

64. Ibid., 42.

65. The other elements are a reduced dropout rate, increased income and assets, and improved health. Schreiner, "A Cost-Effectiveness Analysis of the Grameen Bank of Bangladesh," 369–70.

66. McKernan, "The Impact of Microcredit Programs on Self-Employment Profits, 97.

67. I have noted that our perception of things may also be conditioned by principles.

68. Our perception of things may also be conditioned by our ideas of cause and effect, which may differ between persons.

chapter five.   **Political Analysis of Problems in Bihar**

1. Long, "India's Shining Hopes," 17–18.

2. In 2001 Bihar was split into two states, with the mineral-rich southern portion named Jharkhand. With the exception of the above quote from Simon Long, all references in this chapter are to pre-2001 Bihar.

3. An imperfect obligation is one we should pursue when and how we choose; it does not require a particular action at a particular time; the obligation gets stronger as our capacity to pursue it becomes greater.

4. See, for example, Wade, *Governing the Market* (especially chapter 8 in contrast to chapters 9 and 10), and Kohli, *State-Directed Development*.

5. Rawls, *Political Liberalism*, 93.

6. The rigorous application of rational choice microfoundations, by contrast, leads to a view of social change as a path-dependent unfolding of incentive structures. We can see this influence in Bates's conclusion of his account of Kenya's agrarian development: "When political actors intervene in the economy and seek to restructure economic relations, the policies they choose depend on the incentives generated by the institutional context in which they are made.

Economic forces generate institutions and the structure of the institutions in turn shapes the way in which governments transform their economies. Economy and polity thus interact, generating a process of change. But the process of change is path dependent; the course of the path is shaped by the initial institutional endowment. In this way, each society generates its own history." *Beyond the Miracle of the Market*, 154.

7. Rawls, *The Law of Peoples*, 5; *A Theory of Justice*, 4.

8. Rawls, *The Law of Peoples*, 108.

9. Ibid.

10. Wade, *Governing the Market*, 11; Rodrik, *The New Global Economy and Developing Countries*; Kanbur, "Economic Policy, Distribution and Poverty."

11. Olson, *The Logic of Collective Action*.

12. Bates, *Markets and States in Tropical Africa*.

13. Bates, *Beyond the Miracle of the Market*; Geddes, "Challenging the Conventional Wisdom."

14. Rawls takes the constitutionally governed nation-state to be the effective unit of social cooperation for the purposes of social justice, but since Bihar's development performance is so much worse than that of most Indian states, and since this should be attributed more to state-level mismanagement than to ineffective national government, we can reasonably take the state as a unit of analysis.

15. The poverty line of the Planning Commission of the Government of India is 49 rupees per capita monthly expenditure for rural areas and 57 rupees for urban areas in 1973–74 prices—enough to sustain a diet of 2,400 calories per day in rural areas and 2,100 calories per day in urban areas. This corresponds to an annual income of $73 in rural areas and $84 in urban areas at the 1974 exchange rate. Ravallion and Datt, "Why Has Economic Growth Been More Pro-Poor in Some States of India Than Others?" 397.

16. Datt and Ravallion, "Why Have Some Indian States Done Better than Others at Reducing Rural Poverty?" 18.

17. Sachs, Bajpai, and Ramiah, "Understanding Regional Economic Growth in India," 33; Thakur, *The Making of Laloo Yadav: The Unmaking of Bihar*, 151.

18. Thakur, "Sorry to Spoil Your Sunday."

19. Naik, "Census 2001: Disturbing Inter-State Disparities."

20. Mahatma Gandhi writes, on his first visit to Patna, the state capital: "There was strict untouchability in Bihar. I might not draw water at the well whilst the servants were using it, lest drops of water from my bucket might pollute them, the servants not knowing to what caste I belonged." Gandhi, *An Autobiography, or The Story of My Experiments with Truth*, 306.

21. Based on an early 1980s survey of 2,531 households, Kohli lists upper ("twice-born") castes as comprising 82 percent of Bihar's farmers with over 10

acres of land and 71 percent of farmers with 2.5 to 10 acres. However, upper-caste households made up 25 percent of the farming households surveyed. Kohli, *Democracy and Discontent*, 210. The survey results come from an unpublished report: Prasad and Rodgers, "Class, Caste and Landholding in the Analysis of the Rural Economy," 12.

22. Michel, *Dalits in Modern India*, 12.

23. Nussbaum writes: "Throughout history, certain disgust properties—sliminess, bad smell, stickiness, decay, foulness—have repeatedly and monotonously been associated with, indeed projected onto, groups by reference to whom privileged groups seek to define their superior human status. Jews, women, homosexuals, untouchables, lower-class people—all of these are imagined as tainted by the dirt of the body." *Upheavals of Thought*, 347.

24. Mitra, *Caste Polarization and Politics*, 73.

25. Central Statistical Organisation, *Statistical Abstract of the Indian Union 1965*, 36–40.

26. Kohli, *The State and Poverty in India*, 8.

27. Ravallion and Datt, "Why Has Economic Growth Been More Pro-Poor in Some States of India Than Others?" 393.

28. Prasad, *Bihar Economy Through the Plans*, 16.

29. Bihar has had small-scale artisanal production of iron for centuries, but the state's steel manufacturing was initiated in 1913 by the Tata Iron and Steel Company. Sinha, *Industrial Economy of a Backward Region*, 23.

30. Prasad, *Bihar Economy Through the Plans*, 16.

31. Bihar's Survey and Settlement operations to establish official land records were still not complete as of 1970. Jannuzi, *Agrarian Crisis in India*, 21n.

32. Ibid., 20.

33. According to Jannuzi: "The amendment act of 1959 continued to focus on the primary interests (land revenue and compensation) of the principal antagonists, rather than on the interests of the peasantry having a direct cultivating interest in the land. Nowhere in any of this 'land reform' legislation were the interests of the landless laborers or 'bataidars' (sharecroppers) considered." Ibid., 28. The majority of tenants find their plots changed every year or two so they cannot claim occupancy rights. A 1980–81 study found 28 percent of Bihar's cultivated land under tenancy, mostly in sharecropping arrangements. Although the law sets a maximum of 25 percent of the gross produce for rent, most tenants pay half their crop to the landlord, and up to 75 percent when the landlord shares the cost of inputs. Sharma, "Political Economy of Poverty in Bihar," 2594.

34. Ladejinsky, "The Green Revolution in Punjab," A-73.

35. Ladejinsky, "The Green Revolution in Bihar," A-151.

36. Kohli, *Democracy and Discontent*, 212–13.

37. Ibid., 214.

38. Ibid., 215, 219–20.

39. "Throughout the 1980s, the Congress government was unable to act with even a modest degree of cohesiveness. Much of the leadership's attention was focused on political intrigue. Solving the state's pressing economic and political problems was far from anyone's mind." Ibid., 224.

40. Ibid., 216.

41. Ibid., 230–31.

42. Mitra, *Caste Polarization and Politics*, 86.

43. Rational choice theory can explain any choice as the reflection of the agent's utility function (however oddly shaped), but when the suggested utility function is not related to the agent's interests (as rational choice theorists generally understand them), the connection with rational choice analysis is severed.

44. Jannuzi, *Agrarian Crisis in India*, 134, 148; Singh, "Antecedent Conditions for Collective Violence against Dalits in India," 104–8.

45. Kohli, *Democracy and Discontent*, 231–32.

46. The *Indian Nation* reported on May 28, 1975: "The Bihar government has decided to arm all able-bodied persons in Bhojpur and Patna districts for self-defense to face the extreme menace, who have recently launched an armed struggle. . . . District magistrates of both districts have been asked to visit the affected villages and issue licences [sic] for firearms on the spot to those who were able to possess them. . . . The decision was taken following a spurt of armed attacks on landowners by extremists in these villages." Quoted in Kohli, *Democracy and Discontent*, 218–19.

47. Ibid., 227; Singh, "Antecedent Conditions for Collective Violence against Dalits in India," 46–67.

48. Das, *The State of Bihar*, 100.

49. Steven R. Weisman, "India's Corner of Misery," *New York Times*, April 27, 1987, A1.

50. Ibid., 228.

51. There were 481 caste-related killings in the 1980s and close to a thousand in the 1990s. Thakur, *The Making of Laloo Yadav*, 169.

52. Quoted in Kohli, *Democracy and Discontent*, 226.

53. Wood, "Private Provision after Public Neglect."

54. Thakur, *The Making of Laloo Yadav*, 53–60.

55. Ibid., 72–76.

56. The site is believed to be the birthplace of Rama, a revered Hindu deity.

57. Thakur, *The Making of Laloo Yadav*, 78–82.

58. Das, "Para-Democracy in Bihar," 2959.

59. Thakur, *The Making of Laloo Yadav*, 87; see also Das, "Para-Democracy in Bihar."

60. Chaitanya, "Bihar: Opportunistic Alliances and Shifting Party Loyalties."

61. Sinha, "Social Mobilisation in Bihar," 3287.

62. Joseph, "Lessons from Bihar Fodder Scam," 1687.

63. Election Commission of India, *Statistical Report on General Election, 1995 to Legislative Assembly of Bihar*, 15.

64. Gupta, "Bihar: Elections with a Difference," 790.

65. Thakur, *The Making of Laloo Yadav*, 123.

66. Joseph, "Lessons from Bihar Fodder Scam," 1686.

67. Sachs, Bajpai, and Ramiah, "Understanding Regional Economic Growth in India."

chapter six. **The Ethics and the Politics of Climate Change**

1. Stern, *The Economics of Climate Change*.

2. Nordhaus, *A Question of Balance*. Here Nordhaus updates the analysis in his 2003 publication with Boyer, *Warming the World*.

3. Or 430 ppm of CO_2 equivalent, taking account of other greenhouse gasses as well as carbon dioxide. Stern, *The Economics of Climate Change*, xvi.

4. Alley, "Climate Change 2007."

5. Black, "'Scary' Climate Message from Past."

6. Nordhaus, *A Question of Balance*, 104.

7. So far as it is induced by humans. Those who gain from climate change, such as farmers in cold climates who get longer growing seasons, experience positive externalities.

8. Nordhaus, *A Question of Balance*, 5; Stern, *The Economics of Climate Change*, 28–29. For rational choice theory, see Bates, *Beyond the Miracle of the Market*, 6–8.

9. Stern, *The Economics of Climate Change*, 338.

10. Nordhaus, *A Question of Balance*, 104.

11. Stern, *The Economics of Climate Change*, 337.

12. Nordhaus, *A Question of Balance*, 76

13. Ibid., 104.

14. However, Nordhaus's own model and his model for Stern assume diminishing marginal utility from increasing income at a given point in time.

15. Nordhaus, *A Question of Balance*, 83. The numbers for Stern are attributed to him by Nordhaus.

16. Ibid., 179.

17. "This means that $1,000 worth of climate damages in a century is valued at $20 today." Ibid., 10. The idea is that future costs and benefits should be measured in terms of the investment required today to yield that sum.

18. Stern, *The Economics of Climate Change*, 53, 184.

19. Nordhaus, *A Question of Balance*, 59.

20. Or so-called deadweight losses.

21. Ibid., 148–62.

22. Ibid., 150.

23. Also, note that the *Stern Review* was not subject to peer review. Ibid., 167.

24. Readers familiar with high-level World Bank reports will find the style familiar.

25. Stern, *The Economics of Climate Change*, 319.

26. Ibid., 42–43, 46–61.

27. Ibid., x–xiv, 285–86.

28. Ibid., 143–67, 239–52, 285–308. He notes that he does not account for distributional effects due to lack of time.

29. Ibid., x.

30. Ibid., 65–103, 193.

31. Rawls, *The Law of Peoples*, 10, 88.

32. Nordhaus, *A Question of Balance*, 176.

33. Rawls, *A Theory of Justice*, 266.

34. Ibid., 255.

35. Quoted in Stern, *The Economics of Climate Change*, 179.

36. This would be the case, for example, if low-income regions suffer one-third of world losses, 2 percent in absolute terms, and the weight of these losses is doubled to 4 percent. More recent data, however, indicate that developing countries bear over 90 percent of total economic losses from climate change. Global Humanitarian Forum, *The Anatomy of a Silent Crisis*, 3.

37. Stern, *The Economics of Climate Change*, 179.

38. Ibid., 66–67, 330.

39. Ibid., 330.

40. Ibid.

41. Black, "'Ten Years Remain' to Cut Carbon."

42. Stern, *The Economics of Climate Change*, 87.

43. Global Humanitarian Forum, *The Anatomy of a Silent Crisis*, 1.

44. Stern, *The Economics of Climate Change*, 19.

45. Turner, *Antarctic Climate Change and the Environment*, xxiii. Turner et al. cite the estimate from the Intergovernmental Panel on Climate Change, the source that Stern cites, as 18 cm to 59 cm, indicating a 137 percent rise in the upper boundary.

46. Stern, *The Economics of Climate Change*, 85.

47. Nordhaus, *A Question of Balance*, 107.

48. Global Humanitarian Forum, *The Anatomy of a Silent Crisis*, 24.

49. University of California, San Diego, "Climate Change Effects in California."

50. Black, "'Ten Years Remain' to Cut Carbon." This 2009 analysis is by the United Kingdom Met Office, the national weather service of the United Kingdom. By contrast, Nordhaus in 2008 estimated that CO_2 concentrations could peak at about 480 ppm around 2080 to keep global warming below 2°C (p. 104), so this is another example of newer information indicating greater dangers.

51. World Bank, *World Development Report 2010*, 72, 79.

52. U.S. Bureau of the Census International Database.

53. Total emissions below thirty billion tonnes divided by 9.2 billion people.

54. Stern, *The Economics of Climate Change*, 31, 33.

55. Ibid., 47.

56. Ibid.

57. Nordhaus, on the other hand, criticizes Stern for adopting "Government House utilitarianism," an arrangement in which a utilitarian elite controls a society in which a majority may not itself share those beliefs. He finds this approach misleading for informing the negotiation of policies among sovereign states, preferring instead to formulate an alternative based on real interest rates (Nordhaus's optimal proposal) to a baseline trajectory representing market and policy factors as they currently exist. "When countries weigh their self-interest in international bargains about emissions reductions and burden sharing, they look at the actual gains from bargains, and the returns on these relative to other investments, rather than the gains that would come from a theoretical growth model." *A Question of Balance*, 174–75 including note 14.

58. World Bank, *World Development Report 2010*, 362–63.

59. Global Humanitarian Forum, *The Anatomy of a Silent Crisis*, 1, 4.

60. Stern, *The Economics of Climate Change*, 486.

61. Ibid., 625. This counts incomes and aid from members of the Organization for Economic Cooperation and Development.

62. Emerging industrial economies would push for faster emissions reductions in rich countries and more gradual reductions (after more increases) for themselves.

63. Nordhaus, *A Question of Balance*, 82–83.

64. One tonne of CO_2 has 0.27 tonnes of carbon.

65. Revenues of $2.16 trillion divided by a population of 387 million. Office of Management and Budget, "Historical Tables," Table 1.1, and U.S. Bureau of the Census, *U.S. Census Bureau Announces 2010 Census Population Counts*.

66. In 2010, France, a leader in responding to climate change, is considering a carbon tax of 17 euros ($24) per tonne of emitted carbon dioxide but exempting 93 percent of industrial emissions other than fuel. BBC News, "France to Rethink Carbon Tax Plan."

67. Quoted in U.S. Supreme Court, *Massachusetts v. Environmental Protection Agency*, Justice Stevens at 508.

68. Ibid.

69. "Kyoto Protocol to the United Nations Framework Convention on Climate Change," Annex B, http://unfccc.int/resource/docs/convkp/kpeng.html.

70. Justus and Fletcher, "CRS Issue Brief for Congress: Global Climate Change," CRS-9.

71. Ibid., CRS-6.

72. "Addressing global climate change will require a sustained effort, over many generations. My approach recognizes that sustained economic growth is the solution, not the problem—because a nation that grows its economy is a nation that can afford investments in efficiency, new technologies, and a cleaner environment." Bush, *Global Climate Change Policy Book*.

73. Schwarzenegger, "Executive Order S-3-05"; Marinucci and Martin, "Big Victories," A-1.

74. California's 1990 and 2000 emissions taken from California Energy Commission, "Inventory of California Greenhouse Gas Emissions and Sinks: 1990 to 2004." California's projected 2010 and 2020 population taken from the U.S. Bureau of the Census, "U.S. Population Projections: State Interim Population Projections by Age and Sex: 2004–2030." California's projected 2050 population estimated based on California's proportion of the U.S. population in 2030 and the Census Bureau's estimate for total U.S. population in 2050 (12.77 percent of 419.9 million).

75. Schwarzenegger, "Executive Order S-3-05."

76. Broder, "House Passes Bill to Address Threat of Climate Change."

77. Congressional Research Service, "H.R. 2454: American Clean Energy and Security Act of 2009."

78. Stromberg, "How Washington Failed on Climate Change."

79. Friedman and Samuelsohn, "Hillary Clinton Pledges $100B for Developing Countries."

80. India's per capita emissions are around two tonnes of CO_2e, so India has not yet met the three-tonne target. World Bank, *World Development Report 2010*, 362–63.

81. Pew Research Center, "Fewer Americans See Solid Evidence of Global Warming." The surveys were based on 1,500 adults. The proportion that saw global warming as somewhat serious rose from 29 percent to 30 percent.

82. Both in purchasing power terms for 2008. World Bank, *World Development Report 2010*, 378–79.

83. Global Humanitarian Forum, *The Anatomy of a Silent Crisis*, 9–12.

84. For official development agencies see Sasaki, "Metaevaluation by Formal Evaluation Theory of Aid Evaluation Work"; for U.S. NGOs see Chianca, "International Aid Evaluation."

85. These goals are independently important, and some may help to achieve the primary goal.

86. For example, other things equal, it is more efficient to invest in countries with lower civil strife and lower corruption.

87. Clements, Chianca, and Sasaki, "Reducing World Poverty by Improving Evaluation of Development Aid."

88. Except narrowly and by assumption, as obligations underlying economic transactions are normally expected to be fulfilled. It is hard to ground a broad moral concept of obligation on the narrow model of rational utility maximization used by rational choice theorists and neoclassical economists.

chapter seven. **Kantian Ontology of Practical Reason and Social Science**

1. Kohli, *State-Directed Development*, 6.
2. For example, Wade, *Governing the Market*, 37, and Kohli, *State-Directed Development*, 421–22.
3. Ibid., 233, 235.
4. Ibid., 236–55.
5. Ibid., 238, 239, 243.
6. Ibid., 373.
7. Ibid., 350.
8. The Kuomintang gained its greatest economic and political support from the United States mainly because it was on the U.S. military perimeter with Communist China.
9. Kohli, *State-Directed Development*, 9.
10. Ibid.
11. Ibid., 10–11.
12. Ibid., 421, note 30.
13. Ibid., 421, 423.
14. Nussbaum, *Upheavals of Thought*.
15. Rawlsian political analysis can support the exercise of public reason as Rawls describes it in *Political Liberalism*, but the place and weight of a given principal or interest may depend on a person's comprehensive doctrine. Rawlsian political analysis can elaborate a Kantian comprehensive doctrine.

works cited

Alley, Richard, et al. "Climate Change 2007: The Physical Science Basis: Summary for Policymakers." Geneva: Intergovernmental Panel on Climate Change, 2007.

Amin, Sajeda, Ashok S. Rai, and Giorgio Topa. "Does Microcredit Reach the Poor and Vulnerable? Evidence from Northern Bangladesh." *Journal of Development Economics* 70, no. 1 (2003): 59–82.

Andreoni, James, and John H. Miller. "Rational Cooperation in the Finitely Repeated Prisoner's Dilemma: Experimental Evidence." *The Economic Journal* 103, no. 418 (1993): 570–85.

Bates, Robert. *Beyond the Miracle of the Market: The Political Economy of Agrarian Development in Kenya.* Cambridge: Cambridge University Press, 1989.

———. *Markets and States in Tropical Africa: The Political Basis of Agricultural Policies.* Berkeley: University of California Press, 1981.

BBC News. "France to Rethink Carbon Tax Plan," BBC News, December 30, 2009, http://news.bbc.co.uk/2/hi/europe/8434505.stm.

Bernasek, Alexandra. "Banking on Social Change: Grameen Bank Lending to Women." *International Journal of Politics, Culture and Society* 16, no. 3 (spring 2003): 369–85.

Besley, Timothy, and Stephen Coate. "Group Lending, Repayment Incentives and Social Collateral." *Journal of Development Economics* 46, no. 1 (1995): 1–18.

Black, Richard. "'Scary' Climate Message from Past." BBC News, October 10, 2009, http://news.bbc.co.uk/2/hi/8299426.stm.

———. "'Ten Years Remain' to Cut Carbon." BBC News, December 10, 2009, http://news.bbc.co.uk/go/pr/fr/-/2/hi/science/nature/8405025.stm.

Broder, John M. "House Passes Bill to Address Threat of Climate Change." *New York Times*, June 26, 2009, http://www.nytimes.com/2009/06/27/us/politics/27climate.html.

Bush, George W. "Executive Summary." In *Global Climate Change Policy Book.* Washington, DC, White House news release, 2002. http://www.usgcrp.gov/usgcrp/Library/gcinitiative2002/gccstorybook.htm#Executive%20Summary.

California Energy Commission. "Inventory of California Greenhouse Gas Emissios and Sinks: 1990 to 2004," specifically figure 1: California's Gross GHG

Emissions Trends, ii, http://www.energy.ca.gov/2006publications/CEC
-600-2006-013/CEC-600-2006-013-SF.PDF. Sacramento: California Energy Commission, 2006.

Central Statistical Organisation, Department of Statistics, Government of India.
Statistical Abstract of the Indian Union 1965, Delhi: Manager of Publications, 1966.

Chaitanya, Krishna. "Bihar: Opportunistic Alliances and Shifting Party Loyalties." *Economic and Political Weekly* 31, no. 16–17 (1996): 993–94.

Chaves, Rodrigo A., and Claudio Gonzalez-Vega. "The Design of Successful
Rural Financial Intermediaries: Evidence from Indonesia." *World Development* 24, no. 1 (1996): 65–78.

Chianca, Thomaz K. "International Aid Evaluation: An Analysis and Policy Proposals." Ph.D. dissertation, Western Michigan University, 2008.

Clements, Paul. "A Poverty-Oriented Cost-Benefit Approach to the Analysis of
Development Projects." *World Development* 23, no. 4 (1995): 577–92.

Clements, Paul, Thomaz Chianca, and Ryoh Sasaki. "Reducing World Poverty by
Improving Evaluation of Development Aid." *American Journal of Evaluation*
29, no. 2 (2008): 195–214.

Clements, Paul, and Emily Hauptmann. "The Reasonable and the Rational
Capacities in Political Analysis." *Politics & Society* 30, no. 1 (2002): 85–
111.

Das, Arvind N. "Para-Democracy in Bihar." *Economic and Political Weekly* 30,
no. 15 (1998): 2959–60.

———. *The State of Bihar: An Economic History without Footnotes*. Amsterdam:
VU University Press, 1992.

Datt, Gaurav, and Martin Ravallion. "Why Have Some Indian States Done Better than Others at Reducing Rural Poverty?" *Economica* 65, no.1 (1998):
17–38.

Diamond, Larry, and Marc F. Plattner, eds. *Economic Reform and Democracy*.
Baltimore, MD: Johns Hopkins University Press, 1995.

Election Commission of India, *Statistical Report on General Election, 1995, to Legislative Assembly of Bihar*. New Delhi: Election Commission of India, 1995,
http://eci.nic.in/eci_main/statisticalreports/SE_1995/StatisticalReport
-BR95.pdf.

Elster, Jon. *The Cement of Society: A Study of Social Order*. Cambridge: Cambridge
University Press, 1989.

Evans, Peter. *Embedded Autonomy: States and Industrial Transformation*. Princeton: Princeton University Press, 1995.

Fehr, Ernst, and Urs Fischbacher. "The Economics of Strong Reciprocity." In
*Moral Sentiments and Material Interests: The Foundations of Cooperation in
Economic Life*, edited by Herbert Gintis, Samuel Bowles, and Robert T.
Boyd, 151–91. Cambridge, MA: MIT Press, 2006.

Flood, Merill M. "Some Experimental Games." *Management Science* 5, no.1 (1958): 5–26.

Fogassi, Leonardo. "The Mirror Neuron System: How Cognitive Functions Emerge from Motor Organization." *Journal of Economic Behavior & Organization* 77 (2010): 66–75.

Friedman, Lisa, and Darren Samuelsohn. "Hillary Clinton Pledges $100B for Developing Countries." *New York Times*, December 17, 2009, http://www .nytimes.com/cwire/2009/12/17/17climatewire-hillary-clinton-pledges -100b-for-developing-96794.html.

Friedman, Milton. *Capitalism and Freedom*. Fortieth anniversary edition. Chicago: University of Chicago Press, 2002.

Fujita, Koichi. "Credit Flowing from the Poor to the Rich: The Financial Market and the Role of the Grameen Bank in Rural Bangladesh." *The Developing Economies* 38, no. 3 (1962): 343–73.

Gandhi, Mohandas K. *An Autobiography, or The Story of My Experiments with Truth*. Translated by M. Desai. Ahmedabad, India: Navajivan Publishing House, 1927, http://www.archive.org/details/AnAutobiographyOrTheStory OfMyExperimentsWithTruth.

Geddes, Barbara. "Challenging the Conventional Wisdom." In *Economic Reform and Democracy*, edited by Larry Diamond and Marc F. Plattner, 59–73. Baltimore, MD: Johns Hopkins University Press, 1995.

Gintis, Herbert, Samuel Bowles, and Robert T. Boyd, eds. *Moral Sentiments and Material Interests: The Foundations of Cooperation in Economic Life*. Cambridge, MA: MIT Press, 2006.

Global Humanitarian Forum. *The Anatomy of a Silent Crisis*. Human Impact Report: Climate Change. Geneva: Global Humanitarian Forum, 2009.

Congressional Research Service. "H.R. 2454: American Clean Energy and Security Act of 2009." GovTrack, 2009, http://www.govtrack.us/congress/bill .xpd?bill=h111-2454&tab=summary.

Grameen Bank. "History," http://www.grameen-info.org/index.php?option= com_content&task=view&id=19&Itemid=114.

————. "The Sixteen Decisions," http://www.grameen-info.org/index.php?op tion=com_content&task=view&id=22&Itemid=109.

Gupta, Tilak D. "Bihar: Elections with a Difference." *Economic and Political Weekly* 30, no. 15 (1995): 789–92.

Hashemi, Syed M., Sidney Ruth Schuler, and Ann P. Riley. "Rural Credit Programs and Women's Empowerment in Bangladesh." *World Development* 24, no. 4 (1996): 635–53.

Hauser, Marc D. *Moral Minds: How Nature Designed Our Universal Sense of Right and Wrong*. New York: HarperCollins, 2006.

Honneth, Axel. *The Struggle for Recognition: The Moral Grammar of Social Conflicts*. Translated by Joel Anderson. Cambridge, MA: MIT Press, 1996.

Jain, Pankaj S. "Managing Credit for the Rural Poor: Lessons from the Grameen Bank." *World Development* 24, no. 1 (1996): 79–89.

Jannuzi, F. Tomasson. *Agrarian Crisis in India: The Case of Bihar*. Austin: University of Texas Press, 1974.

Joseph, K. P. "Lessons from Bihar Fodder Scam." *Economic and Political Weekly* 32, no. 28 (1997): 1686–87.

Justus, John R., and Susan R. Fletcher. "CRS Issue Brief for Congress: Global Climate Change." Washington, DC: Congressional Research Service, March 27, 2002.

Kagel, John H., and Alvin E. Roth, eds. *The Handbook of Experimental Economics*. Princeton: Princeton University Press, 1995.

Kalisch, Gerhard K., et al. "Some Experimental N-Person Games." In *Decision Processes*, edited by R. M. Thrall, C. H. Coombs, and R. L. Davis, 301–27. New York: Wiley, 1954.

Kanbur, Ravi. "Economic Policy, Distribution and Poverty: The Nature of Disagreements." *World Development* 29, no. 6 (2001): 1083–94.

Kant, Immanuel. *Critique of Practical Reason*. Translated by Werner S. Pluhar. Indianapolis: Hackett Publishing Company, Inc., 2002 [1788].

———. *Groundwork for the Metaphysics of Morals*. Edited and translated by Allen W. Wood. New Haven: Yale University Press, 2002 [1785].

———. *The Metaphysics of Morals*. Edited and translated by Mary Gregor. Cambridge: Cambridge University Press, 1996 [1797].

———. *Religion within the Boundaries of Mere Reason and Other Writings*. Edited by Allen Wood and George di Giovani. Cambridge: Cambridge University Press, 1998 [1793].

Khandker, Shahidur R. *Fighting Poverty with Microcredit: Experience in Bangladesh*. Oxford: Oxford University Press for the World Bank, 1996.

———. "Grameen Bank: Impact, Costs, and Program Sustainability." *Asian Development Review* 14, no. 1 (1996): 97–130.

Kohli, Atul. *Democracy and Discontent: India's Growing Crisis of Governability*. Cambridge: Cambridge University Press, 1990.

———. *The State and Poverty in India: The Politics of Reform*. Cambridge: Cambridge University Press, 1987.

———. *State-Directed Development: Political Power and Industrialization in the Global Periphery*. Cambridge: Cambridge University Press, 2004.

Knight, Jack. *Institutions and Social Conflict*. Cambridge: Cambridge University Press, 1992.

"Kyoto Protocol to the United Nations Framework Convention on Climate Change," Annex B, http://unfccc.int/resource/docs/convkp/kpeng.html.

Ladejinsky, Wolf. "The Green Revolution in Bihar—The Kosi Area: A Field Trip," *Economic and Political Weekly* 4, no. 39 (September 27, 1969): A147–A162.

————. "The Green Revolution in Punjab: A Field Trip," *Economic and Political Weekly* 4, no. 26 (June 28, 1969): A73–A82.

Ledyard, John O. "Public Goods: A Survey of Experimental Results." In *The Handbook of Experimental Economics*, edited by John H. Kagel and Alvin E. Roth, 111–67. Princeton: Princeton University Press, 1995.

Levi, Margaret. *Consent, Dissent and Patriotism.* Cambridge: Cambridge University Press, 1997.

Long, Simon. "India's Shining Hopes: A Survey of India." Country Survey Insert. *The Economist* 370, no. 8363 (February 21, 2004): 17–18.

March, James G. *A Primer on Decision Making: How Decisions Happen.* New York: The Free Press, 1994.

Marinucci, Carla, and Mark Martin. "Big Victories: Schwarzenegger Re-elected in Landslide, Weathering Anti-GOP Storm," *San Francisco Chronicle*, November 8, 2006, A-1, http://www.sfgate.com/cgi-bin/article.cgi?file=/c/a/2006/11/08/MNGSMM8CR91.DTL.

Marwell, Gerald, and Ruth E. Ames. "Economists Free Ride, Does Anyone Else?" *Journal of Public Economics* 15, no. 3 (1981): 295–310.

————. "Experiments in the Provision of Public Goods: I. Resources, Interest, Group Size, and the Free-Rider Problem." *American Journal of Sociology* 84 (1979): 1335–60.

McKernan, Signe-Mary. "The Impact of Microcredit Programs on Self-Employment Profits: Do Noncredit Program Aspects Matter?" *Review of Economics and Statistics* 84, no. 1 (2002): 93–115.

Michel, S. M., ed. *Dalits in Modern India: Vision and Values.* New Delhi: Vistaar Publications, 1999.

Mitra, Roma. *Caste Polarization and Politics.* Patna, Bihar: Syndicate Publication, 1992.

Monroe, Kristen Renwick. *The Heart of Altruism: Perceptions of a Common Humanity.* Princeton: Princeton University Press, 1996.

Morduch, Jonathan, "The Role of Subsidies in Microfinance: Evidence from the Grameen Bank." *Journal of Development Economics* 60, no. 1 (1999): 229–48.

Naik, S. D. "Census 2001: Disturbing Inter-State Disparities." *Business Line*, April 3, 2001. http://www.thehindubusinessline.in/2001/04/03/stories/01032001.htm.

Nordhaus, William. *A Question of Balance: Weighing the Options on Global Warming Policies.* New Haven: Yale University Press, 2008.

Nordhaus, William, and Joseph Boyer. *Warming the World: Economic Models of Global Warming.* Cambridge: MIT Press, 2003.

Nussbaum, Martha. *Upheavals of Thought: The Intelligence of the Emotions.* Cambridge: Cambridge University Press, 2001.

Office of Management and Budget, "Historical Tables," http://www.whitehouse
.gov/omb/budget/Historicals.

Olson, Mancur. *The Logic of Collective Action: Public Goods and the Theory of
Groups*. Cambridge, MA: Harvard University Press, 1965.

Ostrom, Elinor. *Governing the Commons: The Evolution of Institutions for Collective Action*. Cambridge: Cambridge University Press, 1990.

Pew Research Center. "Fewer Americans See Solid Evidence of Global Warming." Pew Research Center for the People and the Press, October 22,
2009. http://pewresearch.org/pubs/1386/cap-and-trade-global-warming
-opinion.

Pitt, Mark M., and Shahidur R. Khandker. *Household and Intrahousehold Impact
of the Grameen Bank and Similar Targeted Credit Programs in Bangladesh*.
World Bank Discussion Papers, No. 320. Washington: The World Bank,
1996.

———. "The Impact of Group-Based Credit Programs on Poor Households in
Bangladesh: Does the Gender of the Participants Matter?" *Journal of Political Economy* 106, no. 5 (1998): 958–96.

Prasad, Kedar Nath. *Bihar Economy Through the Plans: In Comparison with All-
India and Other States*. New Delhi: Northern Book Centre, 1997.

Prasad, P. H., and G. B. Rodgers. "Class, Caste and Landholding in the Analysis
of the Rural Economy." Population and Labour Policies Programme, Working Paper No. 140, World Employment Programme Research. Geneva: International Labor Office, 1983.

Rahman, Aminur. *Women and Microcredit in Rural Bangladesh: Anthropologi-
cal Study of the Rhetoric and Realities of Grameen Bank Lending*. Boulder:
Westview Press, 1999.

Rawls, John. "Kantian Constructivism in Moral Theory." In *John Rawls: Col-
lected Papers*, edited by Samuel Freeman, 303–58. Cambridge, MA: Harvard
University Press, 1999.

———. *The Law of Peoples*. Cambridge, MA: Harvard University Press,
1999.

———. *Lectures on the History of Moral Philosophy*. Cambridge, MA: Harvard
University Press, 2000.

———. *Political Liberalism*. New York: Columbia University Press, 1993.

———. *A Theory of Justice*. Revised edition. Cambridge, MA: Belknap, 1999.

Ravallion, Martin, and Gaurav Datt. "Why Has Economic Growth Been More
Pro-Poor in Some States of India Than Others?" *Journal of Development
Economics* 68 (2002): 381–400.

Robbins, Lionel. *An Essay on the Nature and Significance of Economic Science*.
London: Macmillan, 1935.

Rodrik, Dani. *The New Global Economy and Developing Countries: Making Openness Work*. Baltimore: Johns Hopkins University Press, 1999.

Sachs, Jeffrey D., Nirupam Bajpai, and Ananthi Ramiah. "Understanding Regional Economic Growth in India." Paper presented at Asian Economic Panel, Seoul, Korea, October 2001.

Sasaki, Ryoh. "Metaevaluation by Formal Evaluation Theory of Aid Evaluation Work." Ph.D. dissertation, Western Michigan University, 2008.

Schreiner, Mark. "A Cost-Effectiveness Analysis of the Grameen Bank of Bangladesh." *Development Policy Review* 21, no. 3 (2003): 357–82.

Schwarzenegger, Arnold. "Executive Order S-3-05 by the Governor of the State of California." http://www.dot.ca.gov/hq/energy/ExecOrderS-3-05.htm. Sacramento: State of California, 2005.

Sen, Amartya. *The Idea of Justice.* Cambridge, MA: Belknap, 2009.

Sharma, Alakh N. "Political Economy of Poverty in Bihar." *Economic and Political Weekly* 30, no. 41–42 (1995): 2587–602.

Shaw, Judith. "A World Bank Intervention in the Sri Lankan Welfare Sector: The National Development Trust Fund." *World Development* 27, no. 5 (1999): 825–38.

Singh, K. P. "Antecedent Conditions for Collective Violence against Dalits in India." Ph.D. dissertation, University of Wisconsin-Madison, 2000.

Sinha, Arvind K. *Industrial Economy of a Backward Region.* Delhi: Capital Publishing House, 1988.

———. "Social Mobilisation in Bihar: Bureaucratic Feudalism and Distributive Justice." *Economic and Political Weekly* 31, no. 51 (1996): 3287–88.

Squire, Lyn, and Herman G. Van Der Tak. *Economic Analysis of Projects.* Baltimore: Johns Hopkins University Press, 1975.

Stern, Nicholas. *The Economics of Climate Change: The Stern Review.* Cambridge: Cambridge University Press, 2007.

Stromberg, Stephen. "How Washington Failed on Climate Change." *Washington Post,* regional edition, July 29, 2010, A23.

Thakur, Sankarshan. *The Making of Laloo Yadav: The Unmaking of Bihar.* New Delhi: HarperCollins India, 2000.

———. "Sorry to Spoil Your Sunday." *Indian Express,* August 25, 2002, http://www.indianexpress.com/oldStory/8240/.

Thrall, R. M., C. H. Coombs, and R. L. Davis, eds. *Decision Processes.* New York: Wiley, 1954.

Todd, Helen. *Women at the Center: Grameen Bank Borrowers After One Decade.* Boulder: Westview Press, 1996.

Turner, John, et al., eds. *Antarctic Climate Change and the Environment.* Cambridge, UK: Scientific Committee on Antarctic Research, 2009.

University of California, San Diego. "Climate Change Effects in California." *ScienceDaily,* April 12, 2009, http://www.sciencedaily.com/releases/2009/04/090401182835.htm. Reprinted with editorial adaptations from materials provided by the University of California, San Diego.

U.S. Bureau of the Census. International Database. http://www.census.gov/ipc/ www/idb/region.php.

———. "U.S. Population Projections: State Interim Population Projections by Age and Sex: 2004–2030," http://www.census.gov/population/www/pro jections/projectionsagesex.html.

———. "U.S. Census Bureau Announces 2010 Census Population Counts— Apportionment Counts Delivered to President," http://2010.census.gov/ news/releases/operations/cb10-cn93.html.

U.S. Government Printing Office. *Economic Report of the President* (February 2008), http://www.gpoaccess.gov/eop/2008/2008_erp.pdf.

U.S. Supreme Court. *Massachusetts v. Environmental Protection Agency*, 549 U.S. 497 (2007).

Verplaetse, Jan, et al. *The Moral Brain: Essays on the Evolutionary and Neuroscientific Aspects of Morality*. Dordrecht: Springer, 2009.

Wade, Nicholas. "Scientist under Inquiry Resigns from Harvard," *New York Times*, July 20, 2011, A17(L).

Wade, Robert. *Governing the Market: Economic Theory and the Role of Government in East Asian Industrialization*. Princeton: Princeton University Press, 1990.

Wahid, Abu N. M., ed. *The Grameen Bank: Poverty Relief in Bangladesh*. Boulder: Westview Press, 1993.

Wahid, Abu N. M., and Atium Rahman. "The Grameen Bank and the Power of Rural Administrative Elite in Bangladesh." In *The Grameen Bank: Poverty Relief in Bangladesh*, edited by Abu N. M. Wahid, 155–73. Boulder: Westview Press, 1993.

Weisman, Steven R. "India's Corner of Misery: Bihar's Poor and Lawless," *New York Times*, April 27, 1987, A1.

Wood, Geof. "Private Provision after Public Neglect: Bending Irrigation Markets in North Bihar." *Development and Change* 30, no. 4 (1999): 775–94.

World Bank. *World Development Report 2010: Development and Climate Change*. Washington, DC: The World Bank, 2010.

Winnicott, Donald W. *The Maturational Process and the Facilitating Environment: Studies in the Theory of Emotional Development*. London: Hogarth, 1965.

———. *Playing and Reality*. London: Tavistock, 1971.

Yaron, Jacob. *Successful Rural Financial Institutions*. World Bank Discussion Papers No. 150. Washington, DC: The World Bank, 1992.

Yunus, Muhammad, with Alan Jolis. *Banker to the Poor: Micro-Lending and the Battle against World Poverty*. New York: Public Affairs, 1999.

index

Rawls on, 29–30, 34–42, 65–66
Sen on, 40–42
social analysis, norms (principles)
as accepted basis for, 12–16,
65–66
prisoner's dilemma experiments,
18–19, 67–68, 70–77, 200n9
problem-based analysis, 93–94. *See
also* climate change
program analysis
concept of, 92–93, 95–97, 105
organizational culture and, 118–20
See also Grameen Bank, program
analysis of
psychopathology, 200n85
public arena, concept of, 187–89
public goods, 70, 76–77, 89–90, 124,
200n9
pure reason, 6, 31–32

Rahman, Aminur, 114–15, 116–17
Rahman, Atium, 117
Rai, Ashok S., 112
Ramiah, Ananthi, 144
rational choice theory (rational utility
maximization), 18–19
analytic limits of, 67–70
Bihar, political economy analysis
of, 121–25, 142, 144, 208n43
as constructive theory, 67, 68–70,
86–92
Friedman and, 70, 87, 90–92
interests as driving force in, 2, 8–9,
43–44, 68
justice, limitations in dealing with,
94
Kantian practical reason and, 184,
191
Kenya, Bates' study of agrarian
development in, 18, 68, 77–80,
205n6

military conscription, Levi's
analysis of, 18–19, 68, 80–86
as positive theory, 67–68
principles, efforts at
accommodation of, 68, 86–87
prisoner's dilemma experiments
and, 18–19, 67–68, 70–77,
200n9
problems with model for social and
political analysis, 2–3
Rawlsian view distinguished from,
14–16
social change, view of, 205n6
Rawls, John
on autonomy, 37–39, 191–92,
198n50
Friedman compared to, 90–92
on the good and the right, 1–2,
38, 195n1
Kantian influence on, 5–10, 17,
29, 37, 45, 50
Knight versus, 15
morality, three stages of, 44,
45–50
original position of (*see* original
position)
primary goods, concept of, 22, 25,
35–36, 39, 93, 108–9, 158–59,
176, 203n34
principles and interests in thought
of, 16, 29–30, 34–42, 44,
45–50, 65–66
rational choice theory distinguished
from, 14–16
Rawlsian political analysis and,
3–4
religious toleration, on
development of, 44, 49–50
Sen versus, 40–42
on theoretical reason versus
practical reason, 31

Rawlsian and economic analyses
compared, 179, 180–81
"strong reciprocity," 57, 199n69
The Struggle for Recognition
(Honneth), 44
Subsidy Dependence Index (SDI),
104–7, 110, 111, 203n26

Taiwan, Kuomintang government in,
186–87, 213n8
Taylor, Frederick, 203n23
Thakur, Karpoori, 132, 138, 140–41
theoretical reason versus practical
reason, 31
A Theory of Justice (Rawls), 17, 35–37,
40, 41, 42, 158, 198n39
theory of mind, 59–60
Todd, Helen, 112, 115
Topa, Giorgio, 112

United Nations Climate Conference,
Copenhagen (2009), 163
United Nations Development
Programme, 175
United Nations Environment
Programme, 171
United Nations Framework
Convention on Climate Change
(1992), 171
United States, political responses
to climate change in, 27, 94,
169–74, 180, 189
U.S. Agency for International
Development, 175

utilitarianism
classical, 34–35, 75, 97, 164, 179,
183, 195n12
neoutilitarianism, 19–25, 66, 122,
185, 188, 193
See also rational choice theory

vaishya caste, 127
values, principles as basis for, 10–12
veil of ignorance, 4, 35, 39, 42

Wade, Robert, 28, 186–87
Wahid, Abu N. M., 117
Waxman, Henry, 172, 173
Weber, Max, 14, 15, 203n23
Winnicott, Donald W., 199n57
women, Grameen Bank microloans
to, 21, 22, 93, 97, 104,
109–10, 113–18, 202n18,
202n21
World Bank, 21, 97, 106, 124, 150,
175, 176–77
World Meteorological Organization,
171
World Wars I and II, military
conscription in Canada during,
18–19, 82–86, 88

Yadav, Laloo Prasad, 139–44,
145–46
Yaron, Jacob, 106
Yunus, Muhammad, 97, 102. *See
also* Grameen Bank, program
analysis of

Paul Clements

is professor of political science at Western Michigan University.